Preparing for Trauma Work in Clinical Mental Health

This workbook is a foundational and unique resource for clinicians preparing to work with clients affected by trauma. Chapters integrate a holistic understanding of the unique client within trauma-specific case conceptualization, promote trainees' identification of personal values and past experiences that could impact their ability to provide safe and ethical services, and offer ways to reduce the risk of occupational hazards such as vicarious traumatization. The trauma treatment process is presented within the tri-phasic framework, which is applicable across settings, disciplines, and various theoretical orientations. Each chapter also provides experiential activities that link the chapter content with clinician reflection and application of knowledge and skills, which instructors and supervisors can easily utilize for evaluation and gatekeeping regarding a student's mastery of the content. An ideal resource for graduate-level faculty and supervisors, this book offers a versatile application for mental-health related fields including counseling, psychology, social work, school counseling, substance abuse, and marriage and family therapy.

Designed for students and professional clinicians, this groundbreaking text fills an important education and training gap by providing a comprehensive and enlightening presentation of trauma work while also emphasizing the clinician's growth in self-awareness and professional development.

Lisa Compton, PhD, LCSW, CFE, is a certified trauma treatment specialist and full-time faculty and trauma certificate coordinator for Regent University, USA.

Corie Schoeneberg, PhD, LPC, RPT-S, NCC, is an author, international presenter, graduate counseling course instructor, and clinical and play therapy supervisor.

Preparing for Trauma Work in Clinical Mental Health

A Workbook to Enhance Self-Awareness and
Promote Safe, Competent Practice

Lisa Compton and Corie Schoeneberg

Routledge
Taylor & Francis Group

NEW YORK AND LONDON

First published 2021
by Routledge
52 Vanderbilt Avenue, New York, NY 10017

and by Routledge
2 Park Square, Milton Park, Abingdon, Oxon, OX14 4RN

Routledge is an imprint of the Taylor & Francis Group, an informa business

Library of Congress Cataloging-in-Publication Data
A catalog record for this title has been requested

ISBN: 978-0-367-33185-6 (hbk)
ISBN: 978-0-367-33184-9 (pbk)
ISBN: 978-0-429-31960-0 (ebk)

Typeset in Bembo
by Apex CoVantage, LLC

For Todd: there is no one who makes me smile more.

You are a pillar of strength and constant encourager to me and our boys.—Lisa

For Rob, who is my greatest gift on this side of Heaven.

Your supportive love has been my companion for every step of my trauma work journey.—Corie

Contents

SECTION I: FOUNDATIONS: CONCEPTS AND PRINCIPLES OF TRAUMA TREATMENT

1 Orientation to Trauma Work: The Triad of Trauma, Client, and Self   3

2 Trauma: Identification and Conceptualization   15

3 The Clinician: Reflexive Practice and Professional Development in Trauma Work   28

4 Parallel Process: Risks and Rewards in Trauma Work   37

5 The Client: Trauma in an Individual and Cultural Context   54

6 The Therapeutic Relationship: Attachment and Connection in Trauma Work   68

SECTION II: CASE CONCEPTUALIZATION: A FRAMEWORK FOR TRAUMA TREATMENT

7 Trauma-Informed Intake: Building a Case Conceptualization   89

8 Trauma-Informed Assessment: Expanding Case Conceptualization   104

9 Trauma-Informed Treatment Plan: Synthesizing Case Conceptualization   120

SECTION III: THE TRI-PHASIC MODEL: A TRAUMA-FOCUSED TREATMENT PROCESS

10 Phase 1: Safety and Stabilization in Trauma Work   135

11 Phase 2: Remembrance and Mourning in Trauma Work   152

12 Phase 2 Enhancement: Creative Treatment Approaches
    in Trauma Work   171

13 Phase 3: Reconnection in Trauma Work   188

14 Beyond the Session: Professional Growth in Trauma Work   205

APPENDICES

Appendix A: Trauma-Related Assessments   216

Appendix B: Professional Organizations for Creative Modalities and Approaches   218

References   220
Index   233

Foundations

Concepts and Principles of Trauma Treatment

Chapter 1

Orientation to Trauma Work: The Triad of Trauma, Client, and Self

I will never forget my first encounter with trauma in a client case. I was in my master's practicum experience, and my client was a nine-year-old boy who had recently disclosed an extensive history of sexual abuse. As I met with his mother during private parent sessions, I listened to the harrowing details of the tremendous fallout that was occurring for the child and his family, and suddenly, all of my class lectures and textbook readings about trauma crystalized into strikingly vivid focus within the painful reality of an actual person. Much like the mother who sat before me, I felt completely overwhelmed and at a loss as to how to help this young boy through his pain and fear. As I listened to this mother's lengthy list of problems that they were experiencing, I thought to myself (but, thankfully, did not say out loud to my client): "Wow, you really need talk to a counselor." This thought was immediately followed by another more alarming thought: "Oh my—*I* am that counselor!"

Moments like these tell us so much about the depths of trauma and the needs of our clients while simultaneously illuminating and bringing to center stage our own cavernous feelings of self-doubt. If we look at this scene again, we can see that there are three aspects that the clinician must attend to in order to help this young client: the clinician must have knowledge of the nature of trauma, knowledge of the individual client, and knowledge of self. Without all three of these elements, the therapeutic process is incomplete.

This text aims to illustrate the full clinical picture by drawing attention to all three elements of the triad (trauma, client, and self), each of which is critical for safe and effective trauma work in mental health. In order to provide the best treatment for these cases, we must understand our client's presenting problems and symptomology through a trauma-informed lens, which requires a proficient understanding of the origins and impacts of trauma on the individual. Despite the prevalence of trauma-related problems across client populations, trauma work is considered a specialty area of mental health as it requires a robust set of functional knowledge and specialized clinical skills that are not covered in most graduate curricula.

Additionally, within the trauma treatment context, we must also carefully consider the individual client, who comes with a unique background of development, diversity factors, personal beliefs, and special history. The diversity of our clients tells us that trauma is not always experienced and manifested in the same way, and it is incumbent upon the clinician to understand the client's uniquely personal interaction with trauma. In many ways, trauma is like a backdrop on a theater stage, and our client is like the main character of the play. In order to fully understand the

3

meaning of the play, we must know the characters as well as the setting and context within which the scenes occur.

However, a client does not engage in his or her trauma work alone. Effective post-traumatic growth and healing occur within the therapeutic relationship, and trauma work, at its core, is a powerful relational interaction that requires the full engagement of both the client *and* clinician. This relational exchange necessitates that the clinician be safe, self-aware, and fully present as, indeed, the clinician cannot help a client go further than he or she has personally gone on the road towards self-growth.

With these three elements—knowledge of trauma, knowledge of client, and knowledge of self—the triad of trauma work is set, with each tip of the triangle relying on the others for support and structure. These three elements must be understood as distinctive forces, yet also considered in relationship to their adjacent parts to form one overall framework. This chapter provides a brief introduction to each of these triadic elements and offers the reader an overview of how these topics will be discussed throughout the text. A summary of the structure of this unique book is provided, and recommendations for how to best utilize this workbook are also outlined.

Trauma: Understanding the First Corner of the Triad

Trauma can be understood as "an experience or event that overwhelms your capacity to depend on or protect yourself. The hallmarks of trauma are feelings of terror, horror, and helplessness" (Schmelzer, 2018, p. 11). While these emotions often define the affective reactions in a traumatic experience, physiologically, trauma is "a stress response . . . outside of a person's normative life experience, and a sufficient condition that the response includes a breakdown of self-regulatory functions" (Krupnik, 2019, p. 259). Trauma ignites emotional and physiological responses from those who are impacted by it, and the lingering effects can be expressed in a variety of ways. Individuals reeling in the wake of trauma often represent some of the most hurting and vulnerable client populations, and as such, clinicians who provide care for these clients are held to a high standard of knowledge and expertise regarding this specialty area in the mental health field.

Competency in Trauma Work

Trauma is ubiquitous in mental health, and according to the National Association of State Mental Health Program Directors (NASMHPD, 2012), more than 90% of clients who access therapeutic services are estimated have been exposed to trauma. Consequently, all mental health professionals will, at some point, work with at least one client who has experienced trauma, regardless of the clinical setting in which they practice. The high percentage of trauma-impacted clients is not surprising to clinicians who have practiced for a significant length of time, as vast numbers of clients present with experiences of abuse, violence, loss, war, betrayal, natural disasters, and many other terrifying events. Very often, important trauma-related history is missing or overlooked in the client's initial discussion of his or her presenting problem, but in cases of unprocessed trauma, trauma-related problems and symptoms are, more often than not, impacting the client's current distress, thoughts, behaviors, and feelings.

Whether your professional identity is in psychology, social work, counseling, psychiatry, marriage and family therapy, school counseling, or any another mental health–related discipline, caring for individuals, couples, and families often means addressing trauma wounds. Two-thirds of adults have been exposed to at least one traumatic event, and many of these individuals experience significant complications, including addictions and problems at work and in relationships (Goodman, 2015). While most individuals who have been exposed to a traumatic event do not meet full criteria for posttraumatic stress disorder (PTSD), lack of an official diagnosis does not mean there is a total absence of trauma symptoms (Kilpatrick et al., 2013; Schubert, Schmidt, & Rosner, 2016). Given the pervasiveness of trauma, clinicians should be thoroughly competent in their abilities to conceptualize cases through a trauma-informed lens.

Unfortunately, without comprehensive trauma-specific training, misdiagnosis occurs frequently for clients who are experiencing trauma symptoms disguised as other mental health disorders. For example, a child experiencing difficulty concentrating in school and fidgeting with her hands in class may be diagnosed with attention-deficit/hyperactivity disorder, or ADHD (American Psychiatric Association, 2013). However, if this same child is experiencing physical abuse at home, these symptoms might better be understood within the context of trauma as her problematic behaviors may be more consistent with the hyperarousal caused by the survival reactions to trauma rather than simply understood as inattention and/or hyperactivity. In another example, an adult male presenting with symptoms of pronounced and desperate efforts to avoid abandonment and who experiences significant and persistent relationship problems may be diagnosed with borderline personality disorder (BPD). However, this man's history of sexual abuse and incest requires an understanding of trauma and attachment ruptures, not a narrow focus on his interpersonal difficulties perceived to stem from an inherently "impaired" personality. If clinicians are not knowledgeable about the many faces and presentations of trauma, inappropriate diagnoses are often assigned and, subsequently, insufficient treatment is provided. A degree in a mental health–related field alone does not qualify someone to be an effective trauma therapist (Langberg, 2003), and a lack of proper trauma training is not only unethical, it is also a preventable healthcare hazard.

Trauma-Informed Care

Over the past decade, **trauma-informed care** (TIC) has received increased attention and discussion. In general, the distinction of being a "trauma-informed" individual or organization indicates that there is an acquired understanding how trauma impacts individuals, families, communities, and societies. In addition to possessing this functional knowledge of trauma, the trauma-informed individual or organization must also demonstrate educated responses towards persons struggling with trauma reactions, which involves responses characterized by care, sensitivity, and trauma-informed accommodations. Trauma-informed care, therefore, implies active efforts to gain knowledge about trauma and mindful efforts to avoid situations that may retraumatize others. A trauma-informed approach provides a framework for various services found in settings such as schools, hospitals, police stations, and counseling offices.

The Substance Abuse and Mental Health Services Administration (SAMHSA, 2014) identified six key principles of trauma-informed care, including (1) safety, (2) trustworthiness and transparency, (3) peer support and mutual self-help, (4) collaboration and mutuality, (5) empowerment, voice, and choice, and (6) cultural, historical, and gender issues. Consideration of these principles within the clinical setting emphasizes a climate of safety for the client through tools such as informed consent, skill-building exercises, and, most importantly, through the development of the therapeutic relationship. Proficient trauma specialists advocate for the integration of trauma-informed care across settings, disciplines, and services in order to provide the safest and most fertile environments for growth and healing for individuals overcoming trauma wounds.

Naturally, trauma is discussed in every chapter of this text. However, many of the chapters explore trauma from different angles and through different lenses. Readers can expect a comprehensive presentation of trauma across the arc of this workbook that begins with primary principles of trauma work and concludes with guidelines for treating trauma all the way to termination. Over the course of this book, the identification and conceptualization process of trauma is discussed, and cultural aspects and diagnostic considerations of trauma are explored. Building on these conceptual foundations, trauma-specific treatment and principles of trauma-informed therapeutic care are also comprehensively presented and illustrated.

The Client: Attending to the Second Corner of the Triad

Individuals who survive traumatic events are often affected by the trauma in numerous ways long after the actual danger ceases. Trauma may cause significant distress and impairment in functioning and can potentially result in a wide range of problems, including psychological, affective, and physiological symptoms (Keck, Compton, Schoeneberg, & Compton, 2017). Emotionally, trauma survivors may experience anxiety, depression, fear, guilt, irritability, and grief, while physical symptoms may include shortness of breath, increased blood pressure, gastrointestinal complications, and nausea. Behavioral changes, such as an increase or decrease in eating or changes in sleeping and sexual activity, may occur in addition to other behaviors, such as difficulty concentrating, isolation, and relationship conflict.

Persons reeling from traumatic experiences often experience **existential crises** and struggle to understand why the painful event occurred. Spiritually, trauma may impact convictions about faith, meaning, forgiveness, and one's sense of control, regardless of an individual's specific religion (Sherman, Harris, & Erbes, 2015). Although not all outcomes of trauma are negative (a positive resolution in trauma recovery may result in enhanced resiliency and posttraumatic growth), trauma has the potential to shatter previously held beliefs about ourselves, other people, and the safety of the world around us (Janoff-Bulman, 1992).

With these multifaceted dimensions of the individual, the impacts of trauma are not uniform but, instead, are personally unique and often complex. A person's developmental stage, previous life experiences, cultural background and worldview, protective and risk factors, and tendencies towards internalizing or externalizing psychological stress all serve to inform the manner in which trauma symptoms are manifested and expressed. Clinicians must develop a strong, working case conceptualization of the unique client in order to accurately identify trauma reactions and tailor appropriate treatment approaches.

The Therapeutic Experience and the Trauma Survivor

Entering into a therapeutic relationship presents many potential challenges for trauma survivors. An incredible amount of vulnerability and trust is required to let down one's defenses and participate in a therapeutic relationship, and this may be the first time the client discloses long-held secrets to another person. The inherent power imbalance in the therapeutic alliance may pose additional challenges, especially when clients have experienced abuse or betrayal by authority figures in the past. Clients may enter the therapeutic process with powerful fears about confronting trauma memories, especially when avoidance has been an active defense against such painful thoughts and feelings. Clients often worry that the horrific details of the trauma will ensue a psychological tidal wave that will engulf his or her own capacity to cope while simultaneously overwhelming the clinician. They may fear that trauma recovery will not be successful and that confronting the traumatic memories is not worth the risk, which can deepen feelings of hopelessness and helplessness. The clinician has the crucial role of recognizing these struggles and providing a safe place for clients to be vulnerable, learn to trust again, and overcome fears that have kept them stuck in the aftermath of trauma.

While this workbook focuses heavily on trauma and trauma-related problems and disorders, trauma is never considered apart from the diverse individuals who experience its impacts. A strong understanding of trauma also requires the clinician to have an equally strong understanding of the unique client. In this text, the interweave of trauma and client culture and diversity is considered, and the influence of client attachment history is examined. These factors, along with other significant client variables, integrate to formulate a comprehensive client case conceptualization. In addition, specific trauma-focused goals, applied through a variety of trauma treatment approaches, are presented and explored.

The Clinician: Enriching the Third Corner of the Triad

Many beginning professionals are extremely eager to soak up the enormous ocean of information regarding trauma, and they are often willing to investigate the client and that individual's uniquely personal and developmental context for the trauma. However, a deep examination into one's self is often overlooked or dismissed as somehow less important, less essential, and less urgent. This tendency, if not addressed, is a great loss for the professional as it is, truly, the clinician *him- or herself* that is the greatest and most critical intervention tool. Our most effective resource to improve attachment, foster resiliency, and heal trauma in the therapeutic setting lies *within ourselves* as clinicians. The unconditional support and relational safety provided in a strong therapeutic alliance buffer the emotional and physiological impact of trauma (Gingrich & Gingrich, 2017; Siegel, 2015). In order to provide safe and effective care for the wounds of trauma, we must be willing to turn our eyes inward in order to enhance the most powerful resource of all: one's self.

Professional Functions of Self-Awareness and Reflection

As a fundamental principle, the ceiling of a clinician's ability to facilitate trauma recovery can be found at the end of his or her personal insight into self. **Self-awareness** is perhaps the most crucial skill for an effective trauma clinician. The ability to be introspective helps clinicians manage the complexities of transference and countertransference issues, self-adjust to the "unexpected" that comes up in therapy, and maintain awareness of the personal impact of exposure to trauma stories. Because the relationship with the clinician is highly influential for clients during trauma work, reflective exercises are necessary to both prepare the clinician for trauma work as well as bolster success for longevity in the field. For example, self-awareness can serve as a tool to monitor our internal world, such as the reflection question, "What am I currently feeling in this session?" Self-awareness through reflection is also necessary to address more complicated questions such as "How do I attend to this client's horrifying story without being triggered myself?" and "I have experienced insecure attachment, so how can I provide secure attachment in this therapeutic relationship?" Ultimately, self-awareness operates as the critical foundation upon which all other trauma work skills are built upon.

At this time, most of current literature on trauma focuses exclusively on a didactic approach to learning trauma, which leans solely on explaining theoretical approaches and various interventions in a narrative format. While the conceptual foundations of trauma are critical, equally essential is the personal processing experience that prepares trainees and beginning clinicians for trauma work through personal reflective practice, which is an optimal format for a career that utilizes "self" as the most influential tool (Wilson & Nojachski, 2016). This book is a *personal* tool of professional development. Therefore, as you go through this workbook, you will notice a significance emphasis on *you* and development of your own self-awareness and insight. As the third element of the triad, attention to the person of the clinician (you, the reader) is critical, and this aspect of development warrants your value in time and attention as well.

Parallel Process Between Client and Clinician

A **parallel process** occurs when a similar experience takes place between two different individuals and across two difference contexts. Parallel process is often used to describe a theme or over-arching experience within the client-clinician relationship or trainee-supervisor relationship (Koltz, Odegard, Feit, Provost, & Smith, 2012). For example, a parallel process occurs when a client worries that she may not be "good enough" as a wife and a mother and, meanwhile, the clinician also questions whether she is "good enough" as a mental health professional. Characteristic of parallel process, both of these individuals share the theme of self-doubt and insecurity, but these feelings are driven by different circumstances and are likely expressed in different ways. In another example of parallel process, a client may have tremendous fears about beginning trauma exposure work, and a novice trauma clinician may also have troubling anxiety about facilitating this process too.

Embarking on the journey of trauma recovery is not for the faint of heart, and the process is not a simple one for the client nor for the clinician. Even though they do so in different ways, both the client and clinician share the parallel process of choosing courage and commitment to see the journey's end in trauma work, and both must steady their feet to navigate through the rocky terrain of trauma memories. This active engagement in trauma work, for both the client and the clinician, is the first of many parallel processes that take place along the road of trauma recovery and healing.

This text serves as a tool for trainees and clinicians, not only to learn about trauma and share the psychoeducation with their clients, but also to develop crucial skills that will help both clinicians and clients remain firmly grounded as painful memories surface and are shared in the therapeutic setting. As you explore the concepts and then personally apply them, powerful lessons can be found in the experience itself through the lens of the parallel process. Many of the end-of-chapter workbook exercises reflect on the similar work clients also engage in during therapy. You are encouraged to pay special attention to *what it is like* to engage in this process. In this way, experience is the teacher and insight is the lesson.

Throughout the chapters in this text, readers will learn about trauma and how trauma interacts with the unique client, but attention will also be directed towards enhancing the reader's self-insight and professional growth. While this aspect is integrated in every chapter, some chapters place particular emphasis on clinician development, including a discussion on the professional use of reflection and its role in safe and effective trauma-focused practice, the professional risks and rewards of trauma work, and aspects of professional development needed for ongoing competency in this field. The activities outlined at the conclusion of each chapter are specifically designed for the reader's roles, as both a person and a clinician, by offering exercises intended to promote self-awareness, expand trauma knowledge, and enhance clinical skills.

Structure of the Workbook: Engaging in the Format

Trauma work transcends disciplines, and the concepts and principles discussed in this text are universal across all mental health specialties. The content of this workbook is inclusive to a variety of professional identities including, but not limited to, psychology, social work, counseling, marriage and family therapy, and psychiatry. In honor of the professional diversity of the readers, we use the term "clinician" in reference to the mental health professional providing therapeutic services. While this book is ideal for students, residents, and supervisees working towards a mental health discipline licensure (referred to as "trainees" in this text), this workbook is also applicable to practicing clinicians who have experience in mental health but who are seeking specific training in trauma work. The unique focus of this workbook centers on clinician development, so this text can be ideally paired with other texts that delve deeper into advanced trauma treatment issues and theory-specific intervention and modalities.

Neuroscience illuminates not only the impact of trauma on the brain but also how we learn. Recent research on neuroplasticity, or the brain's ability to change, has contributed important information to the field of trauma studies on how the connections between neurons strengthen or cease based on use (Siegel, 2012). For clients, this means that counseling can potentially reverse unhealthy cognitive and emotional patterns that developed from a trauma by weakening old neural connections and strengthening more adaptive ones (Gingrich & Gingrich, 2017; Siegel, 2015). For clinicians, this neurobiological principle means that practicing a skill (experiential learning) can aid in the development of new neural connections (Clabough, 2019).

Kolb's experiential learning theory (1984) proposed a four-part learning cycle of knowledge and skill development: concrete experience, reflective observation, abstract conceptualization, and active experimentation (Fewster-Thuente & Batteson, 2018; Kolb, 1984). This workbook utilizes the first three components of the learning cycle (the fourth stage, "active experimentation," is conducted with real clients in practicum, internships, residencies, and supervised clinical experiences). Consistent with the principles of neuroscience and Kolb's (1984) theory of learning, readers will notice the layered approach of this workbook, which is both *didactic and reflectively experiential*.

Case Examples of Trauma Work in Practice

The construction of each chapter begins with a concise narrative of seminal and current information related to the chapter topic. Within this didactic section of the chapter, there are several case studies, which are incorporated to promote practical application and critical thinking about the concepts. These case studies are representative of our combined near 40 years of clinical practice, and the clinical illustrations provide opportunities for application of the information learned throughout the book. Within all case examples, the client names and identifying details have been changed to protect the confidentiality of clients. None of the examples in this book refer to a specific client, and they may represent a combination of cases.

Readers should note that there is a degree of trauma exposure in these case studies, which is intentional and designed to help prepare trainees for clinical work with live clients. Case study examples not only translate the concepts into real-life application, they also help clinicians to identify their own level of comfort or discomfort with certain types of trauma material. While some discomfort is normative, reader reactions to the case examples that are characterized by intensive, ruminating, or distressing thoughts or feelings may indicate a potential trauma trigger or represent a trauma reminder from a trainee's own personal background. When case studies or the material in this text are experienced as especially distressing, readers are strongly encouraged to seek out consultation, supervision, or counseling for themselves. Readers should also be mindful of the emotionally charged nature of some topics in this text and, as such, are strongly encouraged to practice positive self-care throughout and take breaks as needed.

Keyword Assessment

Following the didactic portion of the chapter, the reader will have the opportunity to engage in several activities that target comprehension and concept mastery, experiential learning, and supervisor discussion. Throughout the text, important terms that represent current terminology used in literature and common vernacular within the profession will be boldface for the reader. This is not an exhaustive list of terms; however, the text's trauma work vocabulary will help trainees and clinicians navigate the literature and become familiar with language used within this specialty of practice. The first interactive section of the workbook integrates these boldface terms in the *Keyword Assessment*. This section offers a summary of the important chapter terms, and here, the reader is encouraged to assess his or her comprehension of these concepts by writing definitions of the terms in his or her own words, describing the concept's role in trauma work, listing any questions about the concept, and making notes of important aspects to remember about the concept.

Experiential Activities

To further interact with the information presented in the chapter, the next section of the workbook includes ideas for experiential activities. These activities are divided into exercises that specifically aim to expand the reader's self-awareness, knowledge base, and clinical skills. This section is one of the most important elements for professional growth, as readers have the opportunity to explore self and gain personal insight. Many of these reflective activities are creative and artistic in nature, but no artistic ability is required to complete these types of exercises. In fact, the purpose of utilizing art and creativity in addition to word-based reflection is not to produce aesthetic pieces but to engage the "emotional" and non-verbal parts of the brain (Badenoch, 2008; Malchiodi, 2003). Art, metaphor, and the use of creativity often unveils parts of ourselves that we might not have otherwise become aware of or have access to (Perryman, Blisard, & Moss, 2019), so readers are encouraged to embrace this aspect of the process and avoid the temptation to skip any of the exercises.

Supervisory Discussion

In the final workbook section of each chapter, readers are provided with topics for *Supervisory Discussion*. While the text uses the distinction of "supervisory" as the context for discussion, these discussions are not limited to a supervisor-trainee relationship alone, and this portion of the workbook is applicable for dialogue (or written reflections) with colleagues, faculty instructors, clinical supervisors, or professional peer groups. A significant focus of these discussion questions is based on the reader's insights gleaned from the experiential activities. However, many of the exercises associated with the *Experiential Activities* section address content that is personal in nature, and by separating the *Supervisory Discussion* section from the *Experiential Activities* section of the workbook, the privacy of the reader is protected, and the reader can choose how much to disclose and share in discussion.

The *Supervisory Discussion* section and supervision process (if any) will vary depending on the reader's stage of professional development and professional goals, and readers should follow the guidelines and instructions of their clinical supervisors regarding this aspect of the workbook. For example, a faculty instructor may request that the trainee (or student) write a reflection journal that addresses the prompts of this section as an assignment while a site supervisor may request that the questions are discussed in private supervision and in relationship with the trainee's current cases. Still other readers may meet with colleagues or peer groups and select which prompts they wish to discuss, and still other readers may complete this portion independently through their own private journaling and reflection. Whether you are a beginning trainee meeting with your clinical supervisor or a seasoned clinician seeking consultation from a colleague, professional growth and development occurs most ideally with a dispositional attitude characterized by transparency and openness to feedback. We encourage you to utilize all parts of this workbook to its highest potential.

Conclusion

In trauma work, a tendency exists for trainees to focus on learning the latest "techniques" to gain competency. Whether you are a beginning trainee or seasoned clinician, our hope is that this book will challenge you to increase your reflective capacities, remain open to feedback from supervisors and clients, and seek peer-reviewed literature for evidence-based practice, creative approaches, and current scientific studies. The journey down the path of trauma work is full of unexpected turns, a few plot twists, and some harrowing encounters. However, it is the journey itself, not just the destination, that is rich with surprising gifts, rewarding experiences, and many meaningful moments. Your passion, your courage, and your desire to help others will be some of your greatest traveling companions.

KEYWORD ASSESSMENT

Write definitions in your own words, describe the concept's role in trauma work, list any questions, or make notes of important aspects that you want to remember.

Trauma-Informed Care

Existential Crises

Self-Awareness

Parallel Process

EXPERIENTIAL ACTIVITIES: INTERACTING WITH THE CHAPTER CONTENT

Expand Self-Awareness

1) As you begin your developmental journey as a trauma clinician, reflect on your thoughts, feelings, concerns, and goals regarding this process. Do an internet search for pictures, or utilize calendar photos or magazine clippings to select an image of a road or path that best represents how you are feeling at this time. Reflect on the metaphorical nature of the image and how it portrays your internal experience of starting a new phase in your professional growth.

Expand Knowledge

2) Request to have a professional dialogue with a trauma specialist. Ask this professional what he or she wishes he or she had known before beginning trauma work, what professional goals and learning he or she recommends, and what joys he or she has taken away from this specialty practice. Ask any additional questions or process concerns you have about trauma work practice.

Expand Skills

3) Review the concept of parallel process. Using a film or book, explore situations of parallel process between characters. Identify similar themes, experiences, and feelings that the characters share in different contexts, and then reflect on how an awareness of these parallel processes might impact the characters' relationships with one another. If each character could better relate and understand the other's experience more, what would change? How would the situation be impacted by the insight of parallel process?

SUPERVISORY DISCUSSION: SHARING PERSONAL INSIGHTS AND IDENTIFYING AREAS FOR GROWTH

1) Share the insights you gained by reflecting on your chosen image of a road or path. At the start of this learning process, describe your thoughts, feelings, and concerns.

2) Summarize your discussion with the trauma specialist. What were some highlights of the conversation, insights you gained, and topics that sparked your interest?

3) Describe your learning about parallel process from the activity. What have you noticed about the power of parallel process? Why do you believe reflection on parallel process is important and useful for clinicians in trauma work?

4) Outline your professional goals related to trauma work, and connect these goals with the triad of trauma, client, and self. What do you hope to gain and learn as a result of this experience? What do you believe is most needed in order to provide safe and effective trauma treatment for your clients?

Chapter 2

Trauma: Identification and Conceptualization

Although it was more than 25 years ago, I can still recall a particular discussion during one of my graduate classes. Nick, one of my classmates, asked our professor about a case he was struggling with at his practicum site. Nick's client was a 20-year-old female who had been raped on a college campus in a different state and then returned home due to the extreme distress from her attack. Our professor walked Nick and the class through various interventions that he might apply with his client. Nick took copious notes but still seemed overwhelmed by his client's case. In an attempt provide comfort to Nick and our class, the professor told us, "Don't worry, traumas of this nature are *very* rare." This professor was not intentionally misleading the class but was merely reflecting the view on trauma prevalence at that point in time.

Unfortunately, this inaccurate depiction of the frequency of sexual assaults became strikingly evident to me during my master's-level internship, and I was shocked to come face to face with the overwhelming pervasiveness of sexual abuse and other forms of trauma. For my internship experience, I was given the option between working at an addictions-focused clinic in a low-income neighborhood of the city or taking a position at a private practice located in a wealthy suburb. I was still very new to clinical practice and to curb my insecurities and fears about counseling, I chose the internship that I thought would certainly have "easier" presenting problems. Within the first month of my suburban practice, my wealthy, seemingly high-functioning clients presented with histories of incest, suicidal and homicidal ideations, and even exposure to extreme cult violence. The ubiquitous nature of trauma within mental health became uncomfortably clear. However, trauma was not discussed at length in any of my classes at that point in time. I felt ill prepared to treat such profound issues and ignorant of how these traumas impacted my clients' well-being.

Unfortunately, many clinicians feel swallowed up by the enormity of trauma work as they attempt to navigate the often daunting and overwhelming ocean of information. Effective trauma work begins with a strong conceptualization of trauma itself, which includes practical definitions and distinctions between other adverse experiences. In this chapter, we investigate the first corner of the trauma work triad—trauma—and explore its basic principles and concepts. This chapter offers a research-informed perspective of the pervasiveness of trauma, outlines the *Diagnostic and Statistical Manual of Mental Disorders, Fifth Edition*'s (*DSM-5*'s) criteria for experiences that qualify definitively as "traumatic" in nature, discusses the various types and conceptualizations of trauma, highlights the connections between trauma and physical health, and provides a strengths-based perspective for clinicians when working with clients impacted by trauma.

Prevalence of Trauma: Recognizing the Expanse of Trauma's Presence

Trauma does not discriminate who it affects. Trauma transcends all socioeconomic, race, age, gender, sexual orientation, ethnic, and education boundaries. To put the pervasiveness of traumatic events in perspective, according to the Centers for Disease Control and Prevention (CDC, 2015), every year in the United States, 683,000 individuals are victims of child abuse and neglect, and 10 million women and men are victims of physical intimate partner violence. At some point across the lifespan, an estimated 1 in 3 women and 1 in 4 men will experience sexual violence (CDC, 2019a). Traumatic events also involve loss of life, and every year, roughly 35,000 people die in motor vehicle crashes and 15,000 die of prescription opioid overdoses (CDC, 2015). Additional forms of traumatic events include natural disasters that often cause widespread impact such as floods, tornadoes, and hurricanes. Traumatic events are vast, diverse, multifaceted, and shockingly prevalent, just like the survivors it impacts.

During the past three decades, the field of mental health has experienced a burgeoning interest in trauma. One of the most significant events to legitimize the psychological impact of trauma occurred in 1980 when the third edition of the *Diagnostic and Statistical Manual of Mental Disorders,* or DSM-III (American Psychiatric Association, 1980) included posttraumatic stress disorder (PTSD) as a mental health diagnosis. This was the first professional conceptualization of PTSD in which the damage of trauma was not defined exclusively in conjunction with a physical injury (Goodman, 2015). During the 1980s and early 1990s, traumatic events outside the scope of military combat were considered rare due to a lack of public awareness (Courtois & Gold, 2009). However, in more recent decades, events such as the terrorist attacks on September 11, 2001, Hurricane Katrina, Sandy Hook and other school shootings, and the #metoo movement, have sparked an increase in awareness of the unfortunate commonality of traumatic events, both natural and human-caused. The growing awareness has resulted in an urgency to produce research on the nature and impact of trauma as well as explore the factors related to survivors' levels of distress, functioning, and overall well-being.

Becoming skilled in trauma-informed care requires an understanding of the types of circumstances that are considered to be traumatic in nature, and clinicians must be knowledgeable about how these traumatic experiences impact clients' well-being and functioning, both short-term and long-term. However, these concepts are not clear cut, as there is a high degree of subjectivity in defining what is and what is not traumatic, while also accounting for the great variability across individuals in regard to how trauma affects them. The variability in the unique impact that a traumatic event has on an individual is influenced by many factors, including intrinsic and external factors, the larger psychosocial context surrounding the event, as well as the individual's perception of and meaning derived from the trauma. These variables and their influence on the impact of trauma will be explored in depth throughout the text.

Definitions of Trauma: Making Distinctions and Applying Conceptualizations

There are multiple perspectives on what types of events can be considered traumatic in nature, and, consequently, there is often a lack of consensus in how to best conceptualize and define "trauma." Professional literature and the vernacular in the field is diverse, and terms and concepts associated with trauma can become muddled, unclear, and difficult to differentiate. A strong working knowledge of trauma requires clinicians to undertake the challenge of distinguishing between the diagnostic definition of trauma, conceptually organizing the various types of trauma, and discerning the distinctions between trauma, stress, and adversity.

DSM-5's Defining Criteria for Trauma

For mental health professionals, a place to begin operationalizing a definition of trauma is with the current standard classification system, the *DSM-5* (APA, 2013). As the guiding diagnostic manual, the *DSM-5* provides the descriptive criteria that formally defines an event as "'traumatic' in nature, and this definition is applicable for the diagnoses of acute stress disorder (ASD) and posttraumatic stress disorder (PTSD). The primary distinction between ASD and PTSD differs in terms of the onset and duration of symptoms. In ASD, symptoms present at a maximum of one month or less since the time of the traumatic event, and in PTSD, symptoms persist beyond one month following the traumatic event. Despite these differences in symptom duration, both ASD and PTSD utilize the following characteristics to formally define a "trauma" experience:

Exposure to actual or threatened death, serious injury, or sexual violence in one or more of the following ways:

1. Directly experiencing the traumatic event(s).
2. Witnessing, in person, the event(s) as it occurred to others.
3. Learning that the traumatic event(s) occurred to a close family member or a close friend. In cases of actual or threatened death of a family member or friend, the event(s) must have been violent or accidental.
4. Experiencing repeated or extreme exposure to aversive details of the traumatic event(s) (e.g., first responders collecting human remains; police officers repeatedly exposed to details of child abuse. Note: Criterion A4 does not apply to exposure through electronic media, television, movies, or pictures unless this exposure is work related.) (APA, 2013, pp. 271, 281)

Experiences that meet the *DSM-5* criteria for a traumatic event may include a physical assault, a plane crash, hurricane, torture, or the hearing of details regarding a loved one's sexual assault. While the *DSM-5* provides some parameters for what kind of experiences formally qualify as traumatic, the experience of a traumatic event alone does not warrant a diagnosis. For both ASD and PTSD, the key criteria in assigning a formal diagnosis centers on the trauma-related symptoms that result from the trauma exposure (APA, 2013). A comprehensive discussion of the various presentations of these symptoms is provided in section II of this text.

Type 1 and Type 2 Traumas

Outside of the *DSM-5* definition, Terr (1991) proposed an additional method to classify traumatic events, which is based on the frequency of traumatic experiences. A **type 1 trauma,** also referred to as a **single-event trauma**, refers to a one-time event, such as a car accident or workplace shooting. Conversely, a **type 2 trauma,** also referred to as **complex trauma**, represents a recurring event or multiple traumatic events (often interpersonal in nature) which creates a cumulative impact on the individual and, thereby, increases the person's risk for PTSD. Type 2 trauma may include cases of ongoing physical abuse, perpetual community violence, or multiple rape experiences. For individuals with type 2 trauma, the shock of the first traumatic event is followed by a "subsequent unfolding of horrors [which] creates a sense of anticipation. Massive attempts to protect the psyche and the self are put into gear" (Terr, 1991, p. 15). These psychological defense reactions may include denial, dissociation, emotional numbing, and identification with the perpetrator.

While the delineation between the two types of trauma is helpful for conceptualization, the *DSM-5* does not differentiate between single event and complex trauma, and both type 1 and type 2 traumas may result in PTSD symptom clusters, such as intrusive thoughts (e.g., flashbacks, nightmares), avoidance symptoms (e.g., strongly avoiding any reminder of the trauma), negative changes in cognitions and mood (e.g., extreme negative bias or inability to experience positive feelings), and changes in arousal (e.g., heightened startle response) (APA, 2013). Regardless of whether the client presents with type 1 or type 2 trauma, the formal application of a diagnosis, such as PTSD, is uniform, but clinicians frequently notice that clients with type 2 (complex) trauma often experience increased intensity and pervasiveness of trauma-related symptoms. Complex trauma may be accompanied by significant problems with fragmented self-organization and dissociation, difficulty in emotional regulation and expression, negative self-concept, suicidality and self-harming behaviors, eating disorders, sexual dysfunction, addictions to drugs and alcohol, and pervasive interpersonal challenges. These problems, in addition to the symptoms outlined in the *DSM-5*, often represent responses to the experience of chronic trauma (Brewin et al., 2017; Herman, 1992a).

Trauma Work in Practice: Type 1 and Type 2 Traumas

My 47-year-old client, Jermaine, had enjoyed 15 years of long Sunday afternoon bike rides until one particular afternoon in which he was struck by a car while on his bike near his home. The impact of the car shattered bones in Jermaine's left leg and arm, and he needed extensive physical therapy to recover. Long after his physical injuries healed, Jermaine continued to have recurring dreams of the car accident, and his extremely high degree of hypervigilance while bike riding inhibited him from riding more than a few miles at a time. In my work with Jermaine, I noticed several symptoms consistent with PTSD, including reexperiencing symptoms through his nightmares and hypervigilance in conjunction with trauma reminders. For Jermaine, this single event was powerful enough to propel him into clinically significant trauma-related problems, and his case reflected type 1 trauma.

Another client, Shirley, was a 32-year-old woman who married her high school sweetheart and enjoyed several years of marital bliss until the birth of their first child. After bringing home their newborn son home from the hospital, Shirley's husband began drinking heavily and soon became physically abusive to her. Dependent on her husband financially and with limited options, Shirley feared what her husband might do to their son if she tried to leave him. Consequently, she endured years of abuse, including black eyes, bruised ribs, and other injuries from being pushed and hit. Shirley became socially isolated, depressed, and wrestled with thoughts of suicide. She often stayed up at night and wondered how the abusive environment would impact her young son.

In contrast to Jermaine, Shirley's case reflects type 2 (complex) trauma in which Shirley came to expect or anticipate a reoccurring traumatic experience. For Shirley, she not only experienced symptoms consistent with PTSD, but her presenting problems also compounded into depression and other significant concerns. Unlike Jermaine, with whom I was able to work exclusively on overcoming his singular trauma in counseling, Shirley required additional therapeutic goals that integrated considerations for her safety, depression, self-efficacy, and interpersonal patterns.

Developmental Trauma

Similar to type 1 and type 2 traumas, which are not discussed or considered as defining criteria in the *DSM-5*, developmental trauma is another conceptualization of trauma that is frequently discussed in the literature and trauma field but is not included as part of a formal diagnosis. **Developmental trauma** refers to the cumulative impact of chronic or multiple traumatic events that occurred during the formative developmental years in childhood. Frequently, this type of trauma stems from traumatic experiences within the parent-child relationship, creating attachment problems as well as difficulties in the emotional, behavioral, cognitive, and social domains (Spinazzola, van der Kolk, & Ford, 2018). For cases in which trauma occurs within the parent-child relationship, an attachment disorder, which also falls under the trauma and stress-related disorder category of the *DSM-5*, may emerge, and these attachment-related diagnoses include reactive attachment disorder (RAD) and disinhibited social engagement disorder (DSED). Most often, situations of developmental trauma develop within the context of interpersonal trauma, such as ongoing childhood abuse or neglect, but developmental trauma may also result from a series of multiple, non-interpersonal traumatic events during the early years of life, such as a child who witnesses the death of his parent at the age of 3, survives a house fire at the age of 5, and then endures painful medical treatments for cancer at the age of 6.

Children are often considered resilient, but this developmental attribute can be misleading and may contribute to the myth that young children are immune to or will simply "grow out of" the negative impacts of trauma. In fact, children are actually much more vulnerable to the impacts of trauma during early childhood than during any other stage in the lifespan (Gaskill & Perry, 2012). When confronted with a traumatic situation, children, in comparison to adults, have limited internal resources, such as undeveloped coping mechanisms, low self-insight, and limited capacity to understand the problem, and are restricted in their access to external resources, such as opportunities to receive help and support. Their scarce internal and external resources, coupled with the stage of formative brain development, frequently make children more vulnerable to traumatization (Krupnik, 2019). In cases of developmental trauma, traumatic events compound, combine, and accumulate in a powerful way that often sets the child's orientation to life within a trauma-influenced template.

Childhood trauma may impair self-image, emotional regulation, and interpersonal skills, and the impact of trauma may even cause physiological changes in brain development (Cloitre et al., 2009; van der Kolk, 2005). The potential negative impacts to brain development, repeated use of an over-active stress response system, and altered perceptions of the safety of the world can have enduring consequences and place children at a greater risk for mood, anxiety, personality, and substance abuse disorders in adulthood (Read, Fosse, Moskowitz, & Perry, 2014). Childhood traumas also inhibit children's ability to trust others, especially when the trauma was at the hands of a caregiver, and may result in shame and guilt if they internalize blame for the abuse. Although children do, indeed, possess resiliency to overcome adversity and trauma, without a supportive, empathetic adult to process the trauma and buffer its impact, the long-term effects can be devastating.

In many professional settings, adult clients who have experienced developmental trauma are often referenced as cases of complex trauma (type 2 trauma), and frequently, developmental and complex trauma are often used as synonyms or interchangeably. This overlap often occurs because in the majority of complex trauma cases, the adult client's traumatic experiences began in the early years of life. However, as can be seen in the case of Shirley, complex trauma does not always begin in childhood, nor does developmental trauma always result in ongoing trauma in adulthood. For trauma clinicians, the ability to recognize the overlaps as well as distinctions between complex and developmental trauma is helpful in conceptualization.

Trauma vs. Stress and Adversity

A number of years ago, I decided that I was ready to get into better shape, so I took out a gym membership and was excited to begin exercising and building up my fitness stamina. On my very first workout day, I vastly overestimated my capabilities, and my exuberance to begin at the "advanced" level was quickly met with the sobering reality that my body was not prepared for that amount of stress. Before I knew it, I was sitting on the floor trying not to pass out as a consequence of the overexertion I had just put myself through.

When considering the role of normative stress and its distinctions from trauma, stress operates much like physical exercise: a certain amount of it is tolerable and can even serve a positive purpose (such as propelling growth, providing the motivation to manage challenges, offering immediate feedback, etc.), but too high a degree of stress, either in excess or intensity, can result in injury or damage. All individuals must learn to manage the normative stress that accompanies daily living, but when stress becomes too intense (as it did for me in the gym), we must learn to stop, take breaks, recover, and then readjust our approach to keep going. However, when stress is not managed appropriately, the consequences can be dire, leaving the individual at risk for numerous health problems, such as heart conditions and high blood pressure, as well as creating vulnerabilities to mental health issues, such as trauma-related disorders (von Diwans, Trueg, Kirschbaum, Fishchbacher, & Heinrichs, 2018).

Apart from normative stress, excessive or intense and non-beneficial stress is often referred to as **toxic stress**, which can result in an over-activation of the stress response system and thus possibly affect brain structure and chemistry, increase the risk of illness, and diminish the body's ability to return to a state of equilibrium (Morsy, 2019). Frequently, the term **adversity** is used to describe the circumstances or situations in which a person experiences levels of intense or toxic stress. Adverse experiences often create obstacles for optimum development, functioning, and growth, and as a parallel, the effort to overcome adversity can feel like wearing heavy boots while trying to swim across a pool. Toxic stress and adversity are often out of the control of the individual, and the individual must learn to function in a state of heightened arousal. Adversity and subsequent toxic stress can occur in the daily challenges of living in poverty, enduring repeated bullying, managing chronic and painful illness, or caring for a loved one with extreme and challenging special needs, such as a severe addiction, mental illness, or medical condition. In the *DSM-5*, the fallout of intense or toxic stress stemming from adverse experiences can result in a diagnosis of adjustment disorder (AD), which also falls within the category of trauma and stress-related disorders.

In contrast to stress and adversity, trauma, by its nature, represents a type of stress which "maxes out the machine" with no opportunity to "switch the off button." An experience of trauma means that the stress of the situation has far surpassed the individual's ability to cope and endure. Returning to the metaphor of physical exercise, trauma goes beyond a pulled muscle or sprained ankle resultant from stress; trauma often leaves a significant psychological injury, metaphorically paralleling the devastating physical damage of a slipped disc, broken arm, serious concussion, or paralysis. Unlike stress, trauma is never a "normative" event, and healing and recovery most often does not occur easily or rapidly. Krupnik (2019) summarizes the differences across the trauma and stress spectrum by proposing that in normative stress, the individual is able to return to equilibrium following a stressor, while in situations of toxic stress and adversity, the individual experiences a transition into a less adaptive state of functioning. On the far end of the spectrum, traumatic stress overwhelms the individual to the degree that he or she is not able to return to homeostasis and experiences a breakdown of self-regulating abilities. As clients arrive to session and describe their experiences, the clinician's understanding of these varying shades of stress will lay the foundation for a strong conceptualization.

Trauma and Physical Health: Identifying Connections and Integrating Considerations

Dr. Vincent Felitti worked at the California Kaiser Obesity Clinic in the 1980s, and during his practice, he began to notice that many of the patients who dropped out of the clinic also had a history of childhood sexual abuse. Wondering if there was a possible connection between toxic stress in childhood and adult health, he started to survey patients and confirmed a high occurrence of adverse childhood events among his obesity patients. His work caught the attention of Dr. Robert Anda with the Centers for Disease Control (CDC), and they conducted a joint study with 17,337 participants from 1995 to 1997, which became known as the Adverse Childhood Events (ACE) study (Copeland et al., 2018; Felitti et al., 1998). The study examined childhood experiences, such as emotional, sexual, and physical abuse, as well as occurrences of household dysfunction, such as living with a parent who experienced substance abuse and/or mental illness. Under the umbrella of this construct, the ACE study incorporated the full spectrum of conceptualizations of trauma, including type 1 and 2 traumas, developmental trauma, and experiences of extreme adversity. The ACE study was the first large-scale research endeavor to demonstrate a correlation between childhood trauma and health issues later in adulthood.

The results of the ACE study were significant for several reasons. First, the study revealed that adverse childhood events are an unfortunately common occurrence. Among the predominantly white, middle-class study participants, approximately two-thirds of the participants had experienced at least one adverse childhood event (Felitti et al., 1998). Second, the correlations between a person's ACE score and their later problems with physical health presented in a graded fashion, or a "dose-respondent" relationship, meaning that as a person's number of adverse childhood events (ACEs) increased, so did the individual's likelihood of developing many of the leading causes of death in adulthood, including obesity, smoking, alcohol/drug use, suicide, cancer, and heart disease. Since the original ACE study was published, more than 20 years ago, research has continued to demonstrate the link between trauma and physical, psychological, emotional, relational, and spiritual health (van der Kolk, 2015; Courtois & Ford, 2016). One follow-up study even found that the experience of six or more ACEs as a child decreased life expectancy by an average of 20 years (Brown et al., 2009).

While the link between ACEs and overall health indicates the reality of trauma as a health epidemic, this association does not mean that individuals who have a history of trauma are doomed to inevitably poor behavioral and health outcomes. This research does indicate, however, that clinicians must be able to recognize the influence of adverse events, even long after the trauma has ended. Increased ACE scores represent a risk for health issues related to the leading causes of death in the United States (Espeleta, Brett, Ridings, Leavens, & Mullins, 2018), but other, non–life-threatening conditions may also develop from the physical toll of trauma. The impact of trauma on one's physical health can increase the risk of ailments such as fibromyalgia, chronic pain, and autoimmune diseases (Burke, Finn, McGuire, & Roche, 2017; Voinov, Richney, & Bailey, 2013). Clinicians must be able to accurately recognize the signs and symptoms of trauma in order to provide attentive care, prevent misdiagnosis, and foster early intervention. Additionally, the professional practice of screening clients on their ACE score allows clinicians to gain a sense of the client's history while also prompting the client to begin to identify the resiliency traits that helped him or her survive adverse situations. In this way, trauma or adverse life events can be recognized early in the therapeutic process and aspects of resiliency can be incorporated as strengths in treatment.

A Strengths-Based Perspective in Trauma Work: Integrating a Positive Conceptualization

As discussed previously, the *DSM-5* is utilized as a diagnostic standard in determining which events in a person's life qualify as "traumatic," and the *DSM-5* also defines the symptoms consistent with clinical, trauma-related disorders, such as PTSD and ASD. However, utilizing this narrow definition of trauma raises several questions for clinicians. What are the professional and ethical implications of a clinician describing or labeling something as "traumatic" if it doesn't meet the explicit *DSM-5* standards? On the other hand, how might the clinician's refusal to define an individual's painful experience as a trauma impact the therapeutic alliance and the client's feelings? If using solely the *DSM-5*, which is grounded in a medical orientation, how can a clinician see beyond a medical model of symptom evaluation and effectively connect with and understand the holistic experience of the trauma survivor? These questions are critical for trainees and seasoned clinicians to consider. Although insurance reimbursement necessitates the medical model presented by the *DSM-5* to assign diagnoses to clients in order to receive payment for treatment services, an emphasis on the diagnosis alone may **pathologize** (focus exclusively on deficits/symptoms) clients and infer illness to their experience, which is often in contrast to the perspective that symptoms are also representative of psychological survival responses.

To counter pathologizing tendencies, various mental health disciplines advocate for a holistic view of the client, which includes the wellness model in counseling, positive systems perspective in marriage and family therapy, strengths-based framework in social work, and a positive psychology approach. A **strengths–based approach** considers the client's resiliency, which comprises internal and external resources that contribute to one's ability to heal and often manifests as one's intrinsic motivation, determination, and courage not only to survive, but to thrive despite harrowing circumstances. Clinicians, therefore, need to be skilled in helping the client to view his or her symptoms as normative responses to extremely abnormal events (traumas) while also highlighting the client's strengths and empowering personal resiliency resources as part of the therapeutic process.

Many clients have residual negative effects of their trauma histories, but this should not overshadow the reality that they have demonstrated incredible strengths just to survive their past. In fact, many symptoms that a client now experiences as problematic served, at one time, as a method for coping that helped him or her survive horrific circumstances (Keck et al., 2017). A transformational perspective for trauma clinicians is to view clients as individuals who are doing the best they can at any given point in their healing journey. Unconditional positive regard from clinicians and a hopeful outlook for a client's ability to thrive can help counter much of the shame and despair that accompanies trauma. In fact, one of the central roles of effective clinicians is to bear witness to the strengths demonstrated by clients, not only in their tenacious survival of the traumatic experience, but also in their courageous willingness to return to the pain and work through difficult memories as part of their heroic journey towards healing (Schmelzer, 2018). From a strengths-based perspective, trauma-related symptoms may be reframed as survival reactions to overwhelming events; in other words, they once functioned as safety-ensuring, regulating, or soothing forms of coping during the trauma but eventually, over time, became problematic (Briere, Hodges, & Godbout, 2010; Fisher, 2017; Thompson-Hollands, Jun, & Sloan, 2017).

Trauma Work in Practice: Reframing Symptoms as Survival Resources

For my client, Judy, hypervigilance once provided her with a necessary and protective way to stay "on guard" and avoid an encounter with her perpetrator or someone she perceived to be similar to her perpetrator. However, as Judy's hypervigilance continued to dominate her attention and generalized into many of her interpersonal interactions, Judy arrived for counseling experiencing pronounced anxiety and increasing relational conflict and disconnect. While hypervigilance is now considered part of her symptomology within a PTSD diagnosis, my work with Judy offered her a perspective in which hypervigilance is normalized as an important tool she once needed in the past to survive the trauma. For Judy, her trauma recovery will include a "laying down" of this defense as she begins to recognize and accept that the danger has passed. Through Judy's case, the needed purpose of survival responses to trauma, like hypervigilance, is clear, but equally apparent is the problematic evolution of these mechanisms as they persist over time.

The Trauma Lens: Developing a Holistic Perspective

Although research has provided ample evidence of the profound impact of trauma, there is still a tendency to overlook a person's possible history of trauma and narrowly focus on the individual's behaviors and symptoms, such as seeing only the person's gaps in relationship skills or tendencies towards tantrums and extreme dysregulation. Instead of exclusively centering attention on the problematic behaviors, the clinician can utilize a **trauma lens**, which involves the recognition of an individual's unprocessed trauma as the source that fuels symptoms, exacerbates relationship challenges, perpetuates negative affect, and drives dysregulated states. Behaviors and emotions like these often represent the outpouring of an internal disequilibrium that a traumatic experience has created and may not simply represent poor decision-making, psychopathology, or mental illness.

A trauma lens requires a holistic approach for case conceptualization that extends beyond behaviors and symptoms alone. With a trauma lens in place, the clinician can view the client within a broader context and evaluate the client's external systems, such as the family, community, and culture, while also considering the interplay of physical, mental, and emotional internal systems. The clinician must also consider the client's spiritual well-being in regard to the impact of trauma and appropriately incorporate the client's spirituality as a strength and resource in the healing process (Whitford, Olver, & Peterson, 2008). A trauma lens considers the complexity of individual trauma reactions and recognizes trauma's ripple effects on families and communities.

Conclusion

The complexity of trauma work is immediately apparent as one attempts to differentiate between the various types of trauma and considers the diverse ways in which trauma-related problems develop and emerge. Trauma clinicians must have an accurate awareness of the pervasiveness of trauma and its ubiquitous nature in the mental health field. Clinicians must also hold a strong understanding of the diverse definitions and conceptualizations of trauma and be able to clearly identify the various concepts in regard to overlaps and distinctions. A working knowledge of trauma is only the beginning as trauma clinicians aim to integrate trauma considerations with physical health, reframe symptoms as survival responses, and provide care through a holistic trauma lens.

Between the nuanced trauma conceptualizations and across the spectrum of symptom/ strengths perspectives, a balance exists. Much like walking across a beam, our work as trauma clinicians often involves an incredible balancing act: if we lean too far to one side or the other, footing is lost, and we step off the beam. Effective trauma clinicians rely on a balanced view that considers the client's symptomology alongside strengths, systemic context alongside internal resourcefulness, and personal responsibility alongside the crippling impacts of trauma. As you consider the material presented in this chapter, reflect on your tendencies towards any aspects of imbalance in trauma work. The dynamics of trauma work are vast, and the clinician's careful consideration, reflection, and integration begin right at the start with a comprehensive conceptualization of trauma.

KEYWORD ASSESSMENT

Write definitions in your own words, describe the concept's role in trauma work, list any questions, or make notes of important aspects that you want to remember.

Type 1 (Single-Event) Trauma

Type 2 (Complex) Trauma

Developmental Trauma

Toxic Stress

Adversity

Pathologize

Strengths-Based Approach

Trauma Lens

EXPERIENTIAL ACTIVITIES: INTERACTING WITH THE CHAPTER CONTENT

Expand Self-Awareness

1) Complete and score your Adverse Childhood Events (ACEs) inventory. (The ACEs inventory can be found online.)

Expand Knowledge

2) Using your existing knowledge of historical or well-known figures, identify various individuals who portray examples of type 1 and type 2 trauma, developmental trauma, normative stress, toxic stress, and adversity.

Expand Skills

3) Using a blank piece of paper, list the various symptoms of PTSD and ASD down the middle of the page. On one side of the symptom, identify a functional problem that this symptom creates for the individual. Then, on the other side, write a normalizing perspective of the symptom that identifies ways in which the behavior served as a needed survival response during a traumatic event. Make an additional note of how this survival response might be viewed from a strengths-based perspective in trauma work. For example:

Functional Problem	Symptom	Survival Response/Strength
Unable to develop relationships	Hypervigilance Protection	Strong observation skills

SUPERVISORY DISCUSSION: SHARING PERSONAL INSIGHTS AND IDENTIFYING AREAS FOR GROWTH

1) Sharing to the degree with which you are comfortable, discuss your experience of completing the ACEs inventory. What insights did you gain and what was the process like for you?

2) In the section of the chapter headed "A strengths-based perspective in trauma work," the first paragraph presents several questions for clinicians. What are your thoughts and responses to these questions? How do these questions reflect the importance of maintaining a balanced perspective in trauma work as described in the conclusion of the chapter?

3) A strengths-based perspective is applicable not only to clients but also to clinicians. Identify and discuss at least three of your strengths that will be resources for you as you grow into a trauma clinician.

4) Describe how your conceptualization of trauma has changed as a result of your learning.

The Clinician: Reflexive Practice and Professional Development in Trauma Work

Imagine the type of person that you envision to be the most ideal trauma clinician. Try to identify the specific traits you notice about this person and the qualities that are most outstanding to you. Now, consider how you believe this person developed into such an exceptional clinician. What did this person have to learn? What milestones and steps had to be achieved? What did this person have to overcome? What personal characteristics did this person demonstrate and how were those characteristics fostered?

For many of us, the professionally mature, seasoned, expert trauma clinician is easy to imagine. We pay attention to the attributes that make clinicians like these so exceptional; however, we often neglect to consider the process by which the individual came to be such an outstanding helper. In truth, proficient trauma clinicians didn't walk into their first session as experts. They started out as novice trainees who grappled with the concepts and struggled to understand the therapeutic relationship. These clinicians had to engage in a *process* of development that involved both personal and professional transformation and growth.

Professional development is exactly as it sounds: an evolutionary journey of developmental stages that build on learning and self-reflection. For beginning trauma clinicians, recognizing the process by which their professional development will occur is paramount. While mastery of academic concepts in trauma work is critical, reflection and self-awareness are truly the means by which the process of development is most enhanced. In this chapter, the use of reflexive practice is presented as a framework for enhancing self-awareness, the personal motivations and expectations that bring an individual to trauma work are explored, and the common fears and self-doubt that often accompany the process of professional growth are discussed.

The Development of Self-Awareness: Using Reflexive Practice as a Professional Skill

Jung (1954) described the development of self-awareness as a process in which a wholeness between conscious and unconscious is achieved. For trauma clinicians, developing self-awareness is not a task with the possibility of completion; it is an ongoing process in which one continually seeks to have a greater understanding and appreciation of one's thoughts, emotions, and behavior. This ongoing process of internal self-exploration is referred to as **reflexive practice**, and it is a skill required for competent and ethical trauma work.

While there are many uses and benefits of reflexive practice, one critical function operates within the dynamics of the therapeutic relationship. Reflexive practice is the lens through which clinicians are able to identify transference and countertransference, effectively integrate multiculturalism into the therapeutic process, and avoid assumptions or personal judgments about clients (Rosin, 2015). While the identification of and appropriate response towards the issue of transference and countertransference is essential in working with traumatized clients, the clinician's self-awareness is the fundamental prerequisite for understanding this phenomenon. In many ways, self-awareness, propelled by reflexive practice, is the bedrock for the clinician's ability to manage his or her responsibility for the interpersonal complexities within the therapeutic relationship.

Framework of Reflexive Practice

The concepts developed by Schon (1983) and Wong-Wylie (2010) provide a helpful framework for trauma clinicians as they engage in the process of reflexive practice. Clinicians are encouraged to consider three domains in reflective practice: 1) *reflection-in-action*, which refers to the process by which clinicians make professional decisions in trauma work, 2) *reflection-on-action*, which refers to the clinician's reflection on the outcome of decision and what he/she might have done or will do differently in the future, and 3) *reflection-on-self*, which refers to reflection on the clinician's personal thoughts and feelings that influence professional reactions and attitudes (Rosin, 2015). In short, trauma clinicians must reflect on the way they use information to make clinical decisions, the way these decisions impact the situation, the way their personal factors influence each step of the process, and then, finally, consider the overall professional lessons learned. This reflexive practice enhances the clinician's ability to be effective in the therapeutic process while simultaneously enhancing the value and knowledge of self.

The third aspect of reflexive practice, *reflection-on-self*, represents the most intensive exercise towards self-awareness as it involves deeper reflection on personal beliefs and emotions. Clinicians must be willing to reflect on their own thinking patterns, automatic assumptions, and how one thought leads to another. What we believe about a situation highly influences what we decide to do and how we respond, so exploring one's own "mental map" of a situation is critical for understanding the decision-making process.

Sometimes, however, the "mental map" that we've used in past situations doesn't quite align with the current circumstance. Overwhelming feelings of shock, judgment, or confusion at client stories or at the unexpected behaviors or manifestations of trauma from the client may indicate that our "mental map" has just encountered uncharted territory, and our internal compass is spinning as it attempts to regain an understanding of this contradiction to our assumptions. In moments like this, the clinician is faced with a dilemma in which a previously held belief about the world, self, or others does not reconcile with a presenting problem or situation. Consequently, a mental change in the clinician must take place in order to accommodate the conflicting information. This paradigm shift can sometimes create feelings of disequilibrium and anxiety for the clinician as he or she engages in the process of cognitively reorienting to understand a person, situation, or experience in a totally new way.

These challenges to one's beliefs and personal perspectives—the understanding of an experience—can, at times, be a highly emotional process as the clinician sorts through the rationale for why he or she has a particular belief or assumption. When the tension of this process becomes troubling, trainees may feel the desire to avoid this aspect of self-reflection in order to move away from these challenging incongruities (Rosin, 2015). However, when clinicians are willing to explore self in conjunction with the internal challenges that trauma often brings up, the result is an enhanced ability to work with this population and an opportunity to grow as a person.

Trauma Work in Practice: A Trainee's Experience in Reflexive Practice

Mary is a beginning trauma trainee, and she is asked by her clinical supervisor to conduct a trauma screening inventory for a new client at her site. Mary's client is a 40-year-old Hispanic male, who works as a loan officer in a prestigious local firm. When the client requested counseling services, he described excessive alcohol and substance use as his primary concern, and he did not list any problems overtly connected with a history of trauma. When Mary begins the intake with her new client, she decides in the session to go against the instructions of her supervisor and exclude the trauma screening inventory as, from her perspective, it did not appear relevant for this client's case or presenting problem.

Later in supervision, Mary's supervisor encourages her to engage in reflexive practice about what occurred with the client. Initially, Mary feels highly defensive with her supervisor and does not want to discuss why she didn't administer the trauma screen. Mary struggles to find logic to verbalize her choice to exclude the screener, other than that she has very strong feelings and intuition that this client *did not need* a trauma screening, as trauma is clearly not the problem. Recognizing the powerful dynamic of Mary's feelings in the situation, the supervisor facilitates the reflexive process by helping Mary to explore her feelings and her beliefs about her client, his presenting problem, and the possibility of a trauma history.

Since Mary's strong feelings are the most powerful force for her in the moment, Mary begins with the emotional aspect of *reflection-on-self*, and she realizes that she feels embarrassed to even subtly suggest to her client that trauma could be a contributing factor in his current substance abuse problem. As Mary searches for the internal source that is informing her emotional reaction, she is able to recognize a long-held assumption that she has about the types of people who do and do not have trauma histories. Mary explains to her supervisor that she has a very hard time accepting the idea that a wealthy, successful man could be vulnerable to the impacts of trauma. Through the supervision process, Mary begins to recognize her very rigid ideas of what kinds of people *should* and *should not* experience PTSD, and she leaves supervision feeling frustrated with her supervisor, rattled by her personal revelations, and suddenly doubtful of her abilities to help this client.

In the following week's supervision, Mary's supervisor picks back up with Mary in her journey though reflexive practice. This week Mary feels less defensive and more open to considering the powerful and potentially hazardous impact of her beliefs about trauma, and she has the courage to discuss with her supervisor how she felt at the close of the last supervision session. After further implementing *reflection-on-self* by identifying her personal cognitive and affective influences in the situation, Mary fully engages in *reflection-in-action* and describes her decision-making process regarding her choice to exclude the trauma assessment, which includes her affective rationale in the moment, the assumptive reasons behind her inner disagreement with her supervisor's instructions, and the biased information she used in the session to guide her decision.

Finally, Mary moves to *reflection-on-action*, which requires her to consider the impacts of this decision, which include both her relationship with her client as well as her relationship with her supervisor, and what she might do differently in a similar situation in the future. Though personally challenging, the elements of reflexive practice offered Mary a powerful window into self-awareness, highlighted critical lessons in trauma work, and resulted in new-found professional goals in her development. Mary's experience illustrates the framework of reflexive practice as it targets reflection in the clinical decision-making process, the impacts and takeaways of these decisions, and the role of personal cognitive and affective factors that influence the process of both making and experiencing these decisions.

Motivations to Pursue Trauma Work: Choosing to Sit With Pain

Applying the reflexive process as a framework for developing self-awareness as a trauma clinician is helpful, but it is sometimes challenging to know where to begin in exploring oneself. Usually, the most helpful place to start is right where you are, which is at the beginning of your career in trauma work. The very first professional decision you made in this field was the choice to embrace trauma work and commit to competent practice. However, this decision did not formulate out of thin air. Trauma work is rigorous, challenging, and sometimes overwhelming, and yet, something intrinsic and powerful drew you to this specialty and will sustain you across your years in the field.

Corey and Corey (2003) describe a variety of motivations or personal needs that often contribute to one's decision to pursue a mental health discipline. These motivations include the desire to make an impact in the world, the need to care for others, the wish for prestige and expert status, the need to be needed, the desire to control others, the wish for flexibility and professional diversity, and the need to satisfy one's own personal trauma vicariously through the recovery of others. While many of the motivational factors are altruistic, some are also personal in nature.

At first glance, trainees and clinicians tend to dismiss the idea that a personal need was a central aspect that drew them to trauma work, but in reality, there is a piece of ourselves that finds fulfillment in this specialty area of practice. These personal needs, in and of themselves, are neither positive nor negative, as each brings a unique strength as well as areas of potential hazards to clinicians. The key to competent practice and self-awareness is not to deny that these needs exist within ourselves; rather, the goal is to accept, understand, and manage these needs. For example, the trauma clinician whose central desire is to positively impact the world strives to empower others and is able to offer especially powerful inspiration, passion, and hope to his clients. However, how does this clinician respond when the world doesn't seem to be changing and more and more horrific traumas find their way into his office? The blow of disillusionment may be especially profound for this individual, putting him at risk for burnout or compassion fatigue.

In the same way, the clinician who is driven to the field with the need to mend her own psychological wounds from a past trauma by focusing on the trauma of others, rather than her own, also brings both strengths and potential hazards to the session. The **wounded healer** is a concept in the trauma field that refers to a clinician who holds a personal history of trauma. Often, the personal experience of trauma deeply motivates an individual to help others through similar kinds of pain, and these clinicians may have the greatest levels of empathy and understanding for their client's journey. These clinicians are able to draw from their own painful past as well as from their recovery experience in a way that appreciates clients' suffering and compassionately guides clients through their own healing journey (Zerubavel & Wright, 2012). However, clinicians with this motivation are at risk for operating as an impaired professional if they have not fully processed their trauma. With unhealed trauma wounds, client stories may trigger strong emotional responses in these clinicians, and this type of countertransference can potentially hijack the therapeutic process as the clinician begins to use the client's story as a surrogate for his or her own. Trauma clinicians must be acutely aware of how their personal motivations for entering the field impact them as professionals.

Paralleling development across the lifespan, professionals change and grow, and the personal motivator that drives a clinician towards trauma work today may evolve and transform as he or she also personally and professionally matures. Consequently, reflexive practice on the personal decision to remain engaged in trauma work is a self-reflection process that must be revisited periodically during one's professional career. This practice not only ensures client safety through the clinician's depth of self-awareness, it also serves as a positive force towards maintaining career satisfaction.

Self-Doubt and Trauma Work: Navigating Through the Growing Pains

When I was a young adolescent, I remember waking up in the middle of night, crying with agonizing pain in my legs. My parents empathized but reassured me that I was simply experiencing growing pains and that, while extremely painful, this sensation was a normative part of the physical process of growing up. For mental health professionals, a similar parallel exists as our **professional growing pains** may take the form of self-doubt in our professional abilities, manifest as anxiety about facing traumatic content with our clients, or emerge through feelings of guilt for not being able to help everyone in the way we think we should. For trauma clinicians and trainees, who encounter some of the darkest corners of human existence, this labor of development can be especially arduous.

Becoming proficient in trauma work is challenging in a variety of ways. Trainees must be willing to engage in rigorous academic learning, submit to evaluation through supervision, fully embrace the unique nature of the therapeutic relationship in trauma cases, and continually press further into the journey of self-awareness (Pierce, 2016). Each of these aspects of professional development can be significantly anxiety-evoking, and trainees (as well as seasoned clinicians) often find themselves asking themselves questions like: "Can I do this? Am I enough for my clients? Do I have what it takes to help facilitate the process of trauma recovery?"

Professional growth generates both anxiety and joy as we are confronted with our own limitations while simultaneously feeling new confidence in our clinical skills and therapeutic potential. In the process of professional development, trainees must be willing to acknowledge and accept the emotional spectrum of this process, which can swing from crippling feelings of professional self-doubt to the exhilaration of witnessing another person heal, recover, and thrive. Much like a pendulum, beginning clinicians often vacillate between feeling professionally competent and empowered to feeling very doubtful of their capabilities and inner strength (Pierce, 2016). Professional growth is birthed out of reflection and moving through the tension of these extreme experiences.

As you take on the endeavor of this journey towards becoming a trauma clinician, there will be times in which self-doubt seems to take the wind from your sails. However, when moments like these come, take heart. Worries about one's own capabilities, troubling discoveries in self-awareness, anxieties regarding evaluation, and feelings of isolation are extraordinarily common in the process of professional development. These feelings are, indeed, challenging but normative. Internal challenges and conflicts have the power to either deter us from pressing forward or serve as an existential reminder that "growing pains" are a part of development, empowering us with the awareness that we are on the right track. Simply put, these feelings are signs of professional growth and of impending change.

As emerging trauma clinicians, bravely move forward through the fears of uncertainty and harassing thoughts of self-doubt. Embrace anxiety as a change agent and reflect on what it is like to engage in the unfamiliar and, at times, painful process of positive transformation. On the road to trauma recovery, your clients must courageously do the same as they move through fear and anxiety towards growth and change. May (1983) summarized this process best when he explained,

> Anxiety occurs at the point where some emerging potentiality or possibility faces the individual, some possibility of fulfilling his existence; but this very possibility involves the destroying of present security, which thereupon gives rise to the tendency to deny the new potentiality.
>
> (p. 111)

Trauma recovery moves both clinician and client out of their comfort zones and into uncharted territory, producing growth and transformation.

Conclusion

Becoming an effective trauma clinician is not merely a process of understanding concepts, applying theories, and implementing interventions; professional development is a journey of growth for the whole person of the clinician. This process involves continually engaging in reflexive practice in efforts to achieve increased self-awareness, understanding one's reasons for commitment to this work, and embracing the existential challenges that come alongside personal and professional growth. As you go through this text, these central principles will have a place in every chapter and will accompany every new idea that you encounter. Understanding the process by which you will become a competent trauma clinician is as important as what you will learn along the way.

KEYWORD ASSESSMENT

Write definitions in your own words, describe the concept's role in trauma work, list any questions, or make notes of important aspects that you want to remember.

Professional Development

Reflexive Practice

Reflection-in-Action

Reflection-on-Action

Reflection-on-Self

Wounded Healer

Professional Growing Pains

EXPERIENTIAL ACTIVITIES: INTERACTING WITH THE CHAPTER CONTENT

Expand Self-Awareness

1) Review the list of personal motivations for pursuing trauma work and reflect on which two motivations you believe to be most influential for you at this time in your development. Identify at least three strengths as well as two potential professional cautions that can be associated with each of your motivations.

Expand Knowledge

2) On a piece of paper, draw a rope like those used in a game of tug-of-war, with a flag in the center. At one end of the rope, identify at least two ways that you are currently experiencing professional growing pains. At the other end of the rope, list the ways in which these growing pains can serve a positive purpose in your professional development. Lastly, mark the position of the rope's flag as a reflection of which side is currently "pulling" the greatest influence within you.

Expand Skills

3) Mary's case in the chapter illustrates the use of reflexive practice for professional development in trauma work. Using your own personal experience or by imagining a fictitious situation, think of a clinical experience in which you were faced with a difficult circumstance or decision in trauma work. Apply the three domains of reflexive practice and reflect on your clinical experience through each element of this framework.

SUPERVISORY DISCUSSION: SHARING PERSONAL INSIGHTS AND IDENTIFYING AREAS FOR GROWTH

1) Discuss the insights you gained about your motivations for pursuing trauma work and describe how these motivations can potentially influence your practice both positively and negatively.

2) By reflecting more on the "'tug-of-war" activity, describe how you can manage your professional growing pains on your developmental journey. What do you need in order to overcome feelings of anxiety, self-doubt, guilt, or excessive responsibility?

3) Return to the activity on reflexive practice and discuss your insights or questions about the framework. How can you personally use this framework to expand your self-awareness in trauma work? Which aspect of the framework might be especially challenging for you?

4) In the case example from the chapter, Mary realized some hidden assumptions that she held about the types of people she believed *should* and *should not* have a trauma history. Consider areas in which you might also hold biased assumptions regarding trauma. How might these biases impact your work as a trauma clinician? How can you go about uncovering personal areas of hidden bias to bring into your awareness?

Chapter 4

Parallel Process: Risks and Rewards in Trauma Work

If you travel through the California wilderness to Yosemite National Park and hike the Mist Trail, you will find yourself on a quest to discover Vernal Falls. This 317-foot, strikingly beautiful waterfall cascades over a cliff with power and elegance. However, in order to catch a glimpse of this natural wonder, you must trek one and a half miles, uphill almost the entire way. I remember the awe I felt during my own hike up the trail when I finally viewed the full glory of the waterfall, but I also recall how very challenging the climb was for me. While the Mist trail is moderately strenuous anyway, at the time of my adventure, I was also experiencing a medical condition that made the journey extra challenging and laborious. I was committed to witnessing the magical beauty of the waterfall with my own eyes, but I also realized that this choice required me to commit to some sacrifices of comfort and to persevere through intense physical and mental challenges. In the end, I can attest that the risks of the climb were worth the reward of beholding something truly remarkable, and in trauma work, the same principle rings true.

For many of us, our choice to pursue trauma work is propelled from a perspective that deeply values the beauty of the healing and recovery process. We are in this for the final outcome! Our optimism and trust in the therapeutic process lends us strength and hope to keep going through the profound hazards and hardships that intrinsically accompany this important work. While the rewarding aspects of trauma work should always remain within our sights, we must also acknowledge, honor, and attend to the challenges that we face as professionals. When we take a step back and reflect on the reality that the hope of healing over trauma is inherently coupled with risks and difficulties, we are able to recognize the powerful parallel process that occurs between clinician and client. In the same way that our clients commit to the arduous journey of growth beyond trauma, we, too, find ourselves facing similar challenges that involve knowing and monitoring self, maintaining self-care to keep going, and holding the perspective of hope as a beacon throughout the quest.

In this chapter, the dynamic of professional risks and rewards is discussed as we address the potential occupational hazards and then explore the preventive and protective measures for these challenges. While emotional and psychological risks are inherent when providing care in the aftershocks of trauma, this chapter also highlights the powerful opportunities for rewarding experiences and positive outcomes for the professional. For client and clinician alike, the choice to engage in trauma work presents many challenges but also offers opportunities to discover tremendous meaning and life changing growth.

Occupational Risks: Considering the Strain of the Journey

Trauma work changes us. This specialty area of mental health practice can deepen our appreciation for the good in life but also exposes us to a cumulative amount of human suffering. For those who are willing to enter into the heart of pain, the price of this work can be significant if not carefully managed. In trauma work, clinicians must be ever mindful of the signs and impacts of vicarious traumatization, compassion fatigue, and burnout.

Vicarious Traumatization

Those who personally experience or witness trauma are not the only ones who sometimes suffer the negative consequences that stem from traumatic events. While a person may not be directly involved in a traumatic event, **indirect trauma exposure**, which occurs when a person hears trauma stories and feels compassion for those who are physically, mentally, or psychologically wounded, can be significantly powerful in an individual's life, and this phenomenon should not be overlooked or underestimated. The ripple effect of trauma can impact family members, friends, rescue workers, first responders, and the communities surrounding trauma survivors (Burnett, 2017). For trauma clinicians, this indirect exposure is one of the most significant occupational hazards, and it is now included in the *DSM-5* as a qualifier for criterion A of the PTSD diagnosis: "experiencing repeated or extreme exposure to aversive details of the traumatic event" (APA, 2013, p. 271).

McCann and Pearlman (1990) developed the term **vicarious traumatization** (also referred to secondary traumatic stress) as a descriptor reference for the negative changes in professionals that emerge from caring for trauma survivors and from being directly exposed to traumatic accounts. These troubling, intrinsic changes, which are hallmark characteristics of vicarious traumatization, can include shifts in the clinician's thoughts and beliefs concerning trust, safety, power, esteem, and intimacy. The painful realities shared in trauma narratives can trigger the clinician's own trauma history and also distort the lens of relative safety through which he or she views the world (Killian, 2008). Professionals who hear about tragedy each workday may experience an altered perspective in which they begin to believe trauma is everywhere all the time. Trauma clinicians may also personalize the details of clients' traumas and wonder if such events could potentially happen in their own lives.

Trauma Work in Practice: A Professional Personalization of a Client's Trauma

During the early part of my career, I vividly recall listening to a client describe how her daughter was fondled by a male babysitter. The pit in my stomach grew and seemed to do back flips as I pictured this happening to my own children, and on the spot, I decided never to hire a male babysitter. My fear spiraled, and I began to wonder if molestation might happen with a female babysitter, which eventually snowballed into larger questions about my child's safety at sleepovers or friends' homes. I ached at the thought that there might be danger everywhere, and the drowning sense of potential threat left me feeling fearful and helpless. As I waded through my thoughts and fears, I finally mentally returned to the present moment of my session, and I realized that I had not heard a word that my client said for the past five minutes. The power of personalizing trauma, which was experienced through a moment of vicarious traumatization seen in my sudden hypervigilance, had hijacked my thoughts, consumed my internal resources, and, consequently, left me unavailable for my client.

Vicarious traumatization challenges our previous assumptions about the world, which requires clinicians to restructure their existing belief systems and recalibrate in order to accommodate the realities of trauma found within clients' stories (Lu, Zhou, & Pillay, 2017). As discussed in Chapter 3, one utilizes a "mental map," also referred to as a cognitive schema, to understand the world. Cognitive schemas provide the structure and content for one's internal thoughts, hidden assumptions, and underlying thinking patterns, and schemas are constantly enhanced and reinforced through learning and experiences. In the fallout of trauma, assumptions of safety are shattered, and clients must make adjustments to their cognitive schemas as they attempt to integrate their traumatic experiences into their belief systems and life narratives. Representing a parallel process, both the client and clinician are confronted with the unfairness, uncertainty, and depth of evil unveiled in traumatic events, and individuals may struggle to find understanding and firm footing beneath themselves in a world where such atrocities are possible. For clinicians, the challenge lies in the balance of adjusting our cognitive schemas to make room for the realities of trauma while also protecting our thinking patterns from ingraining a vicariously traumatized perspective.

When vigilance for vicarious traumatization is not maintained, clinicians are at risk for developing cognitive distortions often characterized by a hyper-focus on the dangers within the world and/or chronic feelings of depression or anxiety. These symptoms may develop suddenly or creep in over time. For me, I became aware of my vicarious traumatization when I began to have powerful and very troubling nightmares that reflected themes of my internal conflict surrounding two of my client cases. The dreams alerted me to the deep feelings of powerlessness and rage that I was experiencing in conjunction with my client's trauma. As I continued to reflect, I began to recognize my degree of vicarious trauma and its impacts on my ability to work and engage in the therapeutic relationship.

The impact of vicarious traumatization on clinicians may range from brief but significant moments of emotional and psychological pain to professionally and sometimes personally devastating and debilitating outcomes consistent with the *DSM* criteria for this type of trauma. In order to positively manage this aspect of our work, each clinician must mindfully reflect on his or her own beliefs and consider the meaning and implications of adjusting one's cognitive schemas. These adjustments to personal cognitive schemas often involve accepting the reality of suffering while also recognizing, celebrating, and internalizing the safety and joyful experiences that also exist in the world.

Vicarious traumatization is a risk factor for all mental health professionals, but certain factors increase such risk. Some of these heightened risk variables include status as a beginning clinician, younger age with less exposure to distress, work with traumatized children or child victims, caseloads with a high proportion of traumatized clients, lack of trauma-informed supervision, personal trauma history (especially childhood trauma), insufficient training in trauma work skills and treatment, deficient organizational support, and problematic personal coping with stress (Lerias & Byrne, 2003; Shelby, 2019). For clinicians with increased risk for vicarious traumatization, the importance of self-care, self-reflection, and supervision or consultation is all the more vital.

Below is a trauma clinician's self-reflection guide for signs of vicarious traumatization:

- Do I feel physically, mentally, and emotionally unsafe during or after work?
- Am I experiencing ongoing somatic problems (loss of appetite, headaches, chronic fatigue, lowered immune system, ongoing tension in the body, sleeping difficulties, digestion problems, etc.)?

- Do I see danger, evil, and negativity everywhere?
- Am I experiencing increased feelings of depression, anxiety, or irritability?
- Am I withdrawing from my positive relationships or experiencing increased conflict with my spouse/partner, family, friends, children, co-workers?
- Do I have intrusive or reoccurring thoughts or images of my client's trauma or envision myself within a similar type of traumatic situation?
- Am I avoiding trauma reminders through either active or passive efforts with my clients or in my personal life?
- Am I increasing my use of alcohol or other substances as a way to adjust my mood or thoughts?
- Are my thoughts increasingly negative, unhelpful, or irrational?
- Am I experiencing a deepening loss of hope?

The Intersection of Personal Trauma, Vicarious Trauma, and Countertransference

Vicarious traumatization can occur for any trauma clinician, regardless of a personal history of trauma. However, clinicians who have their own trauma history or who have been significantly impacted by previous vicarious trauma may be especially vulnerable to the risks of additional trauma exposure, even indirect exposure. Commonly discussed in all mental health practice, **countertransference** is a broad term that refers to various clinician reactions to the client, and these conscious or unconscious reactions have the potential to positively or negatively influence the therapeutic relationship. Historically, countertransference has been referred to as the clinician's conscious or unconscious reactions to the client, the client's situation, or the dynamics of the therapeutic alliance (Cureton & Clemens, 2015). Countertransference may be cultivated by emotionally vulnerable or psychologically conflicted areas within the clinician, and while some degree of countertransference is inevitable in any type of mental health work, countertransference can serve as "both a hindrance and a potential aid in treatment" (Gelso & Hayes, 2002, p. 270).

When countertransference is unmanaged or the clinician is unaware of its presence or influence, the therapeutic relationship can be negatively impacted. Many clinicians enter the field with their own personal history of trauma or vicarious trauma, and while some of these clinicians may have positively processed and overcome their trauma, others may have trauma that remains unrecognized and/or unprocessed. When clinicians bring in unprocessed trauma, clients and their traumatic experiences may trigger countertransference issues that have the potential to "leak" into the session, potentially affecting the client's treatment or exacerbating the clinician's risk for vicarious traumatization and resurgence of trauma symptoms.

A clinician's similar experience to a client's story may trigger intrusive thoughts and feelings from the clinician's past and inadvertently impact the ways in which the clinician interacts with the client. For example, countertransference can cause a "silencing response," in which the clinician subtly discourages the client from sharing painful material (Gentry, Baranowsky, & Dunning, 2002). Issues of unresolved trauma may also lead clinicians towards distorted compulsions to vicariously achieve their own healing through attempting to "fix" the client. Countertransference may impact the clinician's priorities and influence treatment in a way that attends to the clinician's psychological desires rather than the client's needs. The reexperiencing feature of trauma may also impact a clinician's choices in treatment. In these situations, a clinician may consciously or unconsciously surround him- or herself with trauma cases as a way to manifest and reexperience aspects of his or her own trauma. Undoubtedly, a clinician's unprocessed trauma can present a serious ethical and professional dilemma, which requires ongoing reflection and, when needed, personal trauma-focused treatment for the clinician.

Countertransference is also frequently connected with the use of self-disclosure. Self-disclosure is a therapeutic tool when it is provided purely for the benefit of the client. As an example, a clinician may recognize his client's sense of isolation in trauma, and to attend to this, he might share that he also survived a similar experience. In this situation, self-disclosure emerged out of the parallel process between the client and clinician's experiences. However, self-disclosure becomes dominated by countertransference when the clinician feels an overwhelming urgency to share with the client, redirects the focus of the session towards his or her experience, or provides excessive details that may retraumatize the client (sharing details of personal trauma should *always* be avoided). Under these characteristics, the purpose of self-disclosure is to fulfill the clinician's desire, not to maintain an emphasis on the client's experience.

Aware of the risks associated with countertransference, many beginning clinicians fear that their personal trauma history may hold them back or impede them from effectively working with clients. All clinicians, both beginning and seasoned, must continually reflect and monitor areas and influences of countertransference, especially in highly emotional trauma cases, but a clinician's personal or vicarious trauma history certainly does not necessarily disqualify an individual from providing effective therapeutic services. Clinicians should seek out supervision and personal counseling for any countertransference issues that may impact their ability to provide quality and ethical therapeutic care.

While countertransference certainly presents some risks, this occurrence can also offer opportunities for clinicians to experience enhanced insight into self, the client, relationship patterns, and case conceptualization (Cureton & Clemens, 2015). When clinicians engage in their own healing journey and continually consider areas of potential countertransference, a history of trauma can be transformed from a clinician's area of vulnerability to a clinical asset when working with trauma survivors. These clinicians can provide profound empathy for their clients, hold an enhanced understanding of the power of trauma on various aspects of life, and offer a deep appreciation for the struggle and hope towards recovery.

Compassion Fatigue

In situations of vicarious traumatization, clinicians develop an adoption of trauma-related symptoms as a result of the indirect trauma exposure, but another phenomenon, compassion fatigue, represents an additional occupational hazard. **Compassion fatigue** is characterized by a depletion of empathy, caring, and connection with clients, and these symptoms may manifest as apathy, rigidity, depression, irritability, preoccupation with trauma, anger, numbness, disillusionment, and worthlessness as the clinician feels helpless to stop human suffering (Badger, Royse, & Craig, 2008; Figley, 2002; Hayuni, Hasson-Ohayon, Goldzweig, Sela, & Braun, 2019). Unlike vicarious traumatization, which can occur with any person who is indirectly exposed to trauma, compassion fatigue is specific to helping professionals who lean on the resource of empathy in order to offer facilitative care and therapeutic services (Elwood, Mott, Lohr, & Galovski, 2011). Geoffrion, Morselli, and Guay (2016) summarize: "Ultimately, the therapist who suffers from compassion fatigue has absorbed the emotional weight of his or her professional identity, personal self, and existential state" (p. 272). The experience of compassion fatigue is often profoundly troubling for helping professionals as we feel robbed of our most precious professional values: compassion, empathy, and a desire to care for the hurting.

For me, I became aware of my compassion fatigue when I began to notice a pattern that as soon as I sat down with my client in a session, I started to yawn and feel sudden and extreme boredom, which made my ability to focus on my client very challenging. My pronounced physiological changes were accompanied by mental thoughts of "wishing the session away" as I longed to just get through it and for the day to be over. These and other symptoms of compassion fatigue may lead to impairments in functioning and inhibit relationships for clinicians both professionally and personally.

Compassion fatigue may be influenced by one's professional identity. Professional identity is the combination of one's professional self-image, culture, past experiences, and workplace factors that shape our perceptions and the meaning we attribute to work roles (Skorikov & Vondracek, 2011). The meaning that clinicians attribute to the client's trauma stories as well as their perceived role of responsibility for the client can either increase or decrease the risk for compassion fatigue (Geoffrion et al., 2016). In many ways, the clinician's perceived role in the trauma recovery process becomes the mental filter and compass through which the clinician hears and responds to the needs of the client.

Trauma Work in Practice: The Influence of the Clinician's Self-Perceived Role

Carla was a new trauma clinician, who just began seeing clients last year. Carla believed she was born to help people and, as a result, she was very committed to her clients. Recently, Carla began to provide counseling for several children and adolescents with histories of abuse. At first, Carla experienced tremendous anger and outrage as she read reports about the crimes committed on these children and personally saw some of their bruises. In her heart, she vowed to "undo" the evil that was done to these children as quickly as possible with her own care and compassion. After a month of intense trauma-focused therapy with her clients, Carla realized she was having nightmares of the traumatic stories and was experiencing a depressed mood on most days. Try as she might, Carla felt utterly helpless to stop the universal pain of child abuse, and she turned her anger and outrage inward and blamed herself for not relieving her clients' pain. Carla believed that it was her role and responsibility to stop her clients from hurting, and when this was not accomplished, she felt an increasing sensation of failure. As time went on and these emotions compounded, Carla found herself feeling very little empathy or connection with her clients, and instead of providing safety and attunement to her clients during her sessions, she began to daydream and fantasize about changing careers to a job in which she could just sit alone in front of a computer. Eventually, Carla began to recognize the distortion and impossibility of her perceived professional self-identity, and she slowly identified her symptoms of compassion fatigue and vicarious traumatization. With this self-awareness, Carla was able to share these feelings with her supervisor, who provided her with help, support, and guidance in self-care and in adjusting her views of her professional responsibly in trauma work. Carla's experience is not uncommon, and her situation shares common themes with those of many trauma clinicians.

Carla's case reflects symptoms of both vicarious traumatization as well as compassion fatigue. While a clinician may experience only one of the challenges at a time, very often these experiences co-occur, and the presence of one professional hazard (vicarious traumatization or compassion fatigue) can increase the risk for the other to develop. Unfortunately, almost every helping professional will experience some degree of compassion fatigue throughout his or her career, and clinicians must learn to recognize the signs of compassion fatigue and vicarious traumatization and take proactive steps to attend to these professional challenges.

A trauma clinician's self-reflection guide for signs of compassion fatigue (Mathieu, 2018):

- Do I chronically feel physically, mentally, and emotionally drained?
- Am I struggling to empathize with my clients or remain attuned during sessions?
- Do I dread my sessions or work with certain clients?
- Am I experiencing reduced patience and increased irritability?
- Do I avoid or mentally disconnect from listening to the problems of my spouse/partner, friends, family members, or co-workers?
- Do I feel increased career dissatisfaction or lack of work enjoyment?
- Am I excessively missing work or taking days off?
- Am I experiencing increased sensitivity or numbed sensitivity to emotional content?
- Do I feel increased challenges with intimacy and connection in my personal relationships?
- Do I feel impaired or immobilized to provide care or make clinical decisions with my clients?

Burnout

Alongside vicarious traumatization and compassion fatigue, burnout is another potential professional hazard in the mental health field, although this challenge differs in several ways. **Burnout** can develop without exposure to traumatic stories and can occur in a variety of professional settings (Cieslak et al., 2014). In contrast to compassion fatigue, which is characterized by a draining of empathy and emotional availability, burnout usually has a gradual onset related to the depletion of personal and professional resources that generalize into the workplace and does not particularly emphasize a reduction in compassion exclusively. In burnout, the cumulative stress and exhaustion are directly related to workplace factors, such as long hours, high caseloads, organizational dysfunction, and lack of fairness or rewards (Pelon, 2017).

In an example of burnout, Herman, a veteran trauma clinician, experienced this professional challenge as a caseworker for a nonprofit organization. The organization required Herman to maintain a high-volume caseload, but Herman was acutely aware that there were too few resources to help with the clients' numerous difficult circumstances. After a year of work at his organization, Herman woke up each morning dreading his workday and found he had little motivation to participate in the recreational activities that he used to enjoy during his days off. Eventually, Herman switched jobs to a different organization that had better hours and more resources, and his feelings of burnout quickly decreased.

A trauma clinician's self-reflection guide for signs of burnout:

- Do I feel overworked, tapped out, and consistently stressed?
- Do I resent or feel isolated within my site, organization, and/or from co-workers?
- Do I feel overwhelmed by my workload, consistently behind, or unmotivated to keep up with my tasks?
- Do I ruminate on systemic flaws within my organization and feel unable to facilitate change?
- Do I feel unsupported as a professional or worried about the lack of resources I am able to provide for my clients?
- Do I frequently job search and daydream about other positions, sites, or careers?

Vicarious traumatization, compassion fatigue, and burnout are powerful occupational hazards for the trauma clinician. Unfortunately, many clinicians become discouraged and question their ability to remain in practice when they experience some or all of these professional obstacles. Our degree of personal vulnerability to occupational challenges waxes and wanes across our professional career, and beginning clinicians often benefit from embracing the perspective that learning to manage these aspects is simply another part of their professional growth and development.

Prevention of Occupational Risks: Pacing the Journey

While the occupational challenges in trauma work can be formidable, clinicians can take heart in remembering that these experiences are a normative part of developing as a trauma clinician, and very often, these risks can be mitigated, attended to, and overcome. For every professional hurdle, there is also a preventative and strengthening counterpart. To combat the powerful presence of professional hazards, managing emotional separation, limiting selected exposure, and engaging in self-care can serve as robust mitigating forces.

Maintenance of Emotional Separation

As a trauma specialist, the single most common question that I am asked by others outside the profession is: "How can you bear to listen to such sad stories and be with such hurting people all day?" In response to this question, my answer is simply that I've learned how to become a container rather than a sponge. Sponges soak up, take in, and internalize all the liquid around them until they are heavy and saturated. In contrast, containers become a storehouse for the material, securely holding the material but remaining differentiated from it. Unlike sponges, when containers take on material, the integrity of the container is unchanged and still intact, and the entirety of the material can be safely poured out somewhere else when needed.

When clinicians are able to emotionally and cognitively differentiate from the client, the risk for the clinician to internalize and personalize client's problems is reduced. Beginning clinicians often enter the field as an outpouring of their profound feelings of compassion, and they sometimes fear that an emotional and cognitive boundary will dilute their sensitivity to their client's suffering. Ironically, clinicians who are able to balance differentiation with compassion are frequently more effective, as a certain amount of distance is necessary to maintain objectivity in trauma work (Day, Lawson, & Burge, 2017). Clinicians must be able to extend powerful empathy to others while simultaneously remaining aware that their clients' trauma stories are distinct from their own lives.

The inability to maintain proper emotional separation while extending empathy to trauma survivors has been shown to be a significant risk factor for compassion fatigue development (Compton, 2013; Corcoran, 1989). Mindfully conceptualizing therapeutic empathy means that the clinician aims to deeply understand the client's inner experiences of trauma without directly feeling the *full* weight of the pain (Hayuni et al., 2019). An **appropriate level of emotional separation** refers to the clinician's professional task to find and maintain the balance between being too connected (enmeshed) and too distant (avoidant/detached) with the client. Emotional separation in trauma work also prompts the clinician to refuse assuming *full* credit for successes, such as when a client achieves treatment goals, or taking on the *entire* responsibility for perceived failures, such as when a client drops out of treatment prematurely. This intentional monitoring and adjusting of connection levels serves as a protective factor for clinicians while still allowing for the development of the therapeutic bond.

One way to maintain proper emotional separation is through maintaining the clinician's own emotional regulation. Regulation often involves the clinician's mindful and active management of his or her personal reactions by positively and effectively working through feelings of anger, fear, and sadness towards client stories, towards oneself, and even towards clients. Developing the regulation skills necessary to deal with the emotional intensity of trauma work requires self-awareness and attention to our own levels of emotional arousal. Prikhidko and Swank (2018) suggest several strategies for emotional regulation that clinicians can utilize both inside and outside of sessions, which include progressive muscle relaxation, verbal and non-verbal emotional expression, and the practice of mindfulness. A clinician's attention to his or her own emotional regulation does not hinder his or her ability to engage in emotional communication but rather enhances the clinician's capacity to remain present and connected with the client and effectively convey genuine understanding and compassion.

In addition to regulation, emotional separation is also achieved practically, and the clinician's separation between work and personal life is crucial for prevention of compassion fatigue. Practical, professional behaviors that facilitate separation are accomplished through the consistent use of boundaries. Seemingly small issues, such as allowing clients to text personal cell phones (distinct from an emergency number for use between sessions) or interacting with clients on social media, permeates the lines between personal and professional life and invades the space necessary to take a break from the intensity of trauma work. Clinicians can model nurturance for clients without crossing professional boundaries (Haddock, 2001). Because boundaries benefit the clinician's emotional wellness and potential longevity in the field, they also serve as an important protection for clients.

Emotional separation involves a regulated and differentiated, rather than enmeshed, approach to trauma work, and this goal can also be accomplished through the use of cognitive restructuring strategies. Cognitive restructuring often involves the use of a conceptual "reframe" of the client and/or the situation. A **reframe** refers to the clinician's mental practice of understanding an aspect of therapeutic work from a different perspective in a way that positively enriches the clinician's therapeutic posture, attitude, or disposition. For example, the clinician who views her client as a victim may benefit from reframing the client as a survivor. Likewise, the clinician who is able to see only his client's tragic and horrific background may benefit from reframing the client's current situation as an opportunity for healing and growth. This strategy, along with the other outlined contributors to emotional separation, reduces the risk of vicarious traumatization, compassion fatigue, and burnout.

Limitations to Elected Exposure

With the inherent risks of trauma work, clinicians can also take practical steps to maintain professional and self-care. By mindfully limiting exposure to trauma material outside of work, clinicians are able to actively reduce their volume of cumulative exposure. While everyone has different tolerance levels, my personal motto, *exposure only for the purpose of healing*, reminds me that my trauma exposure with clients is productive and empowered because it is goal-oriented towards growth and healing. This highly contrasts with the disempowered trauma exposure found in violent movies, TV shows, and books. Excessive and needless trauma exposure only increases my levels of cumulative exposure, and over time, my ability to tolerate purposeful trauma exposure, which helps others heal, may be reduced. Recreationally, I mindfully chose activities that promote joy and laughter and carefully screen all potential shows, movies, and books for trauma content in advance. Taking these precautions also means that I watch out for "clickbait" on the Internet and reduce my exposure to trauma-focused news stories by viewing only the headlines.

Elected trauma exposure spans from personal life to professional choices as well. According to a meta-analysis, the risk of compassion fatigue increased significantly for individuals whose caseloads had a high number of trauma cases (Hensel, Ruiz, Finney, & Dewa, 2015). To integrate this finding into professional practice, clinicians can mindfully limit their amount of indirect trauma exposure by dedicating a percentage of their caseload to other specialty areas, such as marriage or skill-building group therapy. Alternatively, clinicians can creatively limit indirect trauma exposure by reducing the number of clients seen each week and exchanging those therapy hours for time to teach courses, present, supervise, or consult. While all mental health work involves some degree of trauma exposure, the emotional intensity of high numbers of trauma cases may not be for everyone. Every clinician should know his or her personal limits and commit to ongoing and consistent self-care.

Efforts in Wellness and Self-Care

Imagine that you are training to run in a marathon; how might you prepare for this monumental task? Certainly, all of us would agree on the critical importance of simple practices like stretching before and after a run, staying hydrated, and creating a schedule that gradually builds up our muscles. While these strategies are common sense for physical training, we somehow have trouble identifying the self-care parallel with the herculean tasks of trauma work. **Self-care** is one of the most essential needs of trauma clinicians, but, unfortunately, it is also often the most neglected and overlooked in practice.

The hazards of vicarious traumatization, compassion fatigue, and burnout all reflect the reality of our own vulnerabilities, which, in turn, points to the critical importance of self-care. As a metaphor, a pitcher of water can be representative of the need for self-preservation within helping professions. From our pitchers, we can only 'pour out' so much care to others before we become empty, risking our own health while also potentially compromising the treatment we provide for clients. We conserve our supply of energy and empathy through healthy boundaries in our personal lives, and we replenish ourselves by participating in activities and relationships outside of work that "fill our pitchers" once again. Keeping a careful eye on our "pitchers," which includes our emotional, psychological, social, and physical health, requires the self-awareness to know what our personal needs are, and which methods are most effective for everyday practice.

Every clinician's needs are unique, and the type of self-care activities that are most helpful and enjoyable are as diverse as the individuals. Clinicians who are extroverted in nature may benefit from activities that offer social elements, while more introverted clinicians may require solitude to recharge. Religious activities often address the community, cultural, and spiritual needs of clinicians, and other activities, like yoga or aerobic exercise such as walks, can aid in physical and cognitive self-care. Simple activities, such as enjoying a glass of wine with a friend or taking time to create something pleasurable, such as a preparing a meal, gardening, or crafting, can profoundly improve feelings of self-care. Many clinicians worry about the time required for self-care activities, but mindfulness, which can be done briefly and at any point during the day, has been shown to potentially prevent compassion fatigue and improve work morale (Silver, Caleshu, Casson-Parkin, & Ormond, 2018).

Because clinical work can be a very isolating profession, self-care also often involves developing and maintaining supportive professional relationships. While there are some mental health positions that provide frequent interaction and strong support from coworkers, many clinical positions offer minimal to absent opportunities for connecting and consulting with colleagues. A central goal for many trauma clinicians is the development of a peer support circle, which may be highly beneficial for connection and community, consultation on difficult cases, and emotional support for the difficult aspects of trauma work. When clinicians are located in rural or remote settings, peer support groups may come from unconventional places, such as professional connections through social media, email lists sponsored through professional organizations, conference and workshop attendance, and membership with local and national organizations, such as the American Psychological Association (APA), the American Counseling Association (ACA), or the National Association of Social Workers (NASW).

A trauma clinician's guide for self-care:

Cognitive: Engage in positive self-talk, gratitude, reflection on the impacts of professional trauma work, and reframe any short-comings or mistakes as "points for growth"

Emotional: Provide oneself a safe space to cry (outside of session) or utilize other means to release grief, express anger, and recognize and attend to dysregulation

Physical: Consistently care for one's physical body through exercise, nutrition, sleep, taking breaks, and good posture

Social: Make time for fun activities, healthy relationships, boundaries, laughter

Spiritual: Engage in existential thought, meaning-making, faith, and hope, and connect with a spiritual or faith-based community for support and connection

Most clinicians rely on self-awareness and reflection as the primary method for assessing their own emotional and psychological health and self-care practices, but there are many helpful assessments that clinicians can also utilize as resources to monitor personal wellness. Possibly the most well-known wellness assessment is the Professional Quality of Life Scale (ProQOL 5, R-V, Stamm, 2010) which evaluates compassion fatigue, burnout, and compassion satisfaction. Additionally, the Maintenance of Emotional Separation Scale (MESS) is a simple tool to measure the clinician's effective ability to differentiate self from others (Corcoran, 1982). Gratitude and daily spiritual experiences can be monitored by the Daily Spiritual Experiences Scale, or DSES (Underwood, 2011; Underwood & Teresi, 2002). Of course, the same self-report measures used with clients for particular symptoms and strengths can also be used for clinicians' self-monitoring (see Appendix A for a list of additional assessments). These measures may be useful for identifying areas that need additional attention and support.

Clinicians are encouraged to identify areas in which they feel depleted or vulnerable in relation to vicarious traumatization, compassion fatigue, and burnout, and should then create a wellness intervention plan that highlights specific short-term and long-term goals (Turner, 2019). Very often, self-care must go beyond pleasurable activities, and clinicians need focused reflection on specific aspects and challenges of trauma work. Focused reflection may involve targeted conversations with a colleague or supervisor, or these replenishing activities may be more creative, artistic, or experiential in nature.

In American culture, self-care is often viewed as an "indulgence" that we occasionally squeeze into our busy lives, similar to the infrequent treat of chocolate cake or a trip to the beach. However, as professionals who work with some of the most challenging cases, we need to reframe self-care from an optional extravagance to a necessary routine discipline. While trauma work inherently requires attention and care to the needs of others, clinicians must also attend to their own needs as part of an ethical obligation necessary to maintain safe and effective practice and avoid becoming an impaired professional (Hendricks, Bradley, Brogan, & Brogan, 2009; Meany-Walen et al., 2018). In trauma work, an impaired professional is unable to provide competent or adequate levels of therapeutic services for clients due to the high degree of interference from personal issues into professional work.

For trauma clinicians, maintaining a priority and focus on our own mental health is a vital aspect of self-care. The trauma found in our clients' stories is unfortunately not the only exposure to pain and adversity we may face in our lives:

> Contagious trauma is a process not of taking on another's trauma, like vicarious trauma, but rather a compounding of trauma, an expansive process that binds the trauma of witnessing with the often unrelated life trauma of the advocate [clinician] themselves, the stress of work or the hostility of friends and neighbors, the deaths of friends or other buried memories.
>
> (Coddington, 2017, p. 71)

Our own stress and adversity can weaken our ability to maintain healthy boundaries and compound the indirect trauma exposure of our clients' narratives. Unfortunately, many of us are better at instructing our clients on self-care than heeding our own advice. Therefore, clinicians must recognize and prioritize their own needs by engaging in personally effective forms of coping to benefit and protect their mental, emotional, physical, social, and spiritual health.

A trauma clinician's reflection activities for professional wellness (Bradley, Whisenhunt, Adamson, & Kress, 2013; Turner, 2019):

- Draw a line to divide a piece of paper in half. On one side, list or draw representations of aspects of trauma work that you have control over or are responsible for, and on the other side, list or draw representations of aspects of trauma work that you do not have control over or are not responsible for.
- Draw your "pitcher" of compassion and internal resources. Similar to a measuring cup, mark the differing levels of fullness and depletion on your pitcher and then identify and list the internal and external signs that you experience at these levels. Draw images or list replenishing sources that refill your pitcher.
- Select or create a container that represents you as a trauma clinician. At the end of the workday, take time to care for your container by rinsing and washing it out as a metaphorical exercise of removing the trauma residue you encountered during the day. Practice mindfulness and relaxation skills as you clean your container.

Occupational Benefits: Discovering Beauty Along the Journey

Although trauma work is accompanied by occupational risks and hazards, many trauma clinicians also experience the powerful personal rewards that emerge from this unique helping profession. The parallel process between client and clinician rises to its peak when clinicians are able to recognize and co-experience the meaningful process and outcomes of this important work. In this way, clinicians are able to benefit from compassion satisfaction, vicarious resiliency, and vicarious posttraumatic growth.

Compassion Satisfaction

On the opposite end of the spectrum from compassion fatigue, compassion satisfaction offers clinicians inspiration and motivation for their work. **Compassion satisfaction** is the joy and sense of fulfillment that comes from the work of helping others, and this sense of satisfaction enriches and contributes to the clinician's well-being (Stamm, 2002). Compassion satisfaction may serve as a counterbalancing factor against compassion fatigue and may play a key role in career longevity (Anderson, Papazoglou, & Collins, 2018; Pelon, 2017). According to Radey and Figley (2007), whether work with trauma survivors results in a sense of compassion satisfaction and/or compassion fatigue is often determined by the clinician's thoughts and beliefs, affect, resources, and self-care. For example, maintaining higher levels of hope was as a significant predictor of compassion satisfaction in recent research (Browning, McDermott, & Scaffa, 2019). Thus, the belief that clients can heal increases the likelihood of deriving pleasure from our work.

Vicarious Resiliency

Another potential reward associated with trauma work centers on an increase in personal resiliency. The concept of **vicarious resiliency**, originally proposed by Hernandez, Gangsei, and Engstrom (2007), describes the positive impact on clinicians' coping as a result of witnessing their clients' strength to cope with adversity and ability to thrive despite incredibly difficult challenges. Elements that contribute to vicarious resiliency and clinician empowerment include:

- Witnessing and reflecting on human beings' immense capacity to heal
- Reassessing the significance of the clinician's own problems
- Incorporating spirituality as a valuable dimension in treatment
- Developing tolerance for frustration
- Developing the use of self in therapy (Hernandez et al., 2007)

These elements build personal resiliency and inspiration in clinicians. Additional research has shown that witnessing clients' successes in overcoming trauma can increase the clinician's personal strength, optimism, and professional self-efficacy, all of which contribute to one's ability to bounce back and overcome challenges (Day et al., 2017; Sansbury, Graves, & Scott, 2015; Silveira & Boyer, 2015).

Vicarious Posttraumatic Growth

Another benefit of working with trauma survivors is the potential for **vicarious posttraumatic growth**. The concept of vicarious posttraumatic growth emerged out of seminal qualitative research which observed posttraumatic growth outcomes (positive changes in self-perception, interpersonal relationships, and philosophy of life) in clinicians who had witnessed similar posttraumatic growth in their clients' healing journeys (Arnold, Calhoun, Tedeschi, & Cann, 2005; Tedeschi & Calhoun, 1996). For clinicians, this type of growth is born out of their own internal cognitive struggle to make meaning out of clients' trauma experiences while also valuing the opportunity to witness clients thrive despite adversity (Manning-Jones, de Terte, & Stephens, 2017). In a process parallel to their clients' positive trauma outcomes, clinicians may also experience new strengths and assets that exceed internal structures prior to their interactions with trauma survivors (Day et al., 2017; Fedele, 2018). The potential positive by-products that emerge from helping trauma survivors may include "enduring, trait-oriented changes in self, such as increased levels of sensitivity, compassion, insight, tolerance, empathy, and deepened and expanded sense of spirituality" (Michalchuk & Martin, 2019, pp. 146–7).

Trauma Work in Practice: A Clinician's Experience in Vicarious Posttraumatic Growth

In my own journey through trauma work, I have experienced tremendous changes in myself both professionally and personally. This work has brought me face to face with some of the most heartbreaking situations imaginable, and while these tragedies have shaken me, they have also better illuminated the beauty in the world around me. Against the contrast of despair, I am far more grateful for joy and love, and alongside the reality of depravity, I more readily see and deeply value the acts of courage, kindness, and generosity of others. The meaning that I now find in small moments, like the sound of a bird singing during a rainstorm or someone's choice to smile through their tears, touches my heart in the most powerful and transformative ways. Trauma work has taught me to treasure the journey, not the destination, and along the way, I've learned: "Never fear shadows. They simply mean there's a light shining somewhere nearby" (Renkel, 1983).

Conclusion

Trauma work is a great adventure filled with potential hazards and rewards, continuous opportunities for new learning and personal growth, and interactions with survivors who inspire us and allow us front row seats to witness the incredible feat of human resiliency. One clinician described the power of sharing the trauma recovery journey with clients as an experience in which clinicians are "walking in the sacred spaces" (Hunter, 2012, p. 185). These sacred spaces are the places where good triumphs over evil and compassion trumps adversity. When we come alongside our clients in trauma work, it is impossible to not be affected, either positively or negatively. Attending to our own needs requires reflexive practice, self-awareness, and commitment to self-care. Clinicians must balance "compassion for others with a deep kindness and reverence for our own inner self" (Wicks, 2012, p. 6), and taking good care of both ourselves and our clients is mutually beneficial. As we navigate the risks and rewards of trauma work, we must also remember that this is a parallel journey with our clients. The pilgrimage through trauma always involves challenges for the sojourner, but the quest also holds the promise of redemption and growth.

KEYWORD ASSESSMENT

Write definitions in your own words, describe the concept's role in trauma work, list any questions, or make notes of important aspects that you want to remember.

Indirect Trauma Exposure

Vicarious Traumatization (or Secondary Traumatic Stress)

Countertransference

Compassion Fatigue

Burnout

Appropriate Level of Emotional Separation

Reframe

Self-Care

Compassion Satisfaction

Vicarious Resiliency

Vicarious Posttraumatic Growth

EXPERIENTIAL ACTIVITIES: INTERACTING WITH THE CHAPTER CONTENT

Expand Self-Awareness

1) Using the question guides in the chapter and other assessment tools, such as the ProQOL, WAQ, and MESS, investigate your current levels of vicarious traumatization, compassion fatigue, and burnout.

Expand Knowledge

2) Develop a personal wellness and self-care plan that is uniquely designed for your work as a trauma clinician. Your plan should include at least three specific self-care and prevention strategies that you plan to practice for each of the occupational hazards (vicarious traumatization, compassion fatigue, and burnout).

Expand Skills

3) Review the bulleted list of reflection activities for professional wellness. Select and complete one of these reflection activities.

SUPERVISORY DISCUSSION: SHARING PERSONAL INSIGHTS AND IDENTIFYING AREAS FOR GROWTH

1) Describe the personal insights that you gained by examining your current levels of vicarious traumatization, compassion fatigue, and burnout. As you review the factors that increase the risks for these occupational hazards, what have you learned about yourself as a professional?

2) Reflect on your wellness and self-care plan for trauma work. What challenges or obstacles do you anticipate for the implementation of your plan and how will you address these? Also discuss how you will be able to assess whether your plan is effective in managing the professional challenges of trauma work.

3) Share what it was like to complete your selected reflection activity for professional wellness. What insights did you gain from this experience?

4) Discuss your thoughts and feelings regarding the potential occupational rewards of trauma work (compassion satisfaction, vicarious resiliency, and vicarious posttraumatic growth). Share any past experiences you may have had with these benefits and reflect on how you hope to discover these rewards through trauma work.

Chapter 5

The Client: Trauma in an Individual and Cultural Context

During a recent professional trip to Ukraine, I had the opportunity to meet a local nine-year-old girl. She and I were different in so many ways, including language (she a Russian speaker and I an English speaker), and we needed a translator to communicate, yet we found ourselves connecting on many other levels. While we were talking, her curiosity peaked, and she asked where I was from. She knew that I was from the United States, but I could tell that she wanted to know more—she wanted a deeper sense of what my life might be like and to understand the details of my background. I told her that I grew up in Texas, and I asked if she knew anything about Texas. She shook her head no. I then asked her if she had ever heard about cowboys, and her face lit up and she smiled. I explained to her that I am from "the land of cowboys," which seemed to astonish her. Growing up in my small West Texas town, I didn't think there wasn't anything particularly remarkable about big trucks, steel toed-boots and cowboy hats, vast cotton fields, and rattlesnake festivals, but on the other side of the world in Ukraine, talking with this young lady, I realized the truly unique and quite uncommon nature of my cultural history, background, and traditions.

For many of us, culture is so ingrained into our daily living that it can be difficult to recognize, just as it was for me before I explored outside my cultural circle. When we live in the dominant cultural group, we often consider these cultural aspects as just "normal." It's only when we are transported into a different culture or when our culture is not a part of the majority that we start to recognize how vastly important our culture is to us and how much it informs our perceptions, relationships, and feelings about experiences.

Culture also impacts our perspective of trauma. Every client holds culturally based beliefs, value systems, and messages about what constitutes a trauma and how trauma should be resolved, which significantly affects the experience and understanding of the trauma itself as well as informs the course of the therapeutic process. In this chapter, we explore the role of culture and its connection to trauma, identify cultural risk and protective factors in relationship with trauma, acknowledge culture's influence on diagnosis, communication, and desired therapeutic outcomes in trauma work, and discuss the clinician's role in practicing culturally sensitive trauma work.

Cultural Factors: Understanding Foundations in Multiculturalism

Culture can be understood as shared group beliefs, customs, lifestyle habits, attitudes, and norms that are collectively endorsed by the group and passed on over time (McAuliffe, 2013). The idea of culture is so large that sometimes it can become challenging to differentiate between a personal trait and an aspect of one's culture. However, a clear defining marker that distinguishes a characteristic as a **cultural factor** is the characteristic's affiliation with a larger group. To determine whether a characteristic is a cultural factor, a differentiating question might be: "Can this characteristic (trait/behavior/belief/custom) also be assigned to an identified group of people?" With this grouping definition in mind, cultural factors include one's gender, ethnicity, race, sexual orientation, religion, social class, generational age, and physical and mental abilities (Collins & Arthur, 2010). While each of these cultural factors are accompanied by distinctive cultural norms, attitudes, and lifestyle habits, clinicians must be mindful to avoid stereotyping. **Stereotyping** is an outsider's oversimplification, exaggeration, and/or generalization of the *perceived* characteristics of cultural group towards *all* individuals in the group. Stereotyping often leads to global statements and rigid assumptions (either positive or negative), including assumptions such as "all women are emotional," "rural Americans are conservative," or "persons of low socioeconomic status are uneducated" (McAuliffe, 2013).

While clinicians should carefully consider each cultural factor distinctively, these factors should also be considered in conjunction with one another. A clinician might consider a client's faith background, race, and sexual orientation as distinctive forces in the client's life, but the clinician gains much richer insight when these factors are considered in concert with one another. For example, the clinician might reflect on how a client's Christian faith upbringing interacts with her homosexual orientation within an African American racial culture. Each cultural factor brings its own important framework to the table, but the interactions within one's own cultural world also create powerful dynamics.

Trauma in a Cultural Context: Integrating Dynamics

In trauma work, clinicians are faced with the critical task of integrating knowledge of trauma with equally important knowledge of the unique client. Trauma clinicians must consider how a trauma may be experienced very differently depending on unique cultural factors. For example, consider the cultural implications in the experience of a violent home invasion from the perspective of two different clients: the first client is an upper-class, white, Muslim, male immigrant and the second client is a cognitively impaired Hispanic woman, who lives in a low socioeconomic, inner-city area with substantial crime. For these two individuals, the same traumatic event (a violent home invasion) would carry many parallel thoughts, feelings, and reactions as well as remarkably different ways of understanding, personalizing, and making meaning of the experience.

A client's cultural background can have tremendous implications for current trauma symptoms as well as for clinical outcomes. Across all diverse groups, populations, and cultures, trauma universally impacts the individual through fear dysregulation, attention biases, emotional memory impairment, attachment and interpersonal alternations, and negative changes in the appraisal of self, others, and the world (Liddel & Jobson, 2016). While the impacts of trauma are clear, the modulating effect of culture within the trauma response experience is dynamic as culture filters the client's value orientation, possible risk and/or protective factors, and culturally informed support or shame messages (Maercher & Horn, 2013).

Trauma Work in Practice: Culture and the Expression of Trauma Symptoms

In my work with many traumatized children from vast spectrums of cultures, I have noticed that while there are some nuances, all of these children consistently presented with varying degrees of trauma symptomology. However, cultural factors have a significant influence on the expressions of these symptoms. For instance, my client Adam, a six-year-old African American boy, began his life in an inner city and was exposed to a series of traumatic situations during his early childhood. Adam expressed his emotional dysregulation by tremendously powerful outbursts of anger and rage, and many of his cultural factors (African American ethnicity and urban male values) informed his tendency towards large, externalizing behaviors. However, in another case, I worked with a 10-year-old Latina girl, Maria, whose culture also informed her expression of trauma. Maria was highly internalizing and intensely private about her symptoms of re-experiencing trauma, which was consistent with her cultural values. Both Adam and Maria presented with emotional dysregulation and re-experiencing symptoms, but the presentation of these problems was significantly shaped by the client's culture and the culturally informed acceptable ways of emotional and behavioral expression.

Culture and Trauma Risks: Recognizing Cultural Factors for Conceptualization

Some cultural groups are at an increased risk for the development of PTSD or for increased severity of symptoms. These cultural groups share commonality in that they hold less power, have less access to resources, and are often unacknowledged or overlooked in regard to trauma-related problems. At its core, PTSD is a disorder stemming from profound disempowerment, and individuals who belong to cultural groups already experiencing marginalization and disenfranchisement must face trauma with significant and impactful risks and disadvantages.

The negative impact of disempowerment can be so profound and enduring that it spans generations. Trauma occurs not only in the lives of individuals but can also be experienced collectively by entire cultural groups, leaving significant impact on even the children of survivors. As defined by one clinician, **historical trauma** is "cumulative emotional and psychological wounding, over the lifespan and across generations, emanating from massive group trauma" (Brave Heart, 2003, p. 7). Examples of historical trauma include the genocide of more than six million Jews in the Holocaust, the incarceration of Japanese Americans at the start of World War II, and the violent colonization and oppression of the various tribes of Native Americans (Alford, 2015; Brave Heart, 2003; Nagata, Kim, & Nguyen, 2015). Clinicians must recognize the impacts of historical trauma on cultural groups and consider how this legacy of pain and disenfranchisement may compound the current presenting trauma of the individual client. Culturally based discrimination, hate, violence, and historical trauma becomes a part of that group's cultural heritage and story, and as such, this aspect must be integrated as part of the conceptualization for the client in order to provide trauma-focused and culturally sensitive therapeutic goals, methods for assessment, and intervention approaches.

Disempowered Groups

Disempowered cultural groups often experience limited options when confronted with the danger and terror of a traumatic situation. When the reactions to danger or psychological threat are explored, which include the responses of fight, flight, or freeze (dissociation), disempowered individuals such as women and children often do not have the option or ability to fight, due to physical or resource limitations, or to flee the situation, due to lack of alternative options or inability to survive on one's own. As a result, these individuals are often left with freeze, or dissociation, as the only viable option for physically or psychologically surviving in the face of the traumatic event.

Unfortunately, dissociation is a disabling, disempowering, and psychologically disorganizing method of coping, and the use of dissociation during a traumatic event is one of the greatest risk factors for the development of PTSD and trauma-related problems (Boudoukha, Ouagazzal, & Goutaudier, 2017). For example, research consistently shows that men typically encounter up to four times more potentially traumatic events than do women within a lifetime, but, in comparison to men, women are twice as likely to develop PTSD (Christiansen & Elklit, 2008). While there may be a number of explanations for these statistics (such as women's increased likelihood to seek mental health services as well as the magnitude of common traumas, like rape), the rates of PTSD for females may also result from the disempowered status of women in many traumatic situations. The significant role of disempowerment in connection with trauma is evidenced among women from urban minority groups (a doubly disempowered status), who are at a greater risk for interpersonal trauma and who experience higher occurrences of PTSD in comparison to the general population (Powers et al., 2019). Clinicians should note that while research supports a tendency for women and children to use passive forms of psychological defense in the face of extreme trauma and stress (Christiansen & Elklit, 2008; Powers et al., 2019), this does not mean that dissociation is the *only* traumatic response from this population or that men or physically able and resourceful adults do not dissociate or experience strong feelings of helplessness during traumatic situations.

Marginalized Groups

Marginalized groups, which comprise individuals who are discriminated against based on cultural factors (such as sexual and racial minorities), are also at a higher risk for trauma and posttraumatic symptomology. **Insidious trauma** is an identity-based series of harmful events aimed at individuals who belong to minority or marginalized groups. While insidious trauma does not meet the criteria of a traumatic event outlined by the *DSM-5*, insidious trauma, experienced through ongoing discrimination, culturally motivated violence, oppression, and objectification/ dehumanization, may increase the risk of PTSD and negative well-being (Watson, DeBlaere, Langrehr, Zelaya, & Flores, 2016). For example, lesbian, gay, and bisexual teens report significantly higher incidents of abuse, bullying, and victimization, and, consequently, they are five times more likely to experience suicidal ideation in comparison to their heterosexual peers (Gibbs & Goldbach, 2015).

In additional to insidious trauma, individuals who belong to more than one marginalized group, such LGBTQ people of color, may experience **double jeopardy** (Cole, 2009) in which the individual is exposed to discrimination and oppression based on multiple minority identities. Because insidious trauma, which includes racism and sexual objectification, is inherently linked with characteristics of one's identity, many individuals who belong to one or more minority groups experience lower self-esteem, which can even further exacerbate the individual's vulnerability to a trauma (Watson et al., 2016). Very often, the chronic experience of marginalization, insidious trauma, and cultural double jeopardy creates a climate of significant adversity for the individual, which can result in toxic stress and thus increase the individual's vulnerability to mental health issues and PTSD.

Disenfranchised Groups

Disenfranchised groups comprise individuals who are deprived of rights and privileges or who experience diminished social status and resources. Immigrants, as well as other minority groups, such as individuals with cognitive or physical disabilities or low socioeconomic status, experience tremendous barriers to resources and support that are often critical for well-being, leaving them highly vulnerable to the impacts of trauma. These individuals may experience practical obstacles for daily living (language barriers, limited transportation, lack of special education services, etc.) and invisible barriers of withdrawn social support. Many immigrants and refugees often face additional complex traumatic situations, which may include family separations, anti-immigrant environments, and a history of home-country violence, poverty, or war (Goodman, Versely, Letiecq, & Cleaveland, 2017). These multiple traumas, in conjunction with the disenfranchisement in the larger majority culture, place the immigrant group at a pronounced risk for developing trauma-related symptoms. These risks can be seen in a large meta-analysis study which found that refugee Central Americans relocated in a Western country are 10 times more likely to have PTSD in comparison to the population in their home country (Fazel, Wheeler, & Danesh, 2005).

Culture and Protective Factors in Trauma: Honoring Cultural Resources

While many marginalized individuals may feel disempowered due to their minority status, cultural identity, even within groups that face tremendous obstacles, can be a powerful and positive resource. **Ethnic identity strength** is considered a personal exploration of the cultural information and experiences in connection to one's ethnicity as well as a personal commitment of attachment and belonging to one's ethnic group (Phinney & Ong, 2007). Grounded in cultural pride, ethnic identity strength may serve as a protective factor against the negative outcomes that often result from discrimination and marginalization, including trauma-related symptoms (Watson et al., 2016).

Ethnic identity includes the integration of various aspects of culture, such as race, geographical heritage, sexual orientation, spirituality and religion, age, and socioeconomic status. By embracing one's unique cultural differences as a source of pride rather than shame, individuals are able to transform a minority status that may have once felt disempowering into an aspect of life that enhances feelings of belonging, empowerment, and self-acceptance. During challenging moments of discrimination, individuals with a strong ethnic identity are able to more accurately externalize the experience within a larger cultural context rather than internalize the profoundly negative messages that ultimately damage self-esteem and well-being (Watson et al., 2016). When a client's trauma-related concerns are coupled with cultural obstacles, the fostering and bolstering of ethnic identity strength can serve as a powerful protective factor.

Cultural Frameworks of Trauma Symptoms: Communicating in a Cultural Context

While trauma clinicians may have a highly trained ear for the textbook definitions and explanations of PTSD, they must also be attuned to the unique and sometimes culturally distinctive ways in which clients describe living the experience of trauma. **Idioms of distress** (Nichter, 1981) are distinctive ways by which members of a cultural group describe psychological suffering and emotional affliction. For example, Latino clients may describe a response to a traumatic event as *padecer de los nervios* (to suffer from nerves) or *los nervios alterados* (altered nerves) in which the individual experiences ongoing anxiety, depression, somatic problems, and dissociation. Likewise, individuals from the Cambodian culture may describe *khsaoy beh doung* (a weak heart), which is characterized by heart palpations, sleep disturbances, startle responses, and a poor appetite (Hinton & Lewis-Fernández, 2010). Without multicultural sensitivity and awareness, the mismatch description of trauma between client and clinician may, unfortunately, lead to improper diagnosis, disconnect in the therapeutic relationship, and ineffective care.

Idioms of distress are not only critical in an understanding and communicating about trauma symptoms, they also profoundly impact the client's perception of the experience. Many cultures hold their own beliefs about the origins of and reasons for their symptoms, such as demon possession or a serious physical disorder (Hinton & Lewis-Fernández, 2010). Additionally, clients may form a culturally based conceptualization of the problem, which may include distressing ideas such as beliefs that symptoms can eventually lead to "madness" (as with the Latino altered nerves) or cardiac arrest (as with the Cambodian weak heart). Cultural and self-stigma may also be especially profound with certain symptoms, and clients may feel disconnected from their own cultural group and shamed for their experience due to the beliefs surrounding the symptoms and behaviors (Hinton & Lewis-Fernández, 2010). Clinicians must be mindful not only of the unique description of possible trauma symptoms but also of the cultural implications of these symptoms and any possible diagnosis. In order to aid clinicians in this critical cultural task, a "Glossary of Cultural Terms That Indicate Distress" was included in the *DSM-5* as a resource for cultural idioms and descriptors of various disorders (APA, 2013).

Trauma Work in Practice: A Cultural Intersection in Communication

As an example of these cultural impacts, I refer back to my work with Maria, the 10-year-old client who I discussed earlier in the chapter. During my work with Maria, I also worked with Maria's father, Jorgé, who was a recent immigrant from Mexico. Maria's trauma had devastated the entire family, and consequently, Jorgé spent several weeks in an inpatient psychiatric center as a result of his severe, acute distress. I began to work with Maria following her father's discharge from the hospital, and I met with Jorgé to explain to him the therapeutic process as well as provide some psychoeducation on Maria's trauma symptoms. I fully intended to work with Maria in an outpatient, weekly counseling structure, but during my discussion with Jorgé, I began to realize that Jorgé perceived all mental health services to exist only in an inpatient medical setting involving heavy psychopharmacology. Jorgé was highly distraught because he believed I was requesting that Maria be psychiatrically admitted as he had been weeks earlier.

Jorgé had no knowledge or understanding of the kind of mental health services that I hoped to offer Maria, and this was one of our first major cultural crossroads. As the clinician, I had to be much more mindful of assumptions I personally had (that the family would know what I meant by "weekly counseling"), and I had to be extremely clear in communicating about what treatment would and would not involve. Jorgé also had his own cultural beliefs about Maria's trauma symptoms, which included "visits from the dead," and we had to collaborate to come to a mutual understanding of these experiences, which involved the integration of both a clinical and a cultural lens.

Culturally Sensitive Communication About Trauma

Culture may inform how clients engage in the therapeutic process and what they choose to disclose. For example, in collectivistic cultures, suppressing feelings is viewed not as a psychologically destructive defensive mechanism but rather as a way for dealing with emotions and maintaining social harmony (Drožđek, 2010). In these cultures, emotional exposure and humiliation are viewed as incredibly powerful sources of shame and, therefore, these individuals believe it is wiser to keep shameful or sinful deeds hidden (Drožđek, 2010). Within this type of collectivistic culture, a disclosure about an interpersonal trauma may be perceived as a threat to peace. Clients from these cultures often glean their inner harmony from the harmony existing within the greater group, and they aim to keep this harmony intact as a benefit to all.

Apart from collectivistic cultures, other cultural groups may be reluctant to disclose trauma or parts of their trauma. Clients from some cultures highly value stoicism and view lack of emotionality as a strength, and, therefore, these clients prefer to avoid personal details of emotionally charged topics or events. For the stoic client, clinicians must consider congruent treatment approaches that do not feel dishonoring or disingenuous, which carries implications for emotionally focused or highly expressive treatment modalities. As another example, some clients from a Christian faith may be reluctant to share some aspects of their experience due to the postulate of "forgiving and forgetting." These clients may believe that a retelling of a story in which they experienced harm or ill will is a demonstration of "unforgiveness" and is counter to their faith values (Drožđek, 2010). Clinicians must be mindful of these cultural values as they greatly impact the trauma treatment process.

Trauma Recovery in a Cultural Context: Attending to Cultural Values and Meaning

Culture shapes our perspectives of traumatic situations, and it informs the way we initially understand our problems as well as the way we describe and express trauma symptomology. Culture also impacts the trauma recovery process by coloring our beliefs about what trauma recovery *should* look like in our lives. For example, the clinician must be aware of his/her own wishes about how things will turn out for the client, such as culturally informed values about a client's choice to remain in a marriage or divorce, engage in alternative lifestyles, turn towards or against spiritual beliefs, keep or terminate a pregnancy, or maintain cultural traditions (including rigid gender roles, family rules, attitudes towards education, discipline, and emotional expression). While trauma recovery clinically means a mitigation or cessation of trauma symptoms, the idea of recovery also includes the meaning we derive from our experiences and what we believe about the traumatic event itself and about others who may have been involved.

Gender roles, religion and spirituality, ethnic values, and cultural norms significantly influence our perception of recovery and healing. Even the clinical approach to the trauma recovery process itself is structured along cultural values. For example, many Western trauma clinicians emphasize the importance of disclosure and safety seeking as part of psychoeducation regarding sexual trauma and domestic violence. However, in collectivistic societies, in which the group is a higher priority than the individual, a personal disclosure can lead to massive familial and group upheaval. In cultural situations like these, the disclosure may actually prove to be more traumatic and shameful for the individual than the original trauma event itself. While clinicians must always remain committed to safety of their clients, we can easily overlook traumas that occur within a cultural context simply because we, personally, value something else more highly. Clinicians must keep the client's cultural experience as the guiding light in understanding all parts of the situation while remaining cognizant of their own culturally informed priorities.

The client's desired outcome of the therapeutic process, vision of "trauma recovery," and ideas for situational resolution are highly culturally informed, especially in cases of interpersonal trauma. In cases of interpersonal trauma, which involve a human perpetrator or offender (such as in cases of physical or sexual abuse, violence, neglect or maltreatment, homicide, etc.), the client is confronted with the highly complex and challenging task of working through thoughts and feelings about the offender. Clients must begin to sort through tensions between their feelings and personal values, determine their desired outcomes for the situation, weigh beliefs about justice and forgiveness, and make decisions regarding how the relationship will move forward (if at all) in the future. Cultural values and beliefs very often inform a client's value system, in which different outcomes, such as punishment, retribution, or restoration and reconciliation, may be sought and desired. For example, in Western cultures, individuals often seek legal punishment, relational atonement, and/or an apologetic disposition from a person or persons responsible for inflicting the trauma. Conversely, non-Western collectivistic cultures value restorative justice, in which the parties are able to reestablish their relationship and resolve the conflict in manner by which parties reunite (Droždek, 2010). In South African cultures forgiveness is unrelated to reconciliation, which means that a person can seek relational reconnection with the offender while choosing to withhold forgiveness (Dwyer, 2003). For other clients, like those from a Western Judeo-Christian religion, forgiveness may be valued over reconciliation, and these clients may feel a cultural pressure to forgive when this is not a personal desire.

The concepts of *justice*, *forgiveness*, and *reconciliation* are highly complex, culturally distinctive, and unique within the trauma context. As the trauma treatment process evolves, clients must move through a labyrinth of interpersonal questions, conflict in personal and cultural values, and strongly held beliefs about desired outcomes. Clinicians also enter the process with many of their own culturally guided beliefs about how the situation *should* resolve, but they must remain cognizant of their own biases, avoid imposing these beliefs on the client, and seek to understand the client's culturally informed perspective of resolution and what it means to the client personally to have a "positive" situational and relational conclusion. Clinicians must be prepared to honor the client's values regarding beliefs, decisions, and attitudes towards an offender of an interpersonal trauma even when these values run counter to what the clinician may believe is the "right" outcome or stance.

The Clinician's Role: Engaging Culture in Trauma Work

Multicultural competency requires attention to three domains: awareness, knowledge, and skill (Sue, Arrendondo, & McDavis, 1992). Developing **cultural awareness** involves the clinician's recognition and ownership of his or her own cultural background as well as an acknowledgment of and active work towards resolving personal biases, assumptions, and stereotypes held towards other cultures and various groups (McAuliffe, 2013). In connection with trauma work, clinicians are encouraged to reflect on their own cultural messages surrounding trauma. This may include messages and beliefs surrounding what types of events do and do not constitute a trauma, how one *should* respond to trauma, how one *should* and *should not* communicate about traumatic experiences, and what trauma recovery *should* look like. Clinicians must also reflect on the biases, assumptions, or judgments that they may have regarding how certain cultural groups interact with trauma and consider how different cultural messages about trauma impact them personally. The clinician's exploration into personal cultural awareness is the foundation for integrating multiculturalism and trauma work.

Building on self-awareness, trauma clinicians must also intentionally work to gain multicultural knowledge about other worldviews and cultures different from their own (McAuliffe, 2013). In trauma work, this includes gaining knowledge about various cultural experiences, expressions, and understandings of trauma. This knowledge base can then inform multicultural skills that equip trauma clinicians to select culturally appropriate models and interventions that are congruent with each client's worldview and cultural experience of trauma.

Integration of Multicultural and Trauma-Focused Skills

An important aspect of multicultural competence includes a culturally sensitive and attuned multicultural therapeutic alliance (Collins & Arthur, 2010). When the client and clinician come from distinctly diverse cultural backgrounds, the therapeutic relationship may experience barriers, setbacks, or misunderstandings. Many beginning clinicians feel nervous or hesitant to bring in discussions surrounding culture so as not to highlight glaring differences, but an avoidance of the cultural "elephant in the room" only further highlights these differences and eliminates a powerful therapeutic opportunity for a client to feel exceptionally respected and understood.

Clinicians must remember that cultural conversations and cultural integration in trauma work begin with *them*. This means that it is incumbent upon the clinician to initiate culturally based discussions and to model cultural awareness. McAuliffe (2013) outlines a variety of ways that a clinician can initiate a dialogue about culture. Clinicians may point out the cultural differences they share with the client as a way to create a bridge rather than a divide, and they may integrate culturally oriented questions and reflections. Clinicians may also utilize self-disclosure about their thoughts and feelings regarding the cultural dynamics of the therapeutic relationship, and they also lean on culturally informed information-giving and culturally sensitive psychoeducation. Some cultural groups may respond more positively to directive leads, and many minority groups may experience an increase in the strength of the therapeutic alliance when the clinician shows a willingness to participate in advocacy efforts for the client.

Trauma Work in Practice: Culturally Attuned and Trauma-Focused Strategies

Michael, a clinician, is working with Claudia as she processes her lengthy history of trauma, which includes chronic childhood physical abuse by her father, a house fire in early adulthood in which she lost her entire home, and, most recently, a rape by a male friend. Michael and Claudia represent different cultural backgrounds as Michael is a middle-aged Japanese-American, upper-middle-class, heterosexual male and Claudia is a 25-year-old, white, lower-middle-class, lesbian woman. Michael is very mindful that these cultural differences have the potential to significantly impact the therapeutic relationship, and he aims to integrate multicultural skills in the trauma work with Claudia.

STRATEGY 1: Beginning the discussion by using differences as a bridge

MICHAEL: Claudia, one of the most important goals for our time together is to create a therapeutic relationship in which you feel safe, respected, and able to share freely. Sometimes barriers to building this kind of relationship involve differences between the clinician and client and the thoughts, feelings, and worries we each may have about these differences. However, when we can talk openly about these differences, it can actually serve as a way for you to feel more understood and accepted as a unique person with important values. Some of the ways we may be different include our ethnic and racial heritage, spiritual beliefs, socioeconomic status, sexual orientation, gender, and other cultural practices and values. I can see some of the differences between us (like our racial backgrounds and gender), but I'm sure there are other differences too. I'd really like to hear about all the aspects that contribute to your perspective so that I can know and understand you better. I value how your cultural influences have shaped the experience of your traumas.

STRATEGY 2: Broaching the subject through self-disclosure

CLAUDIA: When the fire happened, I lost everything—absolutely everything. I had to go to work wearing the same set of clothes for a week, and I didn't have a charger and couldn't use my phone to call any of the many people that I needed to about all the logistics of house. I had to sleep on my friend's closet floor for six weeks before I could find a new place. No one seemed to understand how bad things were and how much I actually lost.

MICHAEL: You felt really alone during a time when you needed support so badly. You said that no one seemed to understand how difficult it was for you in so many ways. I worry that you may feel that way about me. When our counseling office moved locations, I wonder what it was like for you to see me transition so easily to a new place. I worry that you think I may not understand how painful and distressing it is to be without resources to start over.

STRATEGY 3: Culturally oriented reflections and attunement

CLAUDIA: After the rape, I just stayed in the shower for three hours. I felt so disgusting.

MICHAEL: You felt violated both physically and to the deepest parts of who you are, and the pain and losses feel devastating. While a forced sexual experience is horrific enough on its own, the rape was perpetrated by a male, which adds another dimension to the experience for you. You've said how much you value your lesbian lifestyle and exclusively female sexual relationships, and this aspect of the rape brings another level of violation. Your body felt defiled and so were your values and your expectations about your sexual experiences.

STRATEGY 4: Culturally oriented information gathering for integration

CLAUDIA: As a kid, anytime I was around my father, I just hated myself. I didn't think I was good enough for him; it was my fault that he beat me. Now, I'm starting to feel this incredible anger directed towards him instead of myself, and I'm unsettled by it. I don't know what to do with this anger at him and what it may mean for our relationship. As a religious person, I don't think I should be feeling this way towards my dad—I'm supposed to honor him.

MICHAEL: You feel so much anger towards your father as you begin to see what happened in a new way. It sounds as though you are also feeling conflict between your experiences and your faith. Tell me more about your religious background and your beliefs about the role of parents and children and how you were taught to handle anger.

Conclusion

While some aspects of trauma universally transcend the human experience, many of the unique facets of the trauma experience are informed by our cultural heritage, worldview, and multicultural make-up. The trauma event may be the focal point of a snapshot, but culture provides the context—the setting and background of the scene. In order to provide truly effective and comprehensive care, the trauma clinician must demonstrate and integrate multicultural competency for clients and pursue personal self-awareness with regard to his or her own cultural beliefs, biases, and positions of cultural power. Effective case conceptualization in trauma work always begins with multicultural competency.

Cultural considerations are paramount in effective client care, but culture carries significant influence for clinicians too. In many ways, our personal culture frames the meaning we make from trauma work, and the ethnic identity strength found through embracing our own unique culture is powerful and important for clinicians as well. Multiculturalism in trauma work does not mean that we must cast aside our own cultural values, but, rather, we make space to honor *both* our client's culture in session as well as our culture outside of session.

KEYWORD ASSESSMENT

Write definitions in your own words, describe the concept's role in trauma work, list any questions, or make notes of important aspects that you want to remember.

Culture

Stereotyping

Historical Trauma

Disempowered Cultural Groups

Marginalized Cultural Groups

Disenfranchised Cultural Groups

Insidious Trauma

Double Jeopardy

Ethnic Identity Strength

Idioms of Distress

Cultural Awareness

EXPERIENTIAL ACTIVITIES: INTERACTING WITH THE CHAPTER CONTENT

Expand Self-Awareness

1) Reflect and discuss the *should*'s you believe about trauma. These hidden beliefs become most apparent when you consider a person who feels/thinks/acts/believes differently than you. Reflect on your cultural beliefs as well as the cultural beliefs that may run counter to yours. Consider how you believe that one *should*:

 ■ Talk about and/or express symptoms of trauma
 ■ Think about the origins of trauma
 ■ Demonstrate trauma recovery

Expand Knowledge

2) Interview someone from a different cultural background. Ask them how different types of traumas are perceived and how the various trauma-related problems are managed in their culture.

Expand Skills

3) Role play a therapeutic situation in which you, the "clinician," implement one of the culturally attuned strategies described in the chapter. Switch roles so that you have the opportunity to be in the "client" role as well. Process the experience with each other.

SUPERVISORY DISCUSSION: SHARING PERSONAL INSIGHTS AND IDENTIFYING AREAS FOR GROWTH

1) Describe the insights you gained regarding how culture informs one's understanding and experience of trauma. What would it be like for you to work with a client whose culturally based values in trauma work are fundamentally different than yours? Integrate any ethical dilemmas or considerations that you anticipate.

2) Share your experiences surrounding your interview. What cultural information surprised you, intrigued you, and triggered issues of cultural awareness for you?

3) After practicing a role-play in culturally attuned trauma work, what have you learned about yourself as both a trauma clinician and as a culturally sensitive professional? What aspects of multiculturalism do you anticipate being areas of personal strength and where do you need to the most growth?

4) Reflect on the concept of ethnic identity strength. How might you integrate this aspect into trauma work for your clients and for yourself personally? How can you manage the boundary of honoring your personal culture and the culture of your client?

Chapter 6

The Therapeutic Relationship: Attachment and Connection in Trauma Work

If you have spent much time with toddlers, you have likely had a lesson in the "boo boo" protocol. My active three-year-old daughter tries her best to keep up with her older brothers, and a frequent consequence of her ambition is a scraped knee, jammed finger, or bumped arm. When an injury occurs, a remarkably consistent and uniform process unfolds: my daughter will urgently seek me out, extend her "boo boo" for me to see, and then tearfully recount the tale of the experience. While she faithfully does her part in this ritual, I must also do mine, which is to be empathically attuned to the pain of the "boo boo" and to the accompanying emotions of the experience, such as the fear while falling from a swing or the embarrassment from taking a tumble. I reflect this attunement through my words, facial expressions, and tone of voice while I truly hear her story, and then as the final step, I offer a caring response that provides some form of healing, such as a kiss, an ice pack, or a Band-Aid. Even with very minor injuries, I have noticed that if any of these steps are left out (such as giving her an ice pack without offering her a chance to tell her story or minimizing the pain of her experience and inadequately empathizing), my daughter does not recover as quickly or with the same degree of emotional resolution as she would have if all aspects were addressed in our interaction. While the "boo boo" protocol is not an evidence-based treatment for trauma, this universal behavior in toddlers (empathy seeking, retelling of the narrative, and the need for care in a relational context) tells us so much about the intrinsic needs of humans in our process of recovery from painful experiences. In this way, children are our best teachers about the necessary ingredients for healing, which always begins and ends inside a safe and caring relationship.

When we imagine trauma work, we often picture the stage of treatment in which the client confronts his or her darkest demons of the trauma experience while the clinician provides a facilitative intervention in the trauma-recall process. Using the "boo boo" protocol metaphor, this parallels the "injury story and ice pack" stage. However, many beginning clinicians experience a significant paradigm shift when they begin to conceptualize trauma work as actually the broader, interactive, and comprehensive process of the therapeutic relationship rather than simply a set of interventions. Trauma work is not something that a clinician "does to" a client; rather, trauma work is most appropriately described as the dynamic and healing experiences that emerge from the therapeutic relationship.

In this chapter, the therapeutic relationship is highlighted as the primary modality for trauma work. The unique relationship between client and clinician is often highly complex and informed by layers of interpersonal histories. Trauma clinicians contribute to an effective therapeutic alliance through a variety of facilitative dispositions and skills, which are discussed, and the role of attachment in trauma work is explored. Lastly, methods for navigating the interpersonal dynamics of the therapeutic relationship are considered.

The Therapeutic Alliance: Recognizing the Most Powerful Resource

The therapeutic alliance is the critical foundation for mental health work, and the importance and power of this relationship is universally recognized in all presenting problems, treatment approaches, theoretical orientations, and professional disciplines. Broadly defined, the therapeutic alliance (also referred to as the therapeutic relationship) is the relational connection, mutual affirmation of trust and respect, role investment, empathic resonance, and collaborative bond between the client and clinician as they mutually agree on and engage in the evolving therapeutic tasks, goals, and processes (Chen et al., 2019; McLaughlin, Keller, Feeny, Youngstrom, & Zoelhner, 2014). The client-clinician alliance is perhaps the single most critical element in therapeutic work as it serves as the greatest predictor for treatment outcomes (Horvath, Del Re, Fluckiger, & Symonds, 2011; Miller, Hubble, Chow, & Seidel, 2013; Norcross & Wampold, 2011). Many beginning trauma clinicians are eager to move past the "basics" and learn trauma-focused treatments and evidence-based interventions, but the quality of the therapeutic relationship should always be perceived as the most powerful resource and the single greatest therapeutic tool in treatment.

Qualities of the Therapeutic Relationship and the Dispositions of the Trauma Clinician

The therapeutic relationship represents a major contributing force in whether or not a client remains in treatment and ultimately experiences a successful outcome of decreased symptoms. Across all types of presenting problems, clients who successfully complete treatment frequently describe their clinician as caring, respectful, understanding, and interested (Luedke, Peluso, Diaz, Freund, & Baker, 2016). In addition to these clinician characteristics, clients who present specifically with trauma-related concerns emphasize the importance of the clinician's willingness to titrate intimacy (gaining relational connection and trust slowly and sensitively), the clinician's utilization of the power of the therapeutic relationship, and the clinician's inclusion of the therapeutic function of hope (Lemma, 2010). These characteristics, which are rooted in the clinician's relational orientation and demeanor, facilitate the process of positive relationship-building with the client, thereby contributing to the most essential and important functions in therapeutic work.

These qualities and characteristics reflect an overall **professional disposition**, which is the emotional posture, social approach, consistent demeanor, and guiding mindset of the clinician to the trauma work process and to each client personally. A trauma clinician may be highly trained and competent in the most advanced trauma treatments, but without the professional dispositions and demeanor that facilitate a positive therapeutic alliance, those clinical skills will likely prove to be ineffective. To develop and enhance these essential and facilitative dispositions, the clinician must continually engage in reflexive practice to assess how these professional characteristics are being communicated to the client and what personal barriers may be impacting the process. Below are the professional dispositions most needed for trauma clinicians:

Unconditional Positive Regard: The clinician values and accepts the client as he or she is *right now* and does not value the client any more or any less based on the client's personal choices, behavior, beliefs, background, healing progress, or set-backs throughout treatment.

Reflective Questions for the Clinician: What do I believe about my client's worth as an individual apart from the problems and goals, and what informs my beliefs? Are there aspects of the client or expressions of his/her trauma in which I feel judgement/dislike/irritation/fear/disgust, and if so, how are these feelings impacting the therapeutic relationship and the trauma work process? Do I *need* my client to improve, and if so, what do I fear will be the consequence if my client does not improve in the way I want?

Safety: The clinician presents as reliable, consistent, and dependable in both practical and emotional ways. The clinician creates an open, "safe haven" relationship in which the client can freely and fully express him/herself and the impacts of trauma without the fear that he/she might overwhelm the clinician.

Reflective Questions for the Clinician: Do I provide consistency and predictability in my session and treatment structure for my client, and if not, what are the forces that are influencing this? What are my thoughts and feelings surrounding my client's trauma and my ability to be fully present as a witness to the trauma recovery process? Do I feel frightened or overwhelmed by my client's trauma, and if so, what is the source of these fears? What do I worry might happen if I fully engage in this particular trauma work process, and how can I manage this both for myself and for my client?

Non-intrusiveness: The clinician expresses a willingness and comfortability with allowing the client to share and relationally connect at his or her own pace.

Reflective Questions for the Clinician: Do I have a timeline agenda that is more important than my client's feelings of safety, and if so, what is that agenda and where is it coming from? Why do I feel rushed or reluctant to connect in this relationship or the process? What are the cues that my client is providing to let me know if the pace in the relationship and in trauma work is either too slow, too fast, or on track?

Transparency: The clinician is open and honest with the client about all aspects of the trauma work process, including the course of treatment, problem/diagnostic considerations, issues of confidentiality, and the influence of any competing agendas of other stakeholders, such as family members, agencies (foster care, probation office, etc.), and employers.

Reflective Questions for the Clinician: Are there topics or issues that make me feel uncomfortable to discuss honestly with my client? If so, what dynamics are fueling these fears? Am I able to attend to *here-and-now* issues with my client and openly discuss our relationship, and if not, what is holding me back from this? Do I believe my client can be fully honest with me, and how might I respond if my client is candid about aspects of trauma work or our relationship that are not favorable?

Attunement and Empathy as the Skills for Fostering the Therapeutic Relationship

In addition to consistently providing these facilitative professional dispositions, the trauma clinician must also demonstrate two critical relationship-building skills: attunement and empathy. Attunement is the mindful, relational skill in which one is wholly and fully present for another person by offering cognitive and affective attention in a nonjudgmental manner with the intended purpose of truly understanding another's unique inner world and phenomenological experience (Schomaker & Ricard, 2015). Attunement provides the sensation of being truly seen and heard.

If we consider attunement the "vehicle" for emotional connection, then affective exchanges can be considered the "highway" on which we drive. Affective exchanges are the emotional messages communicated within relationships, and these exchanges are an essential and hallmark feature of a facilitative therapeutic relationship (Luedke et al., 2016). Most affective exchanges take place on a non-verbal level through subtle facial expressions, physical movements, and vocal tones and inflections (Mozdzierz, Peluso, & Lisiecki, 2014).

Non-verbals speak far more than words alone, and a central aspect of attunement is accurately recognizing, identifying, and connecting with these micro-signals communicated through affective exchanges in order to understand a client's feelings about a situation or experience. This is especially noteworthy when the client's verbal and non-verbal messages are not congruent with one another. For example, a client might say "everything's fine", but when she states this, she does so in a low tone of voice and with her head down. Attunement to this affective exchange alerts the clinician that the client is experiencing strong emotions while presenting incongruent messages, and the clinician's curiosity regarding the client's reasons for incongruence is sparked.

Attunement allows us to understand and identify our client's affective world, but empathy is needed to emotionally connect with the client through the attunement process. Empathy is a person's ability to emotionally resonate with and communicate compassion, connection, and understanding of another person's affective experience and lived reality (Bayne & Hays, 2017). As a key characteristic, empathy does not carry judgment regarding the other person's response to an experience, and this differs significantly from sympathy or pity, which are conversely characterized by emotional distance or superiority. Sympathy communicates, "I feel bad for you"; empathy communicates, "I feel this with you."

Trauma Work in Practice: Attunement and Empathy

A number of years ago, I provided child-centered play therapy for a six-year-old boy who had been exposed to domestic violence in his home. In this type of play therapy, children are not required to talk but rather are allowed to express their experience through their play, which is a developmentally sensitive approach for a child this age. My client did not speak during the entire session, but he played out a lengthy play sequence in which a large number of army men attacked a doll house and eventually "lit it on fire." Consistent with play therapy, I verbally reflected the feelings and experience of the toys all throughout the session as he played. As I reflected the toys' feelings of loss and outrage while they watched the dollhouse burn in the play, he suddenly turned to me and exclaimed, "Now you hear what I'm saying!" Contrary to his statement, the child had not said a single word until this point; however, he wanted to acknowledge the powerful sense of understanding that he was feeling with me. In this situation, my client had communicated so much without saying one word, and attunement and empathy enabled me to hear and connect with these important messages. For both child and adult clients, emotions and the power of an experience are not always expressed through words, and as clinicians, we must learn to listen with more than just our ears.

Both empathy and attunement are often propelled by a sense of curiosity. Curiosity leads the clinician to seek out understanding of the client's experience without making presumptions, assumptions, or transposing his or her own personal reactions onto the client's situation. The authentic interest to truly understand communicates to the client that he or she is valuable and worthy of attention and that his or her personal experience is inherently unique and worthwhile (Briere & Lanktree, 2013). While empathy and attunement are needed at every juncture of the trauma treatment process, these clinical skills are absolutely central in the development of the therapeutic relationship, especially during the early stages of trauma work when the client feels highly vulnerable, wary of trusting the clinician, and unsure of the process. Together, the clinician's relational dispositions, in conjunction with empathic and attunement skills, culminate into a powerful message that communicates "I am here, I understand, and I care" (Landreth, 2012).

Dynamics of the Therapeutic Relationship: Integrating the Influence of Attachment

The qualities of the therapeutic relationship are powerful, and they represent philosophies and ideals that are readily embraced by most mental health professionals. However, the devastating impacts and painful scars left by trauma sometimes create challenging relational dynamics between the client and clinician. Previous relationships and interpersonal experiences influence both the client and clinician in ways that propel reactions to one another and generate issues of transference and countertransference. The impact of relational history carries tremendous implications for the therapeutic relationship, and the most meaningful place to begin in understanding these powerful relational dynamics is at the genesis of its development: attachment.

The Development of Attachment Through the Parent-Child Connection

When children are provided with protective, stable, and nurturing relationships within a safe environment, they grow physically, neurologically, emotionally, socially, and academically (Sege, Bethell, Linkenbach, Jones, Klika, & Pecora, 2017). Developmentally, infants begin life psychologically enmeshed, without differentiation between self and the parent, and in many ways, a parent's response to the child during the early years of life informs the child's way of understanding "self" and "self in the world." Through repeated experiences of relational interaction, the infant develops interpersonal expectations of the parent's responses to his or her personal needs for care and comfort. These expectations and patterns are ultimately forged into an attachment style, which represents the individual's generalized core beliefs about self, automatic patterns of relating with others, and overall orientation to interpersonal intimacy (Bowlby, 1973, 1988). The core beliefs that stem from attachment style may result in internal messages such as "I can count on others to help me—I feel loved, and I will be okay"; "Others often become angry with me when I need care—I feel love and comfort only sometimes"; or "I cannot trust or rely on others—it's safer to not ask for love or comfort." From the prenatal stage through the first three years of life, the primary psychological task is to develop an attachment with a parent or primary caregiver, and from the cradle to the grave, this core attachment relationship serves as the interpersonal template on which all other relationships are experienced (Schoeneberg & Zaporozhets, 2018).

In addition to the parent's response to an infant's need for care and comfort, another critical ingredient in the development of attachment is contingent communication. Contingent communication is a person's accurate attunement to a message being sent by another person (either verbal or non-verbal) followed by a response message which communicates an understanding of and connection with the original message (Siegel, 2012). With infants, contingent communication is demonstrated when a baby points at something and smiles, and the mother responds by also looking to see what the baby is pointing at, smiling with the baby, and then engaging with the baby about the experience of seeing the object. Parental engagement like this may go further and include the mother's sharing an affective interaction about the experience of seeing the object together, taking the baby to the object, talking about the object, or showing the baby something else connected with the object. Peek-a-boo, facial mirroring, eye gazing, vocal tone change, and vocal inflection to match the baby's affective state are additional examples of powerful contingent communication, and these relational interactions are hallmark activities in the attachment process. Babies internalize and generalize the experience of these exchanges and develop beliefs such as "I am worthy of attention and others enjoy and understand me"; "Sometimes others don't seem to notice or understand me"; or "I can't count on others to understand me, and I feel emotionally alone."

Parental responses to the child play a major role in the development of an attachment style, however, attachment may also be impacted by other external forces. An **attachment disruption** represents a significant life event during early childhood in which the child was separated, physically and/or emotionally, from a parent or primary caregiver for a substantial amount of time. Attachment disruptions may include events such as the death of a parent, a parent or child's extended stay in a hospital for medical care, the child's placement in foster care, a parent's unavailability to due illness, severe depression, substance abuse, a divorce or separation that resulted in discontinued contact with a parent, or a parent's incarceration or deportation. Attachment disruptions can be thought of as distinctive from abusive or pathological parenting; instead, these events often represent something that occurs beyond a parent's control or ability to manage but still results in problematic attachment patterns for the child. These types of breaks in the parent-child relationship are often referred to as adverse childhood experiences, and attachment disruptions can contribute to the onset or perpetuation of trauma-related disorders for many children.

The Development of the Relationship Template Through Secure and Insecure Attachment Styles

Childhood attachment experiences may result in a variety of different attachment styles with lingering impacts that evolve as the child ages and can carry on even into adulthood. Children with positively attuned parents who provide consistent availability to the child (especially during times of distress), attend to the child's needs, provide contingent communication, and offer a relational experience that is warm, caring, playful, and supportive often develop a **secure attachment style**. Internalizing a relational safe haven to which they can continuously return, these children often exhibit greater confidence to explore the world, demonstrate resiliency in adverse circumstances, grow and achieve their full potential, and engage in more positive, healthy relationships (Bowlby, 1973, 1988). Secure attachment fostered through positive contingent communication also contributes to the internal ability to conceptualize one's life narrative in a linear, consistent flow that integrates personal thoughts, feelings, and experiences of meaning making together (Jeffrey, 2016).

Many infants and children, however, grow up in relational contexts that do not positively contribute to these critical psychosocial attributes. Patterned parental responses to a child that are characterized by inconsistency, ongoing stress, nonavailability, nonresponsiveness, neglect, chaos, violence, intimidation, or fear can lead to insecure attachment styles, which include avoidant, anxious, or disorganized attachment (Ainsworth, Blehar, Waters, & Wall, 1978). Children who are reared in an emotionally impoverished relationship with a parent may develop an **avoidant attachment style**, which often evolves into challenges with intimacy in adulthood and a desire to achieve physical and/or emotional distance from the attachment figure or those who represent an attachment figure (Van Petegem, Beyers, Brenning, & Vansteenkiste, 2013). Individuals with avoidant attachment often emotionally isolate in order to survive, and they develop a strong resistance to intimacy and do not rely on others to meet their emotional needs. Conversely, children who receive unpredictable or negligent parental responses may develop an **anxious attachment style** (also referred to as ambivalent attachment), which is characterized by a "clingy" posture towards the attachment figure in an effort to maintain the caregiver's attention (Beeney et al., 2017). In adulthood, individuals with this attachment style often have an unsatisfied drive for interpersonal closeness and perceive themselves as unworthy of love and support (Van Petegem et al., 2013).

While individuals who develop avoidant or anxious attachments experience significant parent-child relationship problems and subsequently generalized interpersonal challenges in relationships, the **disorganized attachment style** presents as the most detrimental (Siegel, 2004). This attachment style frequently develops in relational contexts of chronic abuse, neglect, exposure to domestic violence, significant separation from a parent, or foster/institutionalized care. Unlike anxious and avoidant attachment styles, which offer a logical response to the deficits and gaps in the attachment figure's parental practices, disorganized attachment does not have a coherent method in relational interaction (Beeney et al., 2017). The hallmark of disorganized attachment is the agonizing paradox of the child's need to seek out the parent for comfort while simultaneously holding the awareness that the parent is the source of the terror or stress. In these circumstances, the child has no solution and is unable to achieve comfort or regulation (Siegel, 2012). Consequently, children with this attachment style demonstrate a constant "push and pull" in relationships by exhibiting contradictory messages of a desire for emotional closeness or distance that may rapidly oscillate or occur concurrently, such as inexplicable outbursts of anger or aggression followed by a request for physical proximity.

Trauma Work in Practice: Disorganized Attachment

Milo was a preschool-age boy whose grandmother brought him to me for counseling due to his significant behavior problems at home and tumultuous relationship with her. The grandmother explained that in his short life Milo had already experienced an abundance of developmental trauma, neglectful parenting from his mother, and various types of abuse from others before finally coming to live with her. When I first met Milo, I entered the waiting room to find him kicking and yelling at his grandmother for reasons that were unclear to all of us. He was clearly very angry, but after a few minutes, when I explained that he and I would be going to a room full of toys, he instantly became nervous and clung to his grandmother. Milo's big eyes, rigid body posture, and extreme hypervigilance told me that his anxiety was very high about the idea of entering a room with me, and I requested that his grandmother accompany us and stay in the room until he was calm and feeling safe. Once we were all in the playroom and Milo had calmed down and began to become interested in the toys, he suddenly began to push and shove his grandmother out the door and aggressively yell for her to leave.

Within just moments of his grandmother's departure, Milo looked at me with urgent eyes and he began to sorrowfully ask repeatedly where she had gone. Milo must have asked me at least 30 times where his grandmother was during that session, but when our time had ended and we returned to the waiting room to find her just where I said she would be, Milo melted into a heap on the floor and began to wail, kick, and angrily scream at her once again. Instead of finding comfort and a joyful reunion with his grandmother, Milo was triggered into massive dysregulation and seemed to be on an emotional island that kept him at great distance from connecting with his grandmother and from meaningful relationships with others. This confusing pattern of push-and-pull, mismatched reactions, and huge relational swings reflected Milo's disorganized attachment style, and this extreme dynamic continued on for several weeks. Eventually, Milo experienced new consistency, safety, attunement, and care with both me, as his clinician, and with his grandmother at home, and he made great gains.

Attachment Problems and Trauma: Identifying Links, Overlaps, and Distinctions

Significant attachment problems are recognized by the *DSM-5* as a part of the trauma and stress-related disorder category (APA, 2013). At their most extreme, insecure attachment styles, especially the disorganized attachment style, are often consistent with the features of reactive attachment disorder (RAD) or disinhibited social engagement disorder (DSED), outlined in the *DSM*. While attachment disorders and PTSD are not synonymous, they are very closely related. Children who meet the criteria for RAD also frequently meet the criteria for PTSD with the only major difference being that children with RAD/DSED have specifically experienced pathogenic and harmful parental or primary care (Owen, 2017). While insecure or disorganized attachment sometimes results in RAD or DSED in children, these attachment problems may evolve into significant interpersonal challenges and other mental health issues later in adulthood, including borderline and other personality disorders.

Developmental Trauma

Introduced in Chapter 2, developmental trauma is not a diagnosis recognized in the *DSM-5*, but this type of trauma is often referred to as the bridge between attachment disorders and PTSD as it highlights the emotional, behavioral, cognitive, somatic, relational, and self-identity problems that are consequential of the combination of interpersonal trauma and the impaired, harmful, or disrupted attachment between a primary parent/caregiver and child (Spinazzola et al., 2018). Developmental trauma suggests that it is not just *what* trauma happens in a person's life, but of equal importance is *when* the trauma(s) occur(s) (Gaskill & Perry, 2017). During the early years of life, children neurologically develop, create associations, and integrate their experiences at incredible rates, which generates a developmental climate in which experiences and events can profoundly impact the individual in a life-long trajectory. Children are often conceptualized as "highly resilient," but a more developmentally and neurologically appropriate conceptualization suggests that young children are the most vulnerable and the most malleable of any client population (Barfield, Dobson, Gaskill, & Perry, 2012). The impacts of early childhood experiences, including aspects of attachment and developmental trauma, extend all the way across the lifespan, and trauma clinicians must consider the influence of these factors regardless of client age at the time of treatment.

The Scope of Attachment: Considering Impacts and Interactions With Subsequent Trauma

Attachment styles have been shown to be a predictor for post-trauma outcomes, functioning, and symptomology (Ogle, Rubin, & Siegler, 2016). Especially in cases of interpersonal trauma, attachment processes are brought back to the forefront as the individual grapples with his or her internal understanding of relationships, and the contributions of one's attachment history significantly impact the way one internalizes and perceives the traumatic event (Lim, Adams, & Lily, 2012). Much like the function of a seat belt during a car accident, a secure attachment serves as a buffer against the impacts of trauma and is utilized as a critical medium in trauma recovery (Owen, 2017). Individuals with a secure attachment base believe in the helpfulness of social supports and are, therefore, more likely to invest in the therapeutic relationship. Conversely, an insecure attachment leaves the individual vulnerable, unanchored, and disconnected from the human relationships that are so desperately needed in the aftermath of a traumatic event.

Attachment history informs how the individual perceives self in the trauma, and it also structures how the individual responds to the critical relational connection and context that is required for posttraumatic recovery. Clients with insecure attachment backgrounds may feel uncomfortable, unsure, or totally unfamiliar with the attunement and empathy provided by the clinician during this time of distress. The trauma clinician must be prepared to engage with a client who holds an attachment style that may filter the therapeutic relationship through a lens that is programmed to find interpersonal maladies, threats, and signs of disconnection.

Attachment and Regulation

Regulation refers to the ability to utilize attention and inner resources to modulate one's own emotions, level of arousal, thoughts, actions, and attention in order to adapt or achieve a goal (Feng, Hooper, & Jia, 2017). Alternatively, **dysregulation** reflects a state of heightened arousal in the lower brain that is accompanied by a cascade of physiological, emotional, behavioral, and attention-related changes (Siegel, 2012). Everyone experiences dysregulation at one time or another, such as the fear and stress that ensues when there is a near-miss car accident, the panic of rushing to avoid missing a flight, or the intense anger that may follow an offensive comment or gesture. When one becomes dysregulated, the process of regulating back to baseline is essentially the process of quieting and calming of the lower, primitive part of the brain, an area in which rational thinking does not occur. This ability to regulate (or calm during moments of dysregulation) is distinctive from coping skills in that regulation is utilized for sudden and intense situations of distress, whereas coping is often a function of daily living and represents ongoing practices that moderate the frequency, power, or intensity of stress. Regulation is tremendously important as it enables us not only to function through distressing events but also provides the base for the broader experience of self-organization and "how we experience the world, relate to others, and find meaning in life" (Siegel, 2012, p. 273).

During infancy, babies depend on their parent for everything, including the ability to regulate. Infants are not physiologically or psychologically capable of regulating on their own, and they require the presence of a safe and attentive caregiver to help them to regulate and calm. Parents provide regulation for their baby through supportive sensitivity and responsiveness, managing the baby's level of arousal and exposure to stimuli, modeling effective emotional regulation strategies, and providing calm physical closeness to baby, which often involves a synchronizing of lowered heartbeats between parent and child through physical holding and rhythmic motions such as patting, rubbing, rocking, and swaying (Feng et al., 2017). For many parents, this responsiveness is intuitive and reflective of their own positive attachment experiences, and such parents do not need to be reminded to hold and rock a baby when he or she cries; they simply make attuned efforts to find what is personally comforting to his/her unique baby until the child emotionally calms.

As the child grows, this external source of regulation (the parent) is eventually transposed as an internal resource, and the child develops personal regulation skills and can practice small amounts of independent calming for him- or herself, commonly referred to as self-soothing.

The ability to regulate is birthed from the nurturing parent-child relational context, but, unfortunately, this is a central problem for many children. When a parent is unavailable as a consistent source of regulation through comfort, calming, and attunement during infancy, children with insecure attachment must find some way to psychologically, emotionally, and even physically survive and regulate their distress. This predicament often requires the child to utilize regulation strategies that are sustaining for the moment but become detrimental across the lifespan. The use of avoidance or denial, dissociation, self-harm, substance use, and outbursts of anger or aggression are leaned upon as methods for managing distress. In the case story above, Milo experienced powerful dysregulation when he reunited with his grandmother in the waiting room, and his attempt to regulate involved aggressive tantrums until his energy ran out and his exhaustion physiologically calmed him.

Dysregulation is especially noteworthy in trauma work because trauma symptoms are essentially representations of ongoing, often unpredictable, and overwhelming occurrences of dysregulation. Clients who have not experienced a safe relationship in which to adopt helpful regulation skills utilize defensive responses that may provide temporary relief but often only exacerbate the negative impacts of trauma and the severity of symptoms, leaving the individual in a spinning cyclone of devastating patterns (Reynolds et al., 2017). For a client with an insecure attachment background, the therapeutic relationship may be a novel and unique interpersonal encounter in which the client can practice and experience positive regulation in the presence of a safe and attuned person.

Attachment, Self-Regard, and Self-Efficacy

Attachment also impacts one's feelings of self-regard, and individuals with insecure attachment styles often question their self-worth. In relation to trauma, positive feelings of self-regard are a key component to post-trauma functioning, which leaves individuals with negative beliefs about self at a greater risk for higher levels of trauma-related symptomology and more pronounced feelings of shame and self-blame (Lim et al., 2012). One's feelings of self-efficacy, which is a person's belief that his or her actions/thoughts/attitudes will result in an intended outcome, are also informed by attachment experiences. For individuals with secure attachment, their relational experiences have taught them that they if they ask for help, they will receive it, and if they are distressed, they will receive care and will eventually regulate again. The opposite holds true for individuals with insecure attachment; they may lose faith in the process of recovery, question whether or not it is possible to find comfort, or doubt the clinician's ability or willingness to sensitively care for them along the way.

Insecure Attachment and Other Mental Health Issues

Attachment problems have been shown to manifest as severe, complex, and chronic bio/psycho/social/spiritual challenges across the lifespan (Spinazzola et al., 2018). Insecure attachment styles can result in challenges to emotional regulation, interpersonal relationship development, identity formation, and executive functioning (Owen, 2017). Some of these problems mature into other *DSM* diagnoses, and clients may present with dissociative disorders, somatoform disorders, eating disorders, sleep disorders, mood disorders, anxiety disorders, psychosis, substance-use disorders, obsessive-compulsive disorder, and personality disorders. The comorbid rates between early childhood trauma and other mental health issues are expansive, and for psychiatric patients who experienced the onset of a mental disorder in childhood, roughly 44% had histories of developmental trauma while approximately 30% of patients with an adult onset psychiatric disorder had a history of developmental trauma (Green et al., 2010). While every mental health issue must be carefully considered, these disorders often represent branches stemming from the most common diagnostic outcome of cumulative developmental trauma: posttraumatic stress disorder (Farina, Liotti, & Imperatori, 2019).

Implications for Trauma Work: Integrating Attachment With the Therapeutic Relationship

Certainly not all clients who present with trauma-related symptoms also have co-occurring attachment problems, but clinicians are prudent to note the extensive overlap between these two types of traumas and how attachment history impacts the client's view of self and the therapeutic relationship as he or she navigates through recovery. Clinicians also come with their own attachment history and areas of interpersonal countertransference. Undoubtedly, this complex interaction of attachment histories directly impacts the current experience and dynamics of the therapeutic relationship in trauma work. For this reason, trauma clinicians must be especially knowledgeable of attachment, developmental trauma, the influences of their own personal history, and the powerful forces within the therapeutic relationship.

The Interaction of the Internal Working Model of Relationships and the Therapeutic Relationship

One of the most notable outcomes of attachment is a person's development of an internal working model of relationships. This internal working model represents an individual's cognitive schema for understanding self and others, and it acts as a guide for interpersonal patterns, emotional regulation, and relational "rules" for interacting during moments of actual or perceived threat or distress (Bowlby, 1969/ 1988). One's internal working model shapes the individual's expectations for others' responses to his or her request for care, attention, and comfort, which has direct implications for the therapeutic relationship (Ogle et al., 2016).

For clients seeking trauma-focused services, the therapeutic relationship is, by nature, an emotionally vulnerable and sensitive interpersonal experience, and often the trauma work process involves uncomfortable or distressing emotions and memories as the client moves through the recovery process. One potentially distressing aspect of trauma work may include the client's encounter with **relational triggers**, which are reminders of painful or even traumatic interpersonal experiences that often stem from insecure attachment dynamics. While this is often referred to simply as general client transference, a relational trigger is more specific in that it represents an interpersonal interaction that brings up a trauma-associated feeling, sensation, or belief.

Individuals who have been victimized in would-be trusting relationships may be relationally triggered by simple relational hierarchy and even subtle power differentials (Gaskill, 2019). Operating from an internal working model that perceives someone with power as threatening or dangerous, which is often a primary reason for difficulties at school and/or work, these clients may react to the clinician with hypervigilance, avoidance, or anger. Once triggered, clients may experience reactivated feelings of abandonment, rejection, fear, or anger, and/or perceive the clinician's demeanor or actions as sexualized, condescending, an abuse of power, malicious, or unsafe (Briere & Lanktree, 2013).

Trauma Work in Practice: Encountering Relational Triggers

For the last four months, LaToya has provided counseling for Tia to help her with the trauma symptoms associated with her long history of physical and emotional abuse and neglect, which began in very early childhood. Building the therapeutic alliance has been an exceptional challenge because Tia has learned to doubt care from others and feels threatened by emotional closeness and connection since this was so exploited for her in the past.

LATOYA: "You look really down today, Tia."

TIA: "Yeah? What would you know about what I feel?"

LATOYA: "I don't know how you feel, but I can see your downcast eyes and sad frown, and I care about how you are feeling right now. I will listen if you want to share."

TIA: (Sighs.) "I just don't see the point. On days when I've told you more stuff than I planned, I leave here just so angry with myself, and then I'm even more upset than before. I spend the whole day telling myself what a fool I am, and I can't even sleep at night thinking that you know so much about me. If talking to you makes me feel worse, I'm just not even sure why I'm here. Maybe you should just back off."

In this exchange, LaToya offers Tia attunement and nonjudgmental acceptance regarding her feelings, but these facilitative dispositions actually function as relational triggers for Tia. LaToya's attunement to Tia's feelings triggers her to feel uncomfortably exposed as though LaToya can see right through her, and Tia feels profound ambivalence about the therapeutic process. On one hand, Tia soaks up the opportunity to finally receive safe acceptance and understanding during her sessions, but her avoidant attachment pattern tells her that dependency on others is dangerous and costly. In this case, LaToya's simple reflection, which demonstrated appropriate attunement, regarding Tia's feelings and mood represented a relational trigger, and this therapeutic relationship waxes and wanes between progress and setback.

Certainly, the most difficult therapeutic challenge clinicians face with interpersonally wounded clients is gaining and maintaining trust. Many times, clients will attempt to confirm their expectations for what they believe will certainly occur in this type of intimate relationship by challenging the clinician, creating relational tension, making sexual advances, or attempting to provoke the clinician. However, when the clinician refuses to take the bait in the client's attempts to reinforce negative interpersonal beliefs, the client has an opportunity to experience the "mismatch" of a new type of relationship, which positively challenges the client's generalized beliefs about relationships. Through this relational experience, the client begins to see that some relationships can, indeed, offer acceptance, understanding, safety, and nurturing support (Briere & Lanktree, 2013).

For clients who present with a singular traumatic experience and who have a secure attachment base, trauma work often progresses according to the textbook description, and the therapeutic relationship is rewarding and energizing. However, the reality is that these clients are the anomaly rather than the norm, and most clients arrive for treatment with a complex trauma history and/or a disrupted attachment base, which sets the scene for these clients to experience much greater challenges in regard to personality, sense of self-identity, and skills for interpersonal relationship development and maintenance. In the work with these clients, trauma clinicians must be prepared for increased obstacles in developing a strong therapeutic alliance, and very often, the clinician's therapeutic demeanors and dispositions are easier said than done. However, when clinicians can recognize and appreciate a client's pain and reasons for his or her interpersonal behavior, patience and understanding comes more readily.

Fisher (2017) summarizes the potential complexity of building the therapeutic relationship:

> While longing to be loved, safe and welcome, many traumatized clients find themselves alternating between anxious clinging and pushing others away, hating themselves or having little patience with the flaws of others, yearning to be seen and yearning to be invisible. Years later, they present in therapy with symptoms of anxiety, chronic depression, low self-esteem, stuckness in life, or diagnoses of PTSD, bipolar disorder, borderline personality disorder, or even dissociative disorders. Unaware that their symptoms are being driven not just by the traumatic events but by an internal attachment disorder mirroring the traumatic attachment of early childhood, the therapist and client have no framework for understanding the chaos and/or stuckness that may elude their best efforts at treatment
>
> (p. 5).

Ruptures in the Therapeutic Relationship: Normalizing Patterns and Attending to Repair

While the challenges in the development and maintenance of the therapeutic relationship may be substantial, these challenges can be perceived as therapeutic opportunities rather than burdensome hardships. Gelso and Carter (1994) theorized that the therapeutic relationship takes on a U shape in its alliance pattern, which means that the therapeutic relationship often begins with a strong sense of alliance and then decreases in collaborative feelings as the challenges of treatment intensify before making another up-swing as these challenges are navigated, resolved, and weathered. Just as in any other relationship, the client and clinician will almost assuredly encounter ruptures in the relationship, which represent relational tensions or a sudden decline in the therapeutic alliance. Ruptures can occur through situations such as the clinician inadvertently making an insensitive comment to the client, the clinician expressing hurt and frustration for the client's continued dismissive tardiness to session, or the client and clinician strongly disagreeing on whether or not to include another party in sessions. In the case example above, LaToya and Tia encountered a relationship rupture when Tia's perception of LaToya's attunement was experienced as a relational trigger, and Tia told LaToya to "back off."

Ruptures in the therapeutic relationship are especially pronounced for clients with insecure attachment backgrounds. For these clients, their relational history has been characterized by ongoing breaks in the attachment relationship, and these relationship breaks were often not attended to, addressed in a positive way, or repaired and recovered. This template of rupture experiences is often transposed onto the therapeutic relationship and manifested as transference towards the clinician. Basically, the client believes that the therapeutic relationship will mirror the patterns of his or her attachment relationship, which involved repeated violations of trust without successful repair. A trauma-informed relational posture requires that clinicians be mindful of the client's perception of a rupture (i.e., a seemingly insignificant event to the clinician may be quite significant to the client) while also remaining patient and sensitive to the client's unfamiliarity with the interpersonal process of relationship repair (i.e., the inclusion of respect, sensitivity, and proactive reconnection in conjunction with the absence of shaming and blaming).

While relationship ruptures may negatively impact the alliance temporarily, clinicians then have the opportunity for **rupture repair**, in which the relational tension, conflict, perceptions, feelings, and problems are addressed and resolved. The clinician may attend to repairing the rupture by noticing the client's change in affect and then initiating relationship-focused dialogue, such as apologizing for an unintended but insensitive comment, disclosing how the clinician is experiencing the client's tardiness and attitude, and framing a disagreement as a chance to truly listen to each other and collaboratively brainstorm and problem-solve towards a mutual goal. In the situation between LaToya and Tia, LaToya could attend the rupture-repair process though the following therapeutic response possibilities:

- *Expressing understanding, acceptance, and normalization of client ambivalence*
  - Example response from LaToya: "Tia, there is a part of you that feels safe enough in the moment to share things with me, but once you leave, you begin to doubt everything and worry that trusting me might be a mistake."
- *Connecting the current experience in the therapeutic relationship with past attachment/interpersonal history*
  - Example response from LaToya: "Tia, I remember you sharing that your mother would often shame and embarrass you whenever you shared something personal with her, like your feelings and other experiences of abuse. I wonder if you are worried that I am going to do something like that too—there is a part of you that is just waiting for me to betray your trust."
- *Acknowledging the client's feelings but resisting the temptation to personalize them*
  - Example response from LaToya: "My statement about how you are feeling felt too close for you right now, and you really want me to know that you feel uncomfortable with me focusing on your feelings that way. I am glad you can express that things just don't feel okay yet."
- *Remaining patient with the client's interpersonal struggles that manifest in the therapeutic relationship*
  - Example response from LaToya: "Sometimes you just don't want to engage in this process or do this process with me, and that's okay. You have learned how to survive even when that was very, very hard, and more than anything, I want you to feel safe in here with me. So, you can hit the brakes whenever you need to, and I will understand and respect what you need."

Many beginning trauma clinicians desire the therapeutic relationship to be smooth, easily maintained, and entirely non-conflictual, and they earnestly hope for the client to continuously perceive them as a positive figure who doesn't make mistakes. Unfortunately, in trauma work, clinicians may be even more likely to encounter relationship ruptures due to the complex interpersonal issues and the natural experience of stress and apprehension the client feels towards confronting traumatic memories and the recovery process overall (McLaughlin et al., 2014). However, these rupture-and-repair encounters actually offer a prime opportunity to engage in healthy interpersonal practices experientially, which presents an incredibly valuable and relationally healing experience for the client. When clinicians normalize the relational ups and downs that are often experienced in the therapeutic alliance, the relationship is enhanced and becomes a reparative tool in itself, and the safety and trust that is established through these relationship exchanges are foundational to effective trauma work (Farina et al., 2019).

Earned Secure Attachment: Transforming Attachment in the Therapeutic Relationship

We begin life naturally seeking attachment and close relationships, but the experiences of trauma reorganize the priorities of the brain to protect rather than connect. Consequently, the experience of a safe, trusting, and empowering "safe haven" relationship is novel and transformative for many clients (Reynolds et al., 2017). When clinicians remain mindful of the sensitive interpersonal dynamics, develop healthy trust, and provide a safe and accepting relationship for the client to rely on during times of distress in trauma work, the therapeutic relationship may generate a new set of client expectations for relationships and perhaps transform interpersonal patterns into an "earned secure attachment" style of relating (Roisman, Padron, Sroufe, & Egeland, 2002).

In situations of **earned secure attachment**, clients with an insecure attachment style experience a meaningful and authentic connection with a safe person in a reparative relationship, which may occur in the relational context of a friendship, mentorship, marriage, or a therapeutic relationship. This safe person provides many of the attachment functions that were deficient or absent during the individual's early childhood, and the relational experience often includes attunement, contingent communication, and nurturing responsiveness to requests for care and comfort. In this way, the therapeutic relationship is the intervention in itself. With collaborative connection at its core, the relational experience gained through the therapeutic alliance can be powerful enough to transform a client's previous insecure attachment style into features and characteristics more consistent with secure attachment. While trauma can leave many bio/psycho/social/spiritual impacts, "trusting relationships and communication have the ability to heal the mind" (Jeffrey, 2016, p. 234).

Conclusion

In this chapter, we explored that vast complexity of the client's interpersonal history as it contributes to the dynamics of the therapeutic alliance. The professional and relational dispositions of the trauma clinician are especially critical when working with clients who enter trauma work with attachment wounds and scars from interpersonal relationships. Considerations for attachment carry tremendous implications for clinicians as they understand the challenges of the therapeutic alliance in a new way, attend to rupture-repair opportunities, and integrate healing through the experience of the therapeutic relationship itself.

In many ways, the client's past relationships inform how he or she may experience the clinician and the therapeutic alliance; however, this phenomenon is not a one-sided coin. Clinicians enter the therapeutic relationship with their own attachment styles, interpersonal patterns, and aspects of relational countertransference. The therapeutic relationship is a dance of dynamics and a vibrant interaction of perspectives and histories. As trauma clinicians, we cannot safely or effectively enter this sensitive partnership with our clients without recognizing, honoring, and attending to our own relationship templates, expectations, and filters of perception. The therapeutic relationship is the most powerful intervention in trauma work, and therefore, we must care for our half of the dyad by also directing our attunement inward and offering understanding and acceptance of ourselves and own personal histories.

KEYWORD ASSESSMENT

Write definitions in your own words, describe the concept's role in trauma work, list any questions, or make notes of important aspects that you want to remember.

Professional Dispositions

Attachment Disruption

Secure Attachment Style

Avoidant Attachment Style

Anxious Attachment Style

Disorganized Attachment Style

Dysregulation

Relational Triggers

Rupture Repair

Earned Secure Attachment

EXPERIENTIAL ACTIVITIES: INTERACTING WITH THE CHAPTER CONTENT

Expand Self-Awareness

1) Review the reflection questions for each of the clinician dispositions in the section headed "Qualities of the therapeutic relationship and the dispositions of the trauma clinician.". Using the reflection questions as a self-awareness tool, identify which disposition stands out as particularly challenging for you and which disposition stands out as an area of professional confidence.

Expand Knowledge

2) In film, television, or literature, find three characters that exhibit the various attachment styles. Consider what events and patterns contributed to these attachment styles, hypothesize the core beliefs the character internalized from these early attachment experiences, and connect attachment style with the character's current interpersonal relationship patterns, including strengths and limitations within these patterns.

Expand Skills

3) In the case example of LaToya and Tia, develop your response to Tia if she were your client and had just made these statements to you. Reflect on the various aspects that influence your response.

SUPERVISORY DISCUSSION: SHARING PERSONAL INSIGHTS AND IDENTIFYING AREAS FOR GROWTH

1) Describe your growing awareness regarding your professional dispositions in conjunction with trauma work. What kinds of client situations do you imagine will be the most challenging for you to maintain and demonstrate each of the dispositions?

2) After exploring how attachment history can impact interpersonal patterns, describe how your approach to trauma work has changed. What will you be more mindful of when working with your clients?

3) Reflect on your own attachment history. Describe how you believe your attachment history influences your interactions with your clients, including both strengths and areas for growth.

4) After reviewing the various responses to Tia in the case example, discuss how you might work through relational ruptures and repairs in professional practice. Describe considerations for this process as well as your beliefs about why this aspect of the therapeutic relationship is especially important in trauma work.

Case Conceptualization

A Framework for Trauma Treatment

Trauma-Informed Intake: Building a Case Conceptualization

A couple of summers ago, my kids, husband, and I attended a family reunion in south Texas. Alongside their uncle, my twin boys set out on a paddle boat to explore their great-granddad's pond, and while doing so, they managed to capture a young bullfrog, which, by miraculous happenstance, jumped into the boat beside them. Despite my resistance and after much emotional petition, this green fella was eventually deemed our new family pet. We created an impromptu habitat out of an old store-bought macaroni salad container, but we quickly realized that the real challenge was to determine what to feed this little guy. As novice frog caretakers, we offered him a fairly large cricket as a meal option, but the tiny frog left the cricket untouched. A quick internet search confirmed that a cricket is indeed an appropriate food choice for bullfrogs, but the frog's young developmental stage carried a significant impact, which we did not account for. This type of cricket will be gourmet dining for him in the future, but the fact was that the cricket was simply too big for our green friend at that particular point in his lifespan.

In trauma work, we find ourselves in a similar situation. Sometimes what "sounds good" (like a cricket given to a frog) and what might even be propelled by evidence-based research may actually not be an effective or appropriate fit for a client due to unique aspects that we overlooked or did not take into consideration. Prior to developing a treatment plan or applying any therapeutic modality, the clinician must engage in a thorough and comprehensive process of case conceptualization, which serves as the foundation by which an understanding of the presenting problem or concern is developed, treatment can be adjusted and tailored, and attuned trauma work can be provided.

A **case conceptualization** is developed through a comprehensive process of information gathering using a variety of methods with the purpose of gaining a holistic understanding of the unique client and presenting problem. This understanding of the client becomes a primary guide for the clinician with "case conceptualization [serving as] the backbone of therapy, providing structure at every point in the treatment process" (Christon, McLeod, & Jensen-Doss, 2015, p. 37). Regardless of the reason for seeking mental health services, all clinicians, both within and outside of trauma work, will conduct various methods and degrees of information gathering in order to develop a case conceptualization.

All throughout the treatment process, clinicians are continuously applying some type of clinical evaluation, through collecting information, assessing via attunement, conducting observations, or utilizing formal methods. This cumulative information helps the clinician identify and monitor the client's symptoms, problems, and resources which, synthesized, inform ongoing case conceptualization. Very often, the initial evaluative activity that builds a case conceptualization is an **intake interview**, which covers broad topics such as current stressors, relational and home life, personal history, and health. In addition to an intake interview, the clinician may incorporate other methods of information gathering, such as formal or informal assessment, which are narrower in content scope, specialized, and aim to explore a targeted area of interest. For the purpose of this text and to help differentiate between these different types of clinical evaluation activities in trauma work, we refer to the *intake interview* as a universally applied method for global information gathering about a client, and *assessment* is referred to as an additive and selected information-gathering activity that has a specific clinical focus and content. While both types of clinically evaluative activities are critical for a comprehensive case conceptualization, this chapter specifically highlights the trauma-related intake interview, and assessment methods, which are representative of the next phase of information gathering beyond the intake, will be discussed in the subsequent chapter.

While the intake interview is a universal practice for all clients with all types of concerns, this chapter specifically targets aspects that directly contribute to the case conceptualization of the client presenting with trauma-related concerns and problems, which frequently arise as topics of focus during an intake. The general format for intake interviews will be discussed and then followed by a deeper exploration trauma-related features and issues that often accompany these domains. Very often, the intake interview is the first encounter that a client has with the clinician, and therefore, the significance and importance of this information-gathering experience is paramount.

The Intake Interview: Beginning a Case Conceptualization

The intake process can be as diverse as the clients seeking mental health services. Different sites, settings, and specialty practices approach the intake process with various procedures, requirements, and structure. Some sites may request that the client complete aspects of the intake information through written or electronic paperwork while other sites address these topics in session. Conversely, other sites may not have the permission or availability to obtain all parts of an intake. With this diversity of professional circumstances in mind, below is a list of the most common domains and topics routinely covered during an intake interview with a structure that is highly applicable for trauma-related cases.

Client's Current Functioning

- Presenting problem(s) (reasons for seeking help now)
- Mental status exam, including client appearance, orientation, demeanor, mood, speech, insight, motivation, and judgment
- Details surrounding the beginning of the presenting problem(s), current intensity, and frequency of problems
- Current living arrangements
- Physical health problems and current medications
- Current substance use

- Additional stressors (perhaps seemingly unrelated to reason for referral): financial issues, family problems, occupational challenges, etc.
- Current safety concerns (suicidal ideation, self-harm, domestic violence, abuse, violence/ threats towards others, risk-taking behaviors, etc.)

Relational Information

- Friendships, intimate relationships, sexual identity, sexual concerns
- Family relationship background
- Emergency Contact

Historical Information

- Previous significant life events, including developmental milestones
- Previous health issues
- Educational and occupational history
- Grief and loss
- Brief history of traumatic events, which is often discussed in categorical form (exposure to physical/emotional/sexual abuse, significant natural disaster, act of violence, military combat, etc.)
- History of mental health services, including dates of service and service provider(s), any diagnoses, hospitalizations, and the client's reactions to the services received
- History of substance use/abuse/addictions
- History of safety concerns: suicidal ideation/attempts, self-harm, aggression/ violence/threats towards others, or risk-taking behaviors (reckless driving, extreme adventure activities void of safety precautions, etc.)

Personal Aspects

- Aspects of culture: race, ethnicity, gender, age, spirituality/religion, socioeconomic status (SES), physical/cognitive considerations, sexual orientation
- Personality traits, interests, hobbies, learning style
- Personal strengths, support systems, available resources

During all times of information gathering, both during the intake interview and when utilizing any other type of assessment, the process of *how* information is gathered is equally as important the information itself. A central principle for an intake interview is that clients should never feel as though they are in an interrogation or being peppered with questions. While the intake interview aims to glean specific treatment-related information from the client, the focus ideally remains on building the therapeutic alliance and engaging clients in the process as much as possible. The relationship with the client should remain the highest priority and valued above obtaining important data for treatment through intake questions. Information can always be gathered, but damage to the therapeutic relationship has the potential to stop therapeutic work entirely.

The Trauma-Informed Intake Interview: Focusing Conceptualization

The domains outlined for an intake interview are often uniformly applied for most clients and for many types of presenting problems. However, much like adjusting the settings of a camera to capture a certain type of image, the trauma clinician may explore some of these topics with a more attuned eye for the signs, features, and considerations of trauma. The impact of trauma goes beyond diagnostic symptoms alone, so trauma clinicians must be knowledgeable of the traces of trauma that may be present within the dynamics of a multitude of important factors. During the intake interview, these trauma-influenced features in the client may be the first clues that a deeper investigation into a possible trauma history is warranted. With this in mind, the clinician's role is to carefully listen to the client's biographical information and then begin to hypothesize as to whether some of the client's features might be an indication of a trauma history. With a trauma-informed lens in place, the following sections revisit the domains of the intake interview, and this time, we consider the implications and impacts of trauma on these specific aspects in a client's life.

Current Client Functioning: Trauma and Daily Living

Presenting Problems

During this initial phase of the intake interview, clients usually begin by providing their reasons for seeking services as well as discussing any additional current problems or pressing issues. Clinicians must remain mindful that very often clients seek mental health services due to the *symptoms* and/or the consequences of the symptoms they are experiencing; clients are often unable to link their symptoms with an etiological source, such as trauma history. This means that it is incumbent upon the clinician to listen for and begin to organize the client's experiences along case conceptualized hypotheses. In fact, one of the main tenets of trauma-informed care is that "the traumatic event or experience is never viewed as irrelevant to understanding and treating behavioral or mental health problems" (Courtois & Ford, 2016, p. 55).

Although clients are frequently unable to explain the origins and propelling forces of their current problems, clients can provide the clinician with clues that direct the treatment focus. Unfortunately, many beginning clinicians become so consumed with the problem that they miss seeing the person—the client. A truly sensitive approach to trauma-informed information gathering during the intake requires the clinician to move away from the question of "What is wrong with this person?" and move towards a disposition that reflects "What happened to this person and what strengths does she or he possess?"

Occupational and Academic Functioning

Also during this phase of the intake, clients may share problems or concerns related to school or their occupation. Clinicians will notice that not all trauma clients will experience the symptoms or difficulty in functioning outlined in these domains. However, trauma clinicians must be highly knowledgeable of how trauma impacts aspects of functioning and should take note of areas in which a client may be experiencing trauma-related fallout. One such area is occupational and academic functioning, which are often impacted by trauma as difficulty in concentrating is common. For adults, occupational probation or loss of employment may be due to a decrease in job performance related to trauma symptoms, and for youth, the likelihood of poor academic performance and/or grade-level failure significantly increases with posttraumatic stress symptoms (Nooner et al., 2012).

Trauma-Informed Intake in Practice: Understanding Presenting Problems

Richard, a 42-year-old client, came to me for career counseling after he was fired from his fourth managerial-level business job in six years. During the intake, he explained that he believed that he lost his jobs due to his inattention and inability to keep up with the details of his work, and consequently, he frequently made mistakes in deadlines and in paperwork. He sought counseling services to help him to either improve his attention problems so that he could perform his job duties or to gain help in selecting a better-fitting line of work. However, rather than assuming this client's case was as straightforward as it sounded, I chose to do a full intake with Richard prior to applying a career counseling model and focus for treatment.

During the intake interview, I learned that Richard had been taken hostage at knifepoint during a robbery seven years ago while he was performing his workday duties at a local store. Richard assumed that he had successfully recovered from this experience, especially after he began work at a different store, but Richard's current inattention problems proved to be reflective of hypervigilance in addition to other unrecognized trauma-related symptoms. Rather than career counseling, I offered Richard trauma-focused treatment, and by the time of termination, Richard was able to return to the work force and perform his job duties successfully without the need to change career fields.

Health and Substance Abuse

Health problems are also frequently correlated with traumatic stress. Clients with PTSD may be at increased risk for problems in blood pressure, respiratory problems (such as asthma), sexually transmitted diseases, as well as irritable bowel syndrome and inhibited gastrointestinal processes (Espeleta et al., 2018; Hopper, Spinazzola, Simpson, & van der Kolk, 2006). For clients who have other health conditions unrelated to psychological trauma, the fear of triggers and desire to avoid trauma reminders may result with reluctance to comply with certain medical treatment or the medical examination process, and the symptoms of PTSD may complicate and even impede optimal recovery in health issues (Waszczuk et al., 2017).

In regard to substance use, many clients use substances to self-medicate their trauma symptoms, very often beginning use in adolescence, and more than 80% of those diagnosed with PTSD also have a comorbid substance-use disorder (Nooner et al., 2012). A toxic feedback loop develops between the client's trauma-related stress, which stimulates a desire to use substances to cope with the pain, and the new need for or addiction to substance use, which, in turn, increases problems in the client's mind, relationships, body, and spirit (Miller, 2002). Stimulant drugs (also known as "uppers"), such as cocaine, meth, and nonprescribed Ritalin, may be used in an attempt to ease feelings of depression and shame that often accompany trauma but can increase anxiety and impulsive behaviors. Conversely, depressant substances (or "downers"), such as alcohol, prescription pain medication, marijuana, and prescription sleep aids, may be abused to combat the trauma symptoms of anxiety, hypervigilance, and psychological avoidance but can increase depression and fatigue.

Substance use and abuse is a common problem for clients experiencing the impacts of trauma, and clinicians must pay careful attention to this aspect as the elements of addiction, risk-taking, and safety concerns significantly increase for clients who attempt to self-medicate through substances. Treatment programs, such as the Seeking Safety model (Najavits, 2002), address the trauma-related mental health symptoms that are being concurrently experienced with addiction symptoms. Acute issues, such as severe substance abuse and other self-destructive behaviors, may need to be addressed prior to moving forward with trauma treatment (Levy, 1998)

Current Dangers, Suicidality, and Self-Harm

This first intake interview domain also involves screening for any current dangers, including victimizing relationships and thoughts of harming self or others. Some helpful safety-oriented questions might include: "Do you feel safe in your current relationships?", "Tell me about your home life," and "Have you had any thoughts of hurting yourself?" Beginning clinicians often fear that bringing up topics such as intimate partner violence and suicidality will be uncomfortable for clients or might put the idea for suicide in their heads. However, empathetically opening the topics of suicidal ideation and other deeply personal information enhances client safety, not only by attaining the information necessary to determine the best level of care, but also by creating an environment in which difficult subjects can be discussed with acceptance, understanding, and a sense of security.

In the United States, suicidal deaths have increased at alarming rates over the past few decades. According to the mortality rates on the CDC website, in 2018 alone, there were 48,344 completed suicides, which is an increase of 1,171 deaths from 2017 (CDC, 2020). Suicidality is a serious mental health issue that requires evaluation at intake as well as an ongoing assessment during all phases of treatment. Clinicians should note that fleeting suicidal thoughts are not uncommon and do not necessarily indicate an immediate risk of attempt. However, these thoughts should openly be discussed in session and a thorough suicide assessment, including the client's intent, plan, access to means, and other risk and protective factors (such as reasons for living), should be conducted. While "no-suicide contracts" have been determined to be ineffective, research has shown promising results with techniques such as Safety Planning Interventions (SPI+), which combines safety planning activities with phone calls and other follow-up components to reduce suicidal behaviors and increase participation in treatment (Stanley et al., 2018). If the clinician determines that a client is at risk of potentially taking his or her own life (or someone else's), then action must be taken immediately, which may include accessing inpatient-level care.

Self-harm is a sign of emotional pain, but this behavior is not necessarily synonymous with suicidality. While certain self-harm actions could pose a health risk or indicate a desire to end one's suffering, other self-harming behaviors reflect problematic coping strategies associated with complex trauma. For example, self-harm may serve as a method to counter one's feelings of numbness and disconnection (commonly associated with a hypoarousal state). For some clients, the pain inflicted by self-harm offers a physiological way to release the endorphins that the body has come to crave as a result of chronic trauma. Alternatively, the act of self-harm may reflect a complicated reaction of self-hatred stemming from the personalization and internalization of aggression associated with a perpetrator (Cairns & Stanway, 2004). Clinicians should attend to any visible signs of self-harm as well as directly ask about behaviors such as cutting, hair pulling, and burning. Client self-harm and suicidality represent some of the most challenging issues in mental health practice, especially when these behaviors are coupled with trauma. Clinicians, no matter what level of expertise, should always consult, seek supervision, and remain current on the legal and ethical components of this dynamic in treatment.

Trauma Reenactment

Sometimes clients arrive for services due to presenting problems that are associated with problematic or, at times, harmful behavior patterns. In cases like these, clinicians need to apply a trauma-informed lens and consider if these behaviors may be related to trauma reenactment. Historically, Freud (1914) used the term *repetition compulsion* to describe the drive to play out or reenact the past in an attempt at mastery or different outcome (Gostecnik, Tepic, Cvetek, & Cvetek, 2009). **Trauma reenactment** refers to an individual's subconscious reliving or recreation of aspects of a traumatic event and/or attachment wounds. In other words, reenactment represents an individual's unprocessed trauma story that is being acted out through external behaviors for the conscious self and others to witness (Miller, 2002). An example of a reenactment includes a woman who seeks out prostitution after suffering childhood sexual abuse. Unconsciously, this woman replays her sexual victimization over and over again through her behavior.

Some forms of reenactment can be highly detrimental for clients and can present significant safety concerns. Reenactment may lead individuals to gravitate towards circumstances that are reminiscent of their past trauma, and these circumstances are often conditions in which the individual is likely to become victimized again. In rarer instances, reenactment occurs when the individual reenacts his or her trauma on others through victimizing behaviors or perpetration. Clinicians should note that the purpose of exploring a client's possible patterns of reenactment is *not* to blame victims nor excuse harmful actions. Instead, promoting the client's understanding of reenactment provides insight into his or her behavior, which often originates from a subconscious drive to acknowledge and master unprocessed trauma.

Levy (1998) proposed four categories of needs related to trauma reenactment. These personal needs often fuel the compelling motivation to reenact, and Levy (1998) offers examples of both adaptive and problematic reenactment behaviors within each category. First, reenactments may represent an attempt at mastery in which the person aims to gain control in the present over aspects that he or she could not control in the past. For example, a man who witnessed his mother murdered may become a homicide detective to fight crime and try to prevent other murders. Second, reenactments may be a result of rigid defenses used to protect the person from future pain. For example, a young woman whose parents and then foster parents neglected and abandoned her may have an ongoing pattern of clingy and controlling behaviors in her intimate relationships, which eventually results in driving her partners away, and, thus, she routinely reexperiences abandonment. Third, reenactments may occur as cognitive and emotional reactions to triggers. For example, a man who witnessed his drunken father come home and beat his mother may subconsciously create a reenactment by hitting a sales clerk when triggered by disproportionate rage after not being allowed to return an item. Finally, in the fourth category, reenactment is an indication of ego deficits. For example, a woman whose father consistently told her she was a loser and would never amount to anything gets fired from her jobs and is unable to advocate for herself in abusive relationships due to her low self-esteem.

Effective trauma work increases clients' awareness of the strong pull of unprocessed or *unmetabolized* trauma memories (Adams, 1999; Schwartz & Masters, 1994). Clinicians can help clients explore the fear associated with trauma memories, and they can help clients make the connection between the unconscious forces of these memories and any destructive behavior patterns (Levy, 1998). As clients recognize their behavior patterns in relationship with trauma and/or attachment deficits, they have a greater opportunity to extinguish undesired and problematic behaviors. Through psychoeducation, expanded self-insight, and focused trauma work, the client can begin to move from patterns of unconscious trauma reenactment to conscious awareness, and, as a result, the client's feelings of empowerment grow and open the door for positive change. According to van der Kolk (1989), although the aim of repetition is often an attempt at mastery, mastery is rarely accomplished by reenactment and, instead, only furthers suffering. Therefore, the clinician's understanding of and sensitive approach towards cases of reenactment is a necessary component of a trauma-informed case conceptualization.

Relational Information: Trauma and Interpersonal Impacts

As the clinician moves through the intake interview, information gathering will move from presenting problems in daily living and to a focus on the client's current relationships and family background. One of the most devastating impacts of trauma involves the ensuing feelings of shame, fear, and profoundly negative emotions. The weight of these feelings can subsequently lead to a personal sense of isolation and alienation, pulling the individual away from social connectivity.

Social connectedness is essential for psychological and physical well-being, and trauma-related problems very often involve relational challenges that are perpetuated by self-identity issues. Those who have experienced trauma may internalize and personalize deep messages of shame that continuously whisper, "This is your fault," "You are dirty and damaged," "You have no worth," or "No one will accept you this way." Negative relational interactions (or the perception of negative interactions) only serve to confirm these devastating beliefs. The process snowballs, and the individual further internalizes these crippling beliefs about self, which may manifest as feelings of inferiority, incompetence, identity diffusion, depersonalization, low self-esteem, an absence of self-agency, and decreased self-worth (Horowitz, 2015). Relationships and intimacy become triggers for these feelings, and the individual may withdraw, mask, or isolate. The consequences of relational disconnect are profound, and loneliness is a significant predictor for depression and even early mortality (Saeri, Cruwys, Barlow, Stronge, & Sibley, 2018).

While social experiences of shaming, blaming, and loss of support are correlated with higher rates of PTSD and poorer outcomes in treatment, alternatively, when an individual receives consistent, positive social support after a trauma, the individual often demonstrates higher resiliency and more rapid recovery from PTSD (Nooner et al., 2012). For individuals who experienced multiple adverse events in childhood, the sense of having one's family stand by them and having someone to talk with about their feelings is strongly associated with lower rates of depression and fewer negative outcomes (Sege et al., 2017). Even if support was not provided in the immediate aftermath of a traumatic event in childhood, the perception of social support in the months or years following the trauma drastically impacts outcomes as "the presence of strong social ties during adulthood can mitigate many of the deleterious influences of early trauma" (Norman, Hawkley, Ball, Bernston, & Cacioppo, 2011, p. 334). An important area of conceptualization is for the clinician to gain a sense of the social and familial reactions, messages, and support that the client received following the trauma, with the understanding that these interactions often influence the severity of trauma-related symptoms and treatment outcomes.

Trauma Work in Practice: Identifying Interpersonal Influences on Client Outcomes

Albert was a 16-year-old client who arrived for counseling with a history of childhood neglect and repeated sexual victimization. Albert's trauma history resulted in overwhelming feelings of depression and shame, and Albert often battled thoughts of suicide. Because Albert presented with a number of complicated concerns, Albert's foster parents were also involved in the counseling process, and I frequently met with them for family sessions. Unfortunately, Albert's foster parents had profound difficulties understanding and empathizing with Albert's concerns, and their highest priority for Albert was to get him back on track with his academic work, which had fallen significantly behind. While Albert wondered whether or not he was worthy of living, his foster parents focused on his math grade. Albert's lack of familial support during this crisis point in his life only compounded the problem, further isolated him in his depression, and increased his trauma symptomology. As Albert's clinician, I recognized this powerful systemic force, and a main goal in treatment included psychoeducation about the impacts of trauma for Albert's foster parents and increased positive affective communication and support from them.

Historical Information: Trauma, Development, and Past Experiences

In this phase of the intake interview, clients often spend time communicating about aspects of life that may seem unconnected to their current issues, but these can provide insight into symptom development as well as offer the clinician a deeper understanding of the client's attachment history, identity formation, and the use of defenses. One such aspect centers on development, including physical and psychosocial milestones, which may be highly impacted by the traumatic events in one's life. A person's ability to manage the impacts of trauma requires a tremendous amount of energy, and consequently, energy can no longer be spared for other areas of growth, which may result in a halt, stagnation, or regression in development as the individual's full armory of resources is dedicated to physical and/or psychological survival. In children, this may include developmental delays in walking, talking, toilet training, fine and gross motor coordination, reading/writing, and play behaviors. For adolescents, developmental delays may be expressed through gaps in social skills, identity formation, and presenting as immature for one's chronological age. For adults, developmental problems may manifest as barriers to intimate relationships, a failure to launch into independent living or self-sufficiency, or adherence to rigid, black/white versus complex thinking (Taylor & Baker, 2007).

For clients who exhibit developmental concerns, treatment should be designed around the client's **developmental age**, not the client's chronological age. For example, I provided counseling for a 13-year-old girl who had experienced years of severe sexual abuse and trauma. While she outwardly appeared as a young teenager, her psychosocial development more closely mirrored that of a 10-year-old. I began work with this client at her current developmental stage by providing her with play therapy interventions that would have typically felt "childish" to many other 13-year-olds. However, this client relished my acceptance of her developmental stage (an acceptance which many other adults were reluctant to offer), and she immediately engaged in the process of play to reclaim some of the developmental opportunities that trauma had stolen from her in childhood. As clinicians, we always begin where the client is, which includes a consideration for developmental stages.

Brief Trauma History Gathering

The totality of historical information, which is essentially a summary of the client's overall life narrative, provides the clinician with much needed contextual information that may illuminate aspects of the current presenting problem and considerations for treatment. A significant portion of this discussion targets the client's history of adverse and traumatic experiences. While this piece in the conceptualization puzzle is extremely relevant for trauma-focused treatment, there are a few important rules of thumb for the clinician to bear in mind. First, research shows that experiences of **interpersonal trauma**, which represent a traumatic event that results from another person's victimizing actions, are more likely to lead to a higher severity of trauma symptoms and increased potential to meet criteria for PTSD in comparison to non-interpersonal trauma (Yoo et al., 2018). As the clinician learns more about a client's trauma history, a notation of the client's various types of trauma (interpersonal vs. non-interpersonal) will aid the clinician in conceptualizing the client's risk for PTSD and other trauma-related problems. For example, a client with a history of attachment disruptions in early childhood followed by experiences of domestic violence in adulthood (interpersonal traumas) will enter treatment with different clinical considerations than a client who presents with trauma symptoms connected with narrowly surviving a category 5 tornado (non-interpersonal trauma).

Another important principle for clinicians to consider is the depth in which trauma history is explored during the intake itself. The intake gathers general information on traumatic event history and symptomology. Regardless of client age or presenting problem, intake questions concerning traumatic events at the beginning of treatment should optimally remain broad, general, and only briefly explored. Engaging clients in a detailed retelling of the trauma can inadvertently send clients into trauma memory work they are not yet prepared for. As the treatment process unfolds, clinicians begin with an emphasis on healthy coping and stabilization techniques in order to establish the client's firm foundation of psychological safety before diving into the deep end of a trauma narrative. During an intake interview, a client may be emotionally and psychologically spilling over and feel eager and, at times, overwhelmed with the need to share his or her trauma story, but clinicians must be very careful to guide the client into manageable disclosure and content during the intake process. With this important principle in mind, specific discussion about the details of the trauma should not emerge until phase two of treatment, which is discussed later in this text.

Trauma-Informed Intake in Practice: Structuring the Intake Discussion of Trauma History

During her intake session, Stephanie shares with her clinician, Marco, that she is seeking services due to "a horrible childhood." Marco hopes to provide a safe structure for Stephanie to offer more information about her history while simultaneously preventing her from becoming flooded or going too deep, too fast. To accomplish this, Marco explains to Stephanie, "In our time together today, we are going to talk briefly about major and significant moments in your life. Think of this like a preview for a movie—we are just getting a quick clip of important events, and we will save the rest of the full movie for later. Does that sound OK with you?" Marco then asks broad questions, such as whether Stephanie experienced abuse or neglect during her childhood. If Stephanie shares that she was molested by her uncle, Marco may respond, "That must have been a very terrifying and painful experience, and I'm sure it had a significant impact on you. This is something we can discuss more in the future during our sessions together." Marco remains mindful not to probe deeper into the details of the molestation until the therapeutic relationship has had time to grow and Stephanie has developed sufficient coping skills to manage the distress that often accompanies traumatic memories.

Personal Aspects: Trauma, Personality, and Supports

A holistic and comprehensive case conceptualization also integrates a larger understanding of the client rather than focusing exclusively on the problems, features, or life events that may be connected with the reason for referral. The discussion of personal aspects during the intake interview provides the client with an opportunity to share important cultural information, qualities about his/her personality, and support systems that may serve as vital resources. The focus highlights the client's interests, hobbies, and learning style, as these factors can be highly informative in selecting future treatment modalities with which the client will likely resonate and connect.

In regard to personality, specific coping habits and personality tendencies have been linked with increased likelihood for PTSD following a traumatic event. For example, the tendency to react with strong emotions to adverse experiences and focus on negative emotionality is correlated with higher rates of PTSD, while the characteristics of extrovertedness (sociability, talkativeness, and positive affect) and conscientiousness (self-discipline, carefulness, and drive for achievement) are linked with lower rates of PTSD or reduced severity of symptoms (Weinberg & Gil, 2016; Yoo et al., 2018). The client's subjective way of perceiving the traumatic event is another factor, specifically regarding the **degree of proximity to the trauma**, which is the sensation of "closeness" to the trauma (such as feeling as though one was "right there" while witnessing a murder versus feeling more like a removed onlooker), as well as the **degree of personal threat**, which is the sensation of imminent personal danger (such as witnessing a murder with the perception that one will be murdered next versus witnessing a murder with sense of being unobserved or removed/protected from the danger). Very often, the greater the degree of perceived proximity and personal threat during the traumatic event, the more likely the client is to experience PTSD symptoms (Weinberg & Gil, 2016). These subjective reactions to a traumatic event and personality tendencies can have a significant influence on the client's risk and propensity to develop trauma-related symptoms.

Apart from aspects of personality, other elements may contribute to risk and protective factors. Pre-trauma history of other mental health issues, especially anxiety, mood, or conduct disorders, places clients at higher risk for the development of PTSD (Milan, Zona, Acker, & Turcios-Cotto, 2013; Sareen, 2014). Other risk factors for PTSD include lower IQ or mild traumatic brain injuries, fear of possible death during the event, peritraumatic dissociation, acute pain and inhibited ability to cope with physical pain (such as coping deficits due to lack of sleep), and financial stress (Sareen, 2014). Clients who have experienced the death of a close loved one (especially in situations of serious disease or critical injury), endured severe physical or sexual abuse, and/ or encountered emotional abuse during childhood are also at higher risk for the development of PTSD during adulthood (Schoedl, Costa, Fossaluza, Mari, & Mell, 2014).

While there are risks associated with the development of trauma-related symptoms, clients also possess protective factors that may mitigate some of the negative impacts of trauma. Specifically connected with PTSD, resilience factors include faith and religion, adaptive and positive coping strategies, and higher socioeconomic levels (Schoedl et al., 2014). For adolescents, the positive presence and support from a stable parent or caregiver has consistently shown through research to facilitate the natural recovery from trauma-related symptoms (Nooner et al., 2012). For children, safe, stable environments, nurturing relationships, positive social engagements, and opportunities to develop, play, and learn have all been linked with resiliency over adverse childhood experiences (Sege et al., 2017).

Conclusion

Case conceptualization is an essential part of the trauma work, and it informs how the clinician understands the client and the presenting problem. Additionally, it builds the foundation upon which a modality for trauma treatment is selected. Case conceptualization often begins with an intake interview, and clinicians must be highly attuned to the profound and often unrecognized or hidden impacts of trauma. In this chapter, we highlighted various aspects of a client's life that may be significantly influenced by the fallout of trauma. These features are not always synonymous with trauma *symptoms*, which is a critical distinction. While no single client presents with trauma-related features in *all* of the domains outlined, many clients, especially those who meet the criteria for a trauma-related disorder, experience at least some of these patterns. Not uncommonly, these trauma-related features, often discussed during the intake interview, are the first signals to the clinician that unprocessed trauma may be playing an active role in the current problem. When the clinician begins to hypothesize that this may be the case, a more in-depth investigation through assessment is warranted. A thorough assessment explores the possible presence of specific trauma-related symptoms, and this next step in case conceptualization is discussed in the following chapter.

As the therapeutic process begins with the intake, the clinician must be sensitive to the personal risk and vulnerability that is required for clients to share the details of their lives, and this is especially relevant for clients who have significant wounds from others whom they believed they could trust. We often expect our clients to come into our office and present themselves as an open book, and we easily forget how difficult, frightening, intimate, and vulnerable this process can feel. As clinicians, we cannot ask our clients to do something that we are unwilling to do, which ultimately involves the rich but sometimes challenging experience of taking a deep look into the narrative of our own life and inner self and then sharing our experiences openly with another person in the hope that we will be accepted and understood.

KEYWORD ASSESSMENT

Write definitions in your own words, describe the concept's role in trauma work, list any questions, or make notes of important aspects that you want to remember.

Case Conceptualization

Intake Interview

Trauma Reenactment

Developmental Age

Interpersonal Trauma

Perceived degree of proximity to traumatic event

Perceived degree of personal threat during a traumatic event

EXPERIENTIAL ACTIVITIES: INTERACTING WITH THE CHAPTER CONTENT

Expand Self-Awareness

1) Trauma is pervasive, and you or someone you know has likely experienced some of the trauma-influenced features outlined in this chapter. Personifying trauma as though it were a person, write a letter to "Trauma" that describes your thoughts, feelings, and reactions to its impacts. Write out what you want to say to "Trauma."

Expand Knowledge

2) Using your nondominant hand, write the last sentence of this chapter on a piece of paper. Notice the changes you experience in your confidence, energy, physical sensations, and time required to complete the task. Reflect on how underdeveloped skills (such as writing with your nondominant hand) affect you and then consider the parallel experiences that may occur for individuals whose development is stagnated by trauma.

Expand Skills

3) Investigate a research-supported suicide intervention, protocol, or assessment, such as the Safety Planning Interventions (SPI+). Practice elements of this intervention in a role-play using hypothetical situations that may arise during an intake.

SUPERVISORY DISCUSSION: SHARING PERSONAL INSIGHTS AND IDENTIFYING AREAS FOR GROWTH

1) Reflect on your experience of writing a letter to "Trauma." What was this like for you?

2) Discuss the experience of writing with your nondominant hand. How does your experience change your perspective on clients who have developmental implications associated with trauma? Describe how you plan to incorporate developmentally sensitive and inclusive approaches into your intake process.

3) Discuss your thoughts, reactions, insights, and questions regarding suicide assessment. When you consider assessment for suicide and other safety concerns (self-harm, abusive relationships), which aspects do you feel confident addressing with your clients and which aspects do you believe you need growth? Describe your plan for assessing these issues with your clients, including an integration of legal and ethical considerations.

4) The chapter discusses the importance of balancing the therapeutic relationship with information gathering. How do you plan to gather information while keeping your client, not the information, the priority? Describe how you intend to approach the intake process with a trauma-informed perspective.

Chapter 8

Trauma-Informed Assessment: Expanding Case Conceptualization

If you're like me, you have had the experience (perhaps numerous times) of trying to get to a new place, only to find yourself completely lost and disoriented. In situations like these, we often phone a friend to recalibrate our compass, and you can probably guess the first question that often comes from the "on-call" directional helper: "Where are you now?" A treatment plan serves as the clinician's road map to the therapeutic process as it outlines each incremental goal and step for the client. However, a map that pinpoints a destination is not helpful if one does not know his/her current location before beginning the journey.

In the previous chapter, you learned about the important role of a trauma-informed intake in case conceptualization. However, the information gleaned exclusively from an intake interview is often insufficient for a comprehensive case conceptualization. In many settings, the intake interview serves as the initial, broad data collection method, and during this process, the clinician may be alerted to client features that indicate possible signs and traces of trauma. During times like these, the clinician may utilize a more focused assessment method to target specific areas of clinical interest, such as trauma-related concerns. **Assessments** (formal and informal) are clinician-selected methods of information gathering that are utilized with the intended purpose of identifying, differentiating, or gaining a greater understanding of certain features within the client and/or the presenting problem and symptoms. This vital information may include a focus on the presenting issues and symptoms, as well as on the client's characteristics, strengths, and resources. Together, the information acquired through both the intake interview and various assessments provides the critical clinical knowledge necessary to make an accurate diagnosis, develop goals and treatment objectives, and understand the context and perspective of each individual client (Kisiel, Summersett-Ringgold, Weil, & McClelland, 2017). Figure 8.1 visually depicts the flow of the information gathering process, which ultimately results in an individualized trauma treatment plan.

In this chapter, we review the process by which trauma-related problems and symptoms develop over time. In mental health, symptoms are frequently organized and summarized through the use of a mental health diagnosis, and an overview of the various trauma-related disorders outlined by the *DSM-5* is provided. Frequently, trauma symptoms present in a variety of ways, and the incorporation of assessments can be a helpful clinician resource in sifting through problems, understanding the client, and developing a holistic conceptualization of client problems and

Intake Interview: Universally applied for all clients to address broad domains of client's experience
Assessments: Specifically selected for clients to learn more about a narrower scope of content
Treatment Plan: Individually developed for the client through the synthesizing of information to identify problems and determine treatment goals

Figure 8.1 Process of Case Conceptualization Towards the Development of the Trauma Treatment

strengths. The various types of assessments are presented, including an overview of the clinical utility and limitations of these types of tools.

The Prequel to PTSD: Understanding Trauma Symptom Development

Some of our most beloved characters in film have a backstory, and often these backstories are depicted in prequel movies. In cases of posttraumatic stress disorder, there is a neurobiological "backstory" that, when considered, helps us to understand the fully developed PTSD we encounter with our clients. The prequel depiction of PTSD opens with a view of the incredible ways in which our minds and bodies respond to danger and attempt to keep us safe. The physiological and biological mechanisms in our brains provide us with remarkable means and strategies to survive potentially life-threatening situations. However, these mechanisms also often become the catalyst for future trauma symptoms.

In order to understand the development of trauma-related symptoms and PTSD, we must start at the earliest and most foundational stage: neurobiology. Tackling the concepts of neurobiology often feels overwhelming, expansive, and professionally disconnected or irrelevant to many beginning trauma clinicians. However, a general working knowledge of neurobiology aids clinicians in better understanding their clients' reactions to situations, such as the **fight, flight, or freeze response**. Neurobiology is vastly complex, but concepts can be simplified and viewed as clinically applicable when explored through practical illustrations.

Fight or Flight Response

To illustrate the fight or flight neurobiological response to danger, imagine a man walking through the park. As the man admires the beautiful landscape, many neurological activities are happening outside his conscious awareness, including breathing, digestion of his lunch, and an automatic scanning of the environment for potential danger, which acts as an internal "secret service" to keep him safe. His conscious thoughts focus on what he might make for dinner that night, until suddenly, he spots a tiger through the trees. The tiger locks eyes with the man, rumbles a low, ominous growl, and charges at the man like lightning. All plans concerning what to make for dinner cease. Immediately, his internal *alarm system* (amygdala) sounds and he goes into *survival mode*, instantaneously determining that flight is his best chance to avoid death. Physiological functions necessary for flight increase, among them faster heart rate to quickly provide blood to his muscles and shallow breaths to improve oxygen intake, and functions not necessary for flight, such as digestion, communication, and reasoning, are restricted. The man begins to run from the tiger, and, miraculously, he is able to jump into a nearby taxi to escape. While in the taxi, his internal secret service lets him know the danger has passed, and he is able to return to the *rest and digest mode* by restoring his digestive processes and allowing the reasoning part of his brain (prefrontal cortex) back online. He attempts to return his thoughts to what to make for dinner, but he finds it difficult to concentrate, and mental image flashes of the charging tiger continue to interrupt his thinking.

For the man in the above example, the encounter with the tiger was a terrifying experience that may cause him to avoid walking through that park in the future or stay away from other triggering settings or situations, like visits to the zoo, which may remind him of the sights, sounds, or smells of the attack. He may have some difficulty communicating all the exact details of the event due to the executive brain functions that went offline during his fight/flight response, and his ability to verbally articulate the experience may be limited. He may also have lingering nausea from his partially digested lunch, feel exhaustion from the heightened arousal of his central nervous system, and experience flashbacks (visual images or feelings) of the tiger chasing him as his brain tries to process the fragmented memories and images.

Impact of Chronic Flight or Flight Response

In many ways, this man's neurobiology and remarkable brain system saved his life, and his symptoms, which involve normal, acute reactions to the serious danger, such as intrusive thoughts or flashbacks, should dissipate in the coming days as his subconscious works through positively processing the event. However, the problems of this system arise when the man's brain is not able to shut off his alarm system or return to his regulated baseline. While this single event was profound enough, consider what would happen if this man's acute reactions did not dissipate or if he encountered a tiger over and over again, which parallels the situation of complex trauma.

Chronic trauma exposure may result in long-term changes to brain circuit areas, such as the amygdala, hypothalamus, and prefrontal cortex, which impact memory processing and retrieval and verbal declarative memory (Bremner, 2006). As the man continuously encounters the tiger, these powerful, biological reactions to stress would become ongoing and more easily triggered, resulting in significant physiological effects such as frequent scanning of the environment for danger (hypervigilance), exaggerated startle responses, fatigue from the stress hormones released during chronic activation, and reinforcement of vivid flashbacks (Fragkaky, Thomaes, & Sijbrandij, 2016). For the man who encounters the tiger repeatedly over time, what should be a temporary, transient physiological *state* of hyperarousal during a trauma-encounter could become an established and enduring physiological *trait* that persists rather than dissipates (Gaskill & Perry, 2012). Constantly seeing danger when there is none, even within interpersonal relationships, can severely impact one's ability to make connections with others, make rational and objective decisions, perform responsibilities and job duties, and maintain a hopeful, optimistic outlook on life.

Freeze Response

There is another survival response in addition to fight or flight: *freeze* (also referred to as a *faint* response due to the parasympathetic response which causes a drop in blood pressure). Freezing occurs when the brain subconsciously determines that "playing dead" ensures a higher likelihood of surviving the danger than a fight or flight response. Fight or flight responses are considered an active defensive mode, but a freeze response is an inactive mode (also known as hypoarousal) in which heart rate is decreased, breathing slows, and endorphins are released to numb any physical pain in order to help the individual remain in a state of attentive immobility (Roelofs, 2017). Freezing may lead clients to experience guilt and self-blame, wondering, "Why didn't I run or scream or fight back?" Other people, including family members, friends, and even clinicians, may also wonder about these questions and unfairly judge the client for immobile reactions to a traumatic event. Clinicians can listen for these often elusive but profound questions and help clients understand that freezing is not a conscious decision or an act of weakness but, instead, represents an automatic response to a threatening circumstance. Clients can then begin to accept that they did not choose which defensive mode was deployed in a traumatic encounter. These responses occur instantaneously and subconsciously without reasoning or logical contributions from the upper, decision-making parts of the brain (prefrontal cortex).

Impact of Freeze Response and Dissociation

The freeze response can be adaptive during traumatic events, especially when it is not possible to fight or to take flight. However, forms of freezing, such as numbing and dissociation, can cause significant symptoms if they continue to be used as mental defenses (Place, Ling, & Patihis, 2018). Many clients who experience dissociative symptoms fear they are "going crazy" (and movies portraying dissociation reinforce this belief) due to the client's gaps in memory, feelings of being disconnected from oneself and/or the present situation, and splits in personality (which only sometimes accompany this coping strategy).

Clients are often relieved to learn that everyone experiences some degree of dissociation along a continuum. An example of mild dissociation at the lower end of this continuum is the disoriented feeling that many people experience after leaving a movie at the theater or finishing a good book (the individual becomes so engrossed in the fantasy world of the story that it takes a few moments to get back in touch with reality). Many people also commonly experience dissociation while driving (being lost in thought), and upon reaching their destination, experience difficulty recalling the drive there.

While these types of mild dissociative experiences are common to most people, midrange and severe dissociation are less common and have the potential to cause significant issues for the client over time. A midrange dissociative experience might involve a client who becomes so caught up in trauma memories during a therapy session that he or she reacts as if the trauma were currently happening (such as experiencing phantom body sensations or flashbacks) and forgets the present safety and reality of the clinical setting. For example, the man from the tiger story may have the sense that he is "back in the moment" of the chase and experience rapid heart rate, muscle tension or tightness, and extreme fear and anxiety during therapy.

At the high end of continuum, severe dissociation may result in dissociative identity disorder (DID), a condition usually caused by extreme childhood abuse and characterized by profound memory gaps, distinctive personalities within the individual, and an inability to integrate all aspects of self together (APA, 2013). The amnesia experienced with DID helps block painful, traumatic experiences but also generates severe fragmentation of the personality and limited access to memory. Dissociation and other trauma-related symptoms are neurobiological expressions of trauma's significant impact on the mind and body (Fisher, 2017).

In summary, the profound neurobiological changes that accompany a trauma may generate gaps in client's memories, create difficulty with verbal expression of the experience, and exacerbate a heightened sense of ongoing danger. Individuals may experience hypervigilance and hyperarousal, numbing and dissociation, or they may vacillate between these two states of emotional dysregulation (Hicks & Dayton, 2019). However, the good news is that healing is possible! Across the lifespan, physiological changes to the brain's structure can improve with **neuroplasticity**, which is the brain's remarkable ability to change by developing new cells and neural pathways (Bingaman, 2013). When clients are able to understand the neurobiology behind their trauma reactions and lingering symptoms, the experience becomes less confusing, more manageable, and less likely to cause feelings of guilt or shame for the client. Clients benefit from learning that chronic activation of fight/flight/freeze responses may be responsible for a variety of symptoms, including dysregulation of emotions, social isolation, inattention, fatigue, and anxiety.

Trauma Work in Practice: Identifying Dissociation as a Goal for Assessment

When 29-year-old Shelly arrived for counseling, she appeared timid but determined to overcome her trauma-related symptoms. Shelly explained that she endured years of physical and sexual abuse from her father, eventually leading her to the decision to run away and live with a friend in another state when she was 16 years old. During the intake, Shelly briefly described her trauma history, but she explained that she could not remember when the abuse started, many details about it, or even how often it occurred. Shelly shared that she remains in contact with her older sister, who recently showed Shelly a photo album of childhood pictures. Shelly was very distressed to realize that she did not remember a considerable number of events from her childhood, especially when she was between the ages of eight and 11. Shelly explained that she is unable to remember much about the house she lived in during that time, who her childhood playmates were, or the significant family events that occurred during that time frame. Shelly's major gaps in memory in conjunction with her trauma history suggest dissociation as a consideration, which warrants further clinical investigation and assessment. The clinician needs more knowledge of Shelly's tendencies towards dissociation and the degree to which she dissociates so that these aspects can be considered in Shelly's treatment and targeted as goals for safe trauma work.

Trauma-Related Diagnoses: Categorizing Symptoms for Clinical Utility

The neurobiological functions of the three types of danger responses (fight, flight, or freeze) serve as the "origin story" for many trauma-related symptoms and problems. For many individuals, these once helpful survival responses persist rather than dissipate, and over time, strategies transform into symptoms. As clinicians work to help these clients resolve trauma-related problems, an important aspect often involves organizing these symptoms as a group of related problems in a summative mental health diagnosis.

For mental health professionals, diagnosing is a way to categorize symptoms and better understand the common characteristics associated with these symptom clusters to guide treatment planning (APA, 2013). In general, the *DSM* uses levels of distress and impairments in functioning to determine whether or not the individual's symptoms are severe enough to meet the criterion for a diagnosis. Clinicians should note that even though a client may not meet the full criteria or level of impairment to warrant a trauma-related diagnosis, the client may still be experiencing powerful impacts of problems associated with trauma. The assignment of a diagnosis is necessary for most third-party reimbursement; however, a mental health diagnosis can be stigmatizing. Clinicians must be sensitive in diagnostic application and mindful of respectful communication to clients about any diagnoses that are assigned.

The Family of *DSM-5* Trauma and Stress-Related Diagnoses

Most of our discussion in this text specifically targets PTSD. However, trauma problems are best viewed under a broader umbrella. PTSD is one of five main disorders listed in the *DSM-5*'s Trauma and Stressor-Related diagnostic category, and these mental health disorders can be considered a "sibling set" within the trauma and stress family. Some of the "siblings" more closely resemble one another than do others, but they are also distinctive and unique. This "family" of trauma and stress-related diagnoses includes reactive attachment disorder (RAD), disinhibited social engagement disorder (DSED), posttraumatic stress disorder (PTSD), acute stress disorder (ASD), and adjustment disorder (AD). Figure 8.2 visually reflects the trauma and stress family of diagnoses, with the more closely related disorders represented in similar shapes.

In order to accurately diagnose, trainees and clinicians must understand the full criteria for each of these disorders, but a summary of each may aid in differential diagnosis. Briefly stated, RAD is diagnosed in children who display inhibited patterns of interaction with caregivers and emotional disturbance as result of problematic attachment that developed during infancy and early childhood. DSED is also a child-specific diagnosis related to attachment and ascribed to children who overly and indiscriminately connect with unfamiliar adults.

In a similar way that RAD and DSED diagnostically and etiologically connect, ASD, PTSD, and AD also parallel each other. PTSD symptoms are the direct result of a traumatic event that happened at least 30 days prior to diagnosis, and these symptoms include aspects of intrusion, avoidance, arousal, and negative changes in thought and mood (and potentially dissociative symptoms). ASD criteria mirrors the symptoms of PSTD, but the ASD diagnosis is distinguished by a time-limited presence of symptoms, which may emerge as early as three days after the traumatic event but dissipate within one month following the traumatic event (if symptoms persist after one month from the time of the event, PTSD or another diagnosis would be considered). Representing the last branch of the tree with both diagnostic overlaps and distinctions, AD symptoms are the direct result of an identified stressor that occurred within three months prior to diagnosis. The DSM provides less stringent criteria for what constitutes a *stressor*, in comparison to the defining qualities of a *traumatic event* in PTSD/ASD. In AD, the client experiences emotional or behavioral reactions at a disproportionate level to the stressor.

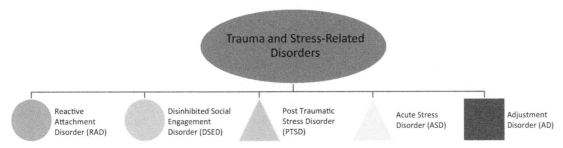

Figure 8.2 The Family of Trauma and Stress-Related Mental Health Diagnoses

Differential Diagnosing

Much like attempting to sort out a basket of tangled yarn, determining a trauma-related diagnosis can be highly challenging. Very often clients with complex trauma have **comorbid** (occurring at the same time) diagnoses, and investigative work may be required to determine the root cause of the client's many and varied symptoms. Clinicians must carefully examine the client's symptomology to determine which symptoms are associated with trauma and which represent a truly distinct set of problems connected with another mental health issue.

For example, the reexperiencing symptoms of PTSD, which include hyperarousal and anxious avoidance, can often mirror or exacerbate the symptoms of generalized anxiety disorder or panic disorder (Sareen, 2014). Other overlaps of symptom presentation can occur alongside disorders such as major depressive disorder (MDD), borderline personality disorder (BPD), and attention deficit hyperactivity disorder (ADHD) (Brewin, 2017; Walton et al., 2017; van der Kolk, 2015). The clinician's ability to apply differential diagnosis and accurately determine comorbidity is critical, as a co-occurrence of PTSD, depression, substance use disorder, and psychosis significantly increases a client's risk for suicidality (Yoo et al., 2018).

For children and adolescents, the application of a differential diagnosis between PTSD and ADHD can be especially challenging. Trauma often causes the symptom of hyperarousal as well as difficulty concentrating due to fragmented memories and intrusive thoughts that restrict one's ability to pay full attention to present situations, and clients who present with these features are often misdiagnosed with ADHD. These clients may indeed be experiencing symptoms best explained by ADHD, or perhaps these symptoms represent the features of PTSD exclusively. Still other clients may experience both PTSD and ADHD in conjunction. However, clinicians must carefully assess to determine if the client's inattention is a result of a trauma experience and better explained by PTSD diagnosis even though the client may meet the ADHD criteria. This complexity in diagnosing requires clinicians to sharpen their assessment skills and increase their tolerance for ambiguity in order to navigate the permeable lines of diagnosis and treatment.

The impact of trauma on distress levels and impairment will vary greatly across clients. Additionally, research indicates that cumulative exposure to trauma significantly increases the complexity of symptom presentation; therefore, clinicians must have a strong working understanding of these disorders as well as knowledge regarding the rates and characteristics of comorbidity with mood disorders and other trauma-related conditions (Cloitre, 2009). Clinicians should be prepared to distinguish between the varied nuances of trauma symptoms and understand their definitive characteristics in comparison to other disorders.

Presentation of Trauma Symptoms and Client Strengths: Developing a Full Picture

Clinician knowledge of the *DSM-5*'s criteria for each of the trauma-related diagnoses is paramount in trauma work, but this is only part of a working conceptualization of trauma symptoms. Trauma clinicians must be able to identify the various manifestations of these broad, clinical descriptions of diagnostic criteria. The presentation of symptoms will range significantly from client to client, and trauma clinicians must seek to learn how trauma is affecting the individual in unique and personal ways. Clinicians must also be mindful of the client's personality, background, and culture and bring balance to searching for client problems as well as strengths.

Identification of Trauma Symptoms

The *DSM* provides a definition of what constitutes a trauma event and categories of symptoms based on the various trauma disorders. However, the following bio/psycho/social/spiritual categories are often how symptoms manifest in real life with real clients. As with the trauma features discussed in the previous chapter, trauma clinicians will notice that each unique client expresses trauma symptoms differently, with no one client experiencing all of these problems or even experiencing problems in all of these categories. Many clients have a tendency towards a cluster of externalizing symptoms (behaviors that are overtly evident to others and expressed outwardly) or internalizing symptoms (psychological, emotional, and/or somatic distress that is not apparent to others). While this is not an exhaustive potential symptom list, these domains and possible expressions of trauma highlight the various signs and symptoms to look for during the assessment process (Briere & Scott, 2015; Place et al., 2018).

- *Behavioral symptoms*: self-mutilation, substance abuse, impulsivity, avoidance of places, people, or physical reminders that may trigger painful memories, and sudden outbursts, tantrums, and significant dysregulation in children
- *Psychological and emotional symptoms*: shame, guilt, anxiety, depression, emotional numbing, hyperarousal (constantly being "keyed up"), anger, excessive fear, hypervigilance, hypoarousal (decreased ability to generate emotional energy or reactions), and developmental regression in children
- *Somatic symptoms*: extreme fatigue, insomnia, stomachaches and headaches with no medical explanation, changes in appetite/eating behaviors, sexual dysfunction, muscle stiffness and increased muscle tone, and rapid resting heartbeat
- *Cognitive symptoms*: memory loss, disorientation, flashbacks, nightmares, and cognitive distortions, difficulty concentrating, and academic/learning/reading delays and regression in children
- *Social symptoms*: difficulty in relationships, dependency, aggression/hostility, misperception of social signals, and isolation
- *Spiritual symptoms*: loss of faith, feelings of betrayal, loss of identity, grief, altered worldview, and loss of meaning

For most individuals, the peak of trauma-related symptoms occurs immediately after the trauma event and then these symptoms often slowly diminish over time. However, up to 25% of individuals experience delayed-onset (at least six months after the traumatic event) PTSD symptoms, and in these cases, symptoms often increase rather than decrease over time (Sareen, 2014). In situations of delayed-onset trauma symptoms, these clients may have even greater difficulty connecting the current problems with the trauma event as months and perhaps even years may have lapsed.

Identification of Client Strengths

In mental health, there is often a tendency to focus on symptomology while overlooking client strengths in assessment. However, a client's strengths provide a buffer for the impact of traumatic events and any potentially ensuing symptoms, and these resources also potentially improve treatment outcomes over time. Client strengths include the various resources that clients can utilize to receive support. Individuals possess their own internal resources which may include resiliency, spiritual beliefs, positive outlook, creativity, adaptability, ego resiliency, and a sense of purpose and goals. External resources include supportive family, romantic partners, friends, religious communities and leadership, cultural associations, school and work connections, and support groups. A comprehensive case conceptualization requires the whole picture of the client, not simply a problem-focused perspective, and the "strengths that are identified through the assessment process can be translated directly into service goals and plans" (Kisiel et al., 2017, p. 439).

Assessments in Trauma Work: Selecting a Type of Instrument

The problems and symptoms of trauma-related diagnoses are expressed through behavioral, somatic, cognitive, psychological/emotional, social, and/or spiritual symptoms; however, identifying, pinpointing, and differentiating between these symptoms can be highly challenging and complex. In other words, we know *what* to look for but may feel unsure of *how* to identify and differentiate symptoms. The clinician often begins with the intake interview as the initial step in conceptually organizing the client's trauma-related problems, but frequently, other assessments must be utilized to target information that may be convoluted, outside of the client's awareness, lost in communication barriers, unacknowledged, or misperceived. There are various types, methods, and formats for assessment work, and each brings unique strengths as well as limitations to the process.

Direct Observation and Collateral Information in Assessment

Case conceptualization and clinical decision making for treatment involves gathering the data from the intake interview and, very often, incorporating other methods that may prove helpful and extraordinarily informative. While we hope that our clients are able to provide us with accurate and reliable narratives of their lives and current functioning, clients frequently lack self-insight or misjudge aspects of their life that feel "normal" to them. These clients often overlook critical aspects of personal information and are simply unaware of the clinical merit of these parts of their lives. Conversely, other clients feel the need to hide, convolute, or protect certain parts of their life and may intentionally mislead the clinician for fear that these parts of themselves will be exposed or exploited. While clinicians may feel tempted to personalize a client's decision to withhold information, a trauma-informed reframe suggests that this behavior is yet another impact of the trauma which the client is attempting to survive in the best way he or she knows how. In either case of intentional or unintentional information withholding, clinicians must remain mindful that the information gleaned from a narrative or single assessment tool alone may be lacking in extremely critical aspects of the client's case.

With this important dynamic in mind, the clinician may implement the use of **direct observation**, which involves observing the client in session and, in some cases, outside the clinical office while the client engages in a normative daily living activity, and the clinician subsequently documents these observations as part of an assessment approach (Quake-Rapp, Miller, Ananthan, & Chiu, 2008). Most frequently, direct observation takes place in session, and in this context, the clinician observes the client's patterns in speech, behavior, mood, and cognitive thought as a primary tool for gaining greater understanding of the client and making clinical hypothesis. For example, I once worked with a client whose self-insight was so low that she was unaware of some of her own behaviors. In one session, I asked my client to complete a brief, written assessment, which was intended to aid in differentiating between some of her presenting problems. As I observed my client attempt to complete the assessment, I noticed her eyes glazed over and she began to engage in invisible writing for several minutes. When I shared this observation with my client, she had no idea that she had done this. In this case, I had intended for my written assessment to provide important information about my client, but, in fact, my direct observation of her carried far more implications regarding her possible diagnoses and care.

Apart from the observation that occurs continuously in session, direct observation may also take place in a naturalistic setting for the client, such as home or school, and this method is exceptionally valuable in learning more about aspects that client either has not or cannot communicate to the clinician. Direct observation in other settings also illuminates aspects that might not otherwise have been noted, such as how elements of the environment interact with and affect the client, and it may also provide the clinician with insight regarding the congruency between the client's perception and the reality of certain situations. Additionally, direct observation may be the assessment tool of choice for systemic work, such as evaluating the dynamics within families, couples, or other important relationships (Faddis & Cobb, 2016). Home visits, family-based techniques, and group interventions all include aspects of powerful direct observation in which the clinician utilizes the context, setting, and relational patterns as a means for gathering information. Direct observation often focuses on the *process* by which clients engage in daily living or within relationships, not just the final product or outcome.

In addition to direct observation, clinicians may also seek **collateral information** from other sources. Collateral information represents important impressions and observations of third parties—individuals who frequently interact with the client or who have helpful knowledge of the client that contributes to a case conceptualization. These additional contextual sources may include teachers, physicians, previous mental health clinicians, family members, spouses and partners, or friends. Collateral information always involves ethical procedures, including obtaining a signed release of information from the client, and the subsequent process of information gathering with these parties may be either formal or informal. Formal collateral information may include objective questionnaires or assessment, such as a teacher observation form, previous medical or mental health records, academic reports, or legal documents. Informal collateral information may include a consultation with a doctor or previous clinician over the phone or involve goal-focused conversations with family members or close friends. Both collateral information and direct observations are especially useful in obtaining information that may otherwise be challenging to retrieve from the client's report alone. Synthesizing the totality of this information generates a much stronger clinical hypothesis about the client's experience and etiology (or origin) of symptoms and other presenting issues.

Objective Instruments

Beyond the intake interview, the clinician may employ an objective instrument to evaluate symptoms as well as identify strengths. An **objective** (or **standardized**) **instrument** is an assessment tool that has been determined through research to have reliability, validity, and clinical utility for the purpose for which it was designed. Very often, objective instruments are nomothetic, which means that the client's individual results on the assessment are compared to a larger population to determine clinical thresholds that can inform risk levels, diagnosis, etc. (Christon et al., 2015). Objective instruments vary in cost (public/free versus commercial/cost), requirements for administration (specific professional licenses, certifications, or additional training), age limits of clients (appropriate for children, adolescents, and/or adults), and level of difficulty in scoring.

While many objective instruments are standardized with established validity and reliability measures developed through extensive research, some instruments may be designed to provide more descriptive information. Idiographic assessments are intended to be used as pre- and post-test tools that compares the individual's results only to him- or herself to monitor changes within the individual (Christon et al., 2015). This type of assessment is especially helpful when the clinician desires to monitor the client's personal progress and individual changes.

An additional benefit of an objective assessment is its utility in aiding a client's educated choice about medications for short-term or long-term use, which can be informed with the data regarding the client's current trauma symptom pervasiveness and severity. There are no medications that "cure" trauma. However, psychotropic medications can reduce many trauma-related symptoms, such as difficulty sleeping and severe anxiety, and thus can help clients move more easily through the treatment process. For example, when clients score in the severe range on the Beck Anxiety Inventory, or BAI (Beck & Steer, 1993) and Beck Depression Inventory, or BDI-II (Beck, Steer, & Brown, 1996), I explain to them what the scores mean and how medications may be effective at decreasing the symptoms of emotional distress and improving overall functioning. Of course, some clients may choose not to take medications for various reasons.

Clinicians should be mindful to maintain a posture of openness regarding the client's choice about medication and avoid stepping outside the professional scope of practice by recommending a specific type of psychotropic. Clinicians may encourage clients to have a thorough discussion with their doctor (preferably psychiatrists, who specialize in psychotropic medications) about the benefits, risks, and limitations of using medications to treat various symptoms. As a best practice, clinicians can collaborate with the prescribing doctor upon receipt of a signed release of information. With clients who are prescribed medication, clinicians should be knowledgeable about the client's ongoing adherence to prescription guidelines as well as continually monitor clients for potential side effects of medications, such as adverse changes to mood, mental status, and increased suicidal ideation. Ultimately, medications aimed at reducing trauma-related symptoms should be understood as an available option for clients as part of the therapeutic treatment process and as a component that requires continual monitoring and consideration by both the medical doctor and the clinician.

While objective assessments are often very helpful in clinical decision making, these instruments also present limitations and considerations. Clients may feel unvalued by "being reduced to a number on a chart" or they may feel pressure to "perform for the test" and worry they might "fail" the assessment. Clinicians should be mindful of other factors that may influence or convolute assessment results, such as the impact of culture, language processing challenges, learning disabilities, and developmental characteristics. Instrument selection also varies according to the client's presenting symptoms and information needed for treatment planning, and clinicians should avoid administering an assessment simply because it is available.

Projective Instruments

In contrast to objective assessment tools, **projective instruments** are a category of assessments in which a client responds to abstract images or instructions with the goal of revealing aspects of the client's personality or personal history (Gregory, 2013). Projective measures usually require additional training to administer because, unlike standardized tests, the interpretation of results is not definitive, and clinicians can inadvertently make subjective errors if not properly trained. A well-known example of a projective instrument is the Rorschach test (Rorschach, 1942), in which clients project their subconscious thoughts/feelings onto a series of inkblot images. Another projective assessment that can be very useful in trauma work is the House-Tree-Person

(HTP) personality instrument (Buck & Hammer, 1969), in which the clinician asks the client to draw a house, a tree, and a person and then interprets the client's inner perceptions and attitudes through these abstract drawings.

Trauma Work in Practice: Utilizing a Projective Assessment

In my professional practice, I utilize the HTP assessment with children and adolescents (although it can be used with adults as well), and I often administer it during various phases of the treatment process as an idiographic assessment to monitor the client's individual changes. During one case, I administered the HTP at the beginning of treatment with a 17-year-old female client, who had experienced severe childhood trauma. In response to the prompt to draw a house, the client drew a home without doors or windows, potentially representative of her feelings of isolation and lack of openness to social interaction. After two years of trauma work and therapy, I repeated the HTP (without discussing the results of the first test), and this time, the client drew a home with a front door, a welcome mat, a path leading to the house, and eight open windows on the front of the house. While interpreting the HTP can be complex, the inclusion of a door and open windows can represent a desire to interact with others, and the path and welcome mat can represent accessibility to the outside world. This projective assessment beautifully illustrated the client's healing and posttraumatic growth reflected in her new openness to life (represented by her drawings) and provided tangible evidence of her progress, which we celebrated during our termination sessions.

Cautions and Considerations for the Application of Assessments

When administering any assessment, there are a number of cautions for clinicians to keep in mind. Clinicians should note which assessments are intended to be utilized diagnostically and which are intended for general information-gathering purposes. Additionally, a crucial rule of thumb centers on the pacing of assessments, which means that clinicians should not administer too many instruments at one time. Inappropriate pacing of assessment administration has the potential to overwhelm the client and also impact the results. Clinicians should not administer an assessment simply because it is available. Multicultural aspects must always be considered regarding the suitability of the assessment in congruence with the client's abilities, development, vocabulary (including cultural slang), and cultural appropriateness. At all times, trainees and clinicians are cautioned to consider their own level of competency, ethical considerations, and corresponding state laws, and clinicians must always seek supervision when learning how to administer a new clinical test.

When utilized effectively, assessments can be a tremendous and much needed resource in trauma work, and there are vast numbers of helpful and problem/strength tailored instruments that can be utilized. Appendix A in this text provides a chart listing many trauma-related and other helpful assessment tools that can be applied in trauma work. A comprehensive assessment utilizing various assessment measures not only provides vital information for the clinician in treatment planning but can also be therapeutic by enhancing clients' self- reflection and understanding (Whiston, 2017).

Conclusion

In order to provide effective and ethical clinical treatment, clinicians must learn how to conduct a thorough (and ongoing) assessment, be familiar with *DSM* diagnoses, and monitor client needs and progress throughout treatment. This chapter highlighted the origins, development, and presentation of PTSD and trauma-related symptoms as well as the types and utility of various assessment methods in trauma work. These clinical skill sets are developed over months and years of experience, and the clinician can learn what is most effective through observing clients' progress in treatment. In addition, clients become wonderful teachers of what is most effective by providing feedback.

The task of case conceptualization in trauma work is complex and often involves equal parts of clinical skill and therapeutic art. Across the course of one's career, all clinicians, ranging from novice to the most senior, experience "impostor syndrome," in which one's knowledge and expertise feels remarkably insufficient and lacking. An important way to for us as clinicians to overcome fears of professional inadequacy and resist giving in to the pressure that we are fully responsible yet insufficient to rescue clients from their pain, is to increase our comfort level with the ambiguity and complexity of trauma work. Assessment of our own positive attributes as clinicians helps us to attend to our potential for growth and better view ourselves as burgeoning professionals (Bell, 2003). While we may lack competency in some areas (and should do our best to gain competency and continue to grow throughout our careers), we also bring our own set of strengths to clinical practice and should consider these traits as we assess ourselves and our clients within the therapeutic process.

KEYWORD ASSESSMENT

Write definitions in your own words, describe the concept's role in trauma work, list any questions, or make notes of important aspects that you want to remember.

Fight Response

Flight Response

Freeze Response

Neuroplasticity

Comorbid Diagnoses

Assessment

Direct Observation

Collateral Information

Objective Instrument

Projective Instrument

EXPERIENTIAL ACTIVITIES: INTERACTING WITH THE CHAPTER CONTENT

Expand Self-Awareness

1) Recall situations in which you experienced each of the distinct fight/flight/freeze responses. These situations may be feeling anxious before public speaking, the fear of almost being hit by a car, an aggressive response to someone, or physically or emotionally fleeing a tense situation. On a blank "gingerbread man" image, select different colors representative of each of the three physiological responses and then color and identify where you felt each type of activation in your body.

Expand Knowledge

2) Using Appendix A as a resource, research the various types of assessments: objective, projective, nomothetic, and idiographic. Select at least two of these assessments and ask a peer to role-play taking these with you.

Expand Skills

3) Sort through the various trauma symptom expressions and connect at least eight of these symptoms with a neurobiological danger response (fight, flight, or freeze) and identify whether you believe the expression is an internalizing or externalizing symptom. Note your rationale for your connections.

SUPERVISORY DISCUSSION: SHARING PERSONAL INSIGHTS AND IDENTIFYING AREAS FOR GROWTH

1) Discuss what you learned about yourself regarding how survival responses manifest within your body. What changes do you notice in yourself when each of these responses is activated?

2) Discuss the learning you took away from investigating and role-playing the assessment instruments. What are some important cautions and considerations for these particular tools?

3) Review the concept of "impostor syndrome," which is presented at the conclusion of the chapter. Reflect on your connections with impostor syndrome and share the aspects of trauma work that most make you experience this phenomenon. How can you manage the feelings associated with impostor syndrome when they arise?

4) Review the case of Shelly from the chapter. In regard to the concern about her dissociative tendencies, where would you go from here? How might you assess this aspect in Shelly, and what might be some considerations or implications for trauma work with this client?

Chapter 9

Trauma-Informed Treatment Plan: Synthesizing Case Conceptualization

Whenever I am in New York City, I always relish the opportunity to visit various art galleries. In contrast to the bustle and grind of the city outside, the talent, skill, and grace of artistry becomes so alive and palpable. I recall one trip to a gallery in which a series of impressionist paintings were on display, including works by Monet. I was familiar with many famous Monet paintings that I had seen through images in books and film, but I was simply in awe to see these masterpieces in person. As I took in Monet's work, I noticed that if I was physically very close to the painting, the image became muddled, indistinct, and blurry. Up close, I struggled to even gain a sense of the general focus or content of the painting; the colors seemed to simply swirl together. However, when I stepped further back and took in the whole painting from a more removed vantage point, the image was pristine, lifelike, and absolutely magical. For this type of art, the power is in the entire picture, designed to be seen from a distance, as opposed to examined for up close details.

In trauma work, there are times when details are critical, and much of the intake and assessment process aims to illuminate the distinct shades and variations of a client's history and symptomology. However, at other times, trauma work requires the clinician to move back, examine the picture broadly, and view the whole process from a comprehensive, overall perspective. In academic terms, we often refer to this as **synthesizing**: the process of combining and unifying many distinct elements of a client's case to form a comprehensive conceptualization. This chapter highlights the process of synthesizing the client's information within the broad framework of trauma treatment. As a metaphorical parallel, we can think of the information gleaned from the intake and assessment as the colors on the painter's palette, and from these colors, the whole image of the trauma treatment process is seen more clearly when we take a step back and view all the parts into one comprehensive picture.

In this chapter, we discuss the conceptual organization and scaffolding for a strong case conceptualization in trauma work and how this conceptualization then informs the trauma treatment plan. Trauma treatment itself is also introduced as a process that develops along three general stages through the tri-phasic model. The client's unique information coupled with knowledge regarding the progressive evolution of trauma treatment aids clinicians in determining goals, establishing a hierarchy of treatment priorities, and navigating through the overall process of trauma work.

A Four-Factor Framework for Conceptualization: Synthesizing Client Information

The completion of the intake and any applied assessments is a major goal, and yet, obtaining information from the client is only as helpful knowing how to synthesize and utilize it. At this point in the process, the clinician is faced with the challenge of making sense of the information from a treatment-oriented perspective. Christon et al. (2015) provide a framework for clinicians in regard to the next step in case conceptualization. Generally, the clinician can explore each piece of client information, including details of each domain in the intake and any assessment data, using a four-factor conceptual framework. This four-factor conceptual framework includes 1) predisposing factors, 2) precipitating or causal factors, 3) perpetuating or maintaining factors, and 4) protective factors. This framework provides a conceptual scaffolding to organize the intake and assessment data in a way that delineates what is happening within and around the client, how these factors may be influencing trauma symptoms, and how these factors may be incorporated for treatment decisions. The clinician must synthesize case conceptualization by hypothesizing a client's:

- *Predisposing Factors*: Risk factors, areas of vulnerability, historical precedents
  - This may include a personal history of generational trauma, family history of significant mental health issues, or history of other adverse events.
- *Precipitating or Causal Factors*: Factors surrounding what immediately proceeds the presenting problem/symptoms, contextual elements (when and how problems present), and aspects that influence the problem/symptoms
  - This may include the trauma event, exposure to trauma triggers that exacerbate symptoms, ongoing harmful relationships, toxic stress, and reenactments that lead to "reliving" the trauma and/or revictimization.
- *Perpetuating or Maintaining Factors*: Dynamics and aspects that contribute to symptom/problem severity and/or provide energy for the problem to be ongoing
  - This may include client substance abuse, self-harming behaviors, physiological patterns (hypo- or hyperarousal) that induce established and problematic habits of coping, lack of familial and/or relational support, negative patterns within the client's systemic framework (family, school, work, community, etc.), or additional stressors outside of trauma-related concerns.
- *Protective Factors*: Areas of client strengths, resources, and support that mitigate the problem/symptoms
  - This may include the client's cultural community, faith/spirituality, positive family relationships and environment, educational/career goals and/or success, or personal feelings of self-worth and empowerment.

These four factors provide conceptual domains for the clinician to consider and hypothesize how various forces in the client's life are influencing what is occurring. This becomes important in regard to treatment priorities and decisions. As a clinical example, imagine that the fairy tale character of Cinderella comes to you for therapeutic services, with the hope that you will help her cope with her strained home life. You notice in the intake that Cinderella is experiencing ongoing abuse in her family, and she presents with several trauma-related symptoms, including hypervigilance, excessive fear around failing to meet unrealistic expectations, frequent nightmares, depression and hopelessness, and tendencies to dissociate while performing abuse-connected tasks, such as cleaning.

After completing the intake and any other assessments, you apply the four-factor model to synthesize the conceptualization of Cinderella's case. For Cinderella, some predisposing factors might include the death of her father as an adverse childhood experience and her long-term social isolation. Precipitating/causal factors for Cinderella's symptoms include daily emotional and sometimes physical abuse from Cinderella's stepmother and stepsisters. The perpetuating/maintaining factors that exacerbate Cinderella's symptoms include her physical exhaustion, which likely contributes to her feelings of depression, and the limitations the stepmother enforces regarding connections to external resources, including her refusal to allow Cinderella to develop social connections outside the family or have access to finances. However, Cinderella also presents with many protective factors, including her appreciation for beauty in the world, her supportive relationships with animals, and her practice of self-care through singing. Cinderella's case demonstrates how the four-factor model provides a framework on which the clinician can better examine dynamics of the client's case, and it provides the clinician with a conceptual orientation to begin identifying effective treatment goals.

Client Readiness for Change: Integrating Client Variables for Treatment Approach

In addition to this four-factor framework for conceptualizing the client's information, clinicians must also consider the client's readiness for change in regard to how he or she is feeling towards the presenting problem. Trauma treatment models and therapeutic interventions facilitate the *process of change* for the client, but the clinician must first consider the client's ***stage of change***, which reflects the client's readiness, willingness, and acceptance to confront the presenting concern and subsequently adapt in new ways. The client's stage of change is paramount in understanding the client's *current* needs in treatment, which frequently include attending to issues and barriers that prevent the client from moving forward in the therapeutic process. In fact, the variations in treatment outcomes are most highly attributed to the client's readiness for change, and research shows that these factors may be more influential on outcomes than even the quality of the therapeutic relationship or the treatment techniques and modalities (Prochaska & Norcross, 2010).

Norcross, Krebs, and Prochaska (2011) provide a summary of the client stages of change and the therapeutic considerations for each of these stages.

- *Precontemplation stage*: The client is unaware or not fully aware of the problem, and the client has no intention to change behavior at this time.
  - Role of the clinician: Empathize with the client's resistance, which includes recognizing the implications and challenges that may accompany the client's acknowledgment or awareness of the trauma and/or trauma-related problems.
- *Contemplation stage*: The client is aware of the problem and its impacts and is considering the option of working towards overcoming it but has not committed to the work. The costs (energy, time, resources, emotional/psychological investment, etc.) required to work on the problem do not yet seem worth it to the client.

- Role of the clinician: Encourage the client to gain insight into his/her own situation and goals and provide psychoeducation and information about trauma as an aid in the process.
- *Preparation stage*: The client is planning for changes and is taking small, active steps in working on the problem. The client is experimenting with the idea of change.
  - Role of the clinician: Provide structure for the client regarding the ways in which trauma recovery might occur and provide empathy and information on what the process of trauma-focused treatment might be like for the client.
- *Action stage*: The client is invested and active in modifying personal behavior, the environment, and personal approaches to daily living. The client is motivated for change in self and/ or the problem, and overt effort reflective of investment, commitment, and energy is evident.
  - Role of the clinician: Offer facilitative skills that aid the client in reaching goals in trauma recovery and provide reflection and feedback on how the client is experiencing these changes.
- *Maintenance stage*: The client has effectively managed the problem and met identified goals and is now working to prevent relapse and consolidate gains.
  - Role of the clinician: Provide information, reflection, encouragement, and feedback regarding the client's posttraumatic growth and trauma recovery changes and also illuminate any anticipated challenges that may create setbacks for the client.

These stages of change can significantly influence the client's willingness to engage in trauma treatment, and clinicians should be mindful that most clients are not in the action stage of change when they arrive for the intake interview. Roughly 40% of clients arrive to their first session in the precontemplation stage, 40% arrive in the contemplation stage, and at the time of intake, only 20% of clients are in the preparation stage and are ready to enter the action stage (Norcross et al., 2011). Skilled clinicians work to recognize the client's current stage of change and then adjust to the client's needs regarding self-insight, ambivalence, and the personal investment required for trauma work and lasting change. Clients may also move back and forth through the stages during trauma treatment, and clinicians can recognize this as a normative part of the process of change rather than viewing it as a major setback or a sudden loss of client investment (Norcross et al., 2011).

Stages of Change and Determining Appropriate Treatment Goals

Stages of change also help inform realistically attainable goals for the client. In the case of Cinderella, who arrives for therapeutic services in the preparation stage, the clinician can offer a treatment plan that matches Cinderella's pace by bolstering her existing protective factors and positive coping habits, offering psychoeducation about trauma, and providing her with a foundation for empowerment in overcoming her symptoms and situation. However, imagine if Cinderella's stepmother was mandated by the Prince to seek treatment for her abusive behaviors. Based on the stepmother's historically antisocial disposition and the Prince's mandate that she enter counseling, her treatment goals would likely focus on tasks more consistent with the pre-contemplation stage of change, which might begin with goals that simply focus on increased self-insight and awareness and the practice of multi-perspective taking. Treatment goals that begin with action stage work and intensive changes, such as immediate focus on the step-mother's communication patterns, exploration into her own trauma history and personality tendencies, and a targeted relationship repair process with Cinderella, will likely prove ineffective as these goals are mismatched with the step-mother's readiness for change at this time. Stages of change help clinicians to determine appropriate and facilitative goals that target the client's current state, not the tasks that the clinicians *hopes* the client is ready to accomplish.

Very often, clients' successful completion of treatment goals mirrors their development across the stages of change. Continuing in our case example, this means that if Cinderella's step-mother can successfully reach those initial goals of self-insight and multi-perspective taking, this milestone will likely represent her growth into the contemplation stage of change. While we hope that all clients can successfully move through all the stages of change during our work with them, sometimes development from just one stage of change to the next is all that the client is ready to do in that point in his or her life. Clinicians must honor and recognize the growth that clients make, even if that growth not as far as or as much as we might have hoped.

Client Readiness for Change and the Clinician

Client stages of change are also invaluable for clinicians to consider in regard to countertransference issues that may arise. For many of us, when we imagine facilitating powerful trauma work with our clients, we envision clients who are engaged and invested in the process. From a stages-of-change perspective, we are picturing a client who is fully immersed in the action stage of change. These are the client cases that fuel us, invigorate us, and remind us of why we chose this profession.

On the other hand, all clinicians, no matter how skilled or experienced, encounter clients who are staunchly in the precontemplation or contemplation stage of change. These clients do not want to be in treatment, they often transfer their negative feelings about the process onto the clinician, and sessions often feel like "pulling teeth" as the clinician butts up against the client's resistance. For client cases like these, clinicians often feel tempted to personalize this dynamic, and they wonder "Why doesn't this person like me?," "Are my skills just not good enough?, or "Am I a fool to think that I can do this kind of work?" These questions cross the mind of every clinician, but most often, this dynamic reflects the client's stage of change and not an inherent flaw on the part of the clinician or a significant lack of facilitative skills. When clinicians are mindful to reflect on the client's stage of change, they are much better able to meet the client where he or she is at, remain patient and understanding of resistance, and keep personal feelings of insecurity in check.

The Trauma-Informed Treatment Plan: Moving From Conceptualization to Specific Goals

The synthesized case conceptualization provides the clinician with bird's-eye view of the dynamics occurring within and around the client, and at this point, the clinician can begin to generate a plan of action to address symptoms and problems. Structured around the holistic understanding of the client, treatment goals (desired outcomes) and corresponding objectives (specific steps to meet the goals) can begin to be developed in the client's treatment plan. A **treatment plan** is a written, goal-directed outline of the proposed progression of treatment that specifically addresses the client's presenting problems, and this "living" document can be modified and adapted as needed over the course of therapy. The treatment plan is often a working document that is continuously updated and adjusted, but planning early in the clinical process aids in defining the problems that need attention, estimates the clinical timeframe, formalizes expectations of both the clinician and the client, and contributes to appropriate theory and intervention selection in the next phase of treatment. The development of therapeutic goals should be a collaborative process with clients to include their voices in decision making and to ensure their motivation in meeting the treatment goals. Even children can and should participate in deciding what they hope to get out of the therapeutic process.

Trauma Treatment Goals

Treatment goals are the identified changes the client would like to achieve as a result of treatment. Goals are often representative of a reduction in the specific trauma-related and other associated symptoms (such as depression or shame) that the client is experiencing, and often these identified problems are based on the data gleaned from client report and/or assessments. While goals may reflect symptom reduction, treatment goals may also include adoption of positive behaviors that will enhance the client's therapeutic growth towards overall wellness healing (Foa, Keane, Friedman, & Cohen, 2009).

MacLeod (2012) developed the **SMARTER approach for goal setting** within health care systems as a format that can be included in trauma-focused treatment plans. In this approach, goals are *specific, measurable, achievable, relevant, timely, engaging, and rewarding*. Vague and unmeasurable goals, such as "the client will improve at work," make it difficult to determine how treatment is progressing. Additionally, goals that are unachievable or irrelevant can frustrate clients and inhibit participation. Goals should use time-bound wording to make expectations clear and include identifiable results that foster motivation for treatment and improve overall well-being. SMARTER goals provide criteria for both clinician and client to determine the success of treatment. The following goals represent examples that are consistent with the SMARTER treatment goal approach.

GOAL 1: Reduce panic attacks from six per week to two or less per week based on client self-report by July 1.

GOAL 2: Decrease depressive symptoms from moderate to minimal based on the Beck Depression Inventory (Beck et al., 1996) within the next four months.

GOAL 3: Engage in three new social activities that the client reports as feeling safe and enjoyable by October 1.

Trauma Treatment Objectives

Treatment goals outline where the client hopes to go in treatment, but these goals often seem distant and out of reach. **Treatment objectives** are the small, incremental steps that clients take to reach their broader goals of symptom reduction and adaption of positive coping. The objectives inform decisions regarding treatment modality selection and are ideally expressed in behavioral language so that they can be measured and used to evaluate progress (Jongsma, 2014). Consideration for the client's lifestyle, culture, personality, stage of change, and other personal factors should be included when formulating these steps.

For example, in connection with the trauma treatment goal number 1 outlined above, the goal indicates that the client will reduce the occurrence of panic attacks, which may include objectives such as (a) consult with medical doctor, (b) research the stages of panic attacks and identify at least three personal triggers and patterns, (c) keep a journal for two weeks about panic symptoms, coping strategies, and effectiveness of applied coping strategies, (d) practice personally effective relaxation exercises three times daily, including deep breathing and progressive muscle relaxation, and (e) identify at least two irrational thoughts that contribute to panic symptoms.

While treatment goals generally transcend all approaches and theoretical orientations, objectives are theory-informed. Objectives reflect *how* the client is going to reach his or her treatment goal, and this process should always be grounded in an identified theory that will be applied in treatment. For example, returning again to the client goal of reducing panic attacks, one example objective included the identification of at least two irrational thoughts that contribute to panic symptoms. This objective mirrors a clinical approach that is based in cognitive-behavioral theory. Alternatively, a clinician who ascribes to a systems orientation might list an objective for this goal as "identify at least two relational or environmental factors that influence or are influenced by the client's panic attacks." Since objectives very much parallel the work of therapeutic treatment, clinicians must reflect on the structure of the treatment plan and review its congruence with the applied theory of choice, appropriateness for the client's culture, and its suitability for addressing the presenting problems.

Hierarchical Order of Treatment Goals and Objectives

Both treatment goals and objectives should be hierarchical. This means that the treatment plan structure should offer a "first things first" approach in the ordering of the most urgent, immediate, or foundational treatment goals and objectives. For example, the treatment goals that aim to "eliminate suicidal thoughts and ideation" should precede any goals and objectives that address "the reduction of trauma symptoms through trauma exposure work." Clinicians should craft the treatment plan according to the client's layered needs so that the document mirrors the order of treatment. Structuring the treatment plan sequentially also allows for ongoing treatment evaluation. Progress towards treatment goals should be monitored throughout the course of treatment, with goal completion documented in the treatment plan, and objectives can be modified based on the client's needs during different phases of therapy. Once goals and objectives have been established in the treatment plan, the therapeutic process continues with an explanation to the client.

Therapeutic Collaboration: Sharing Conceptualizations and Treatment Plans With Clients

Several years ago, I ordered a large set of stereo equipment, but when I received the box in the mail, the instructions for assembly were missing. I sat in the floor surrounded by dozens of parts and pieces with no idea what any of them were nor how to put them together to make the whole system work. In a very similar way, many clients arrive for treatment feeling lost, overwhelmed, and unsure of how the therapeutic process works, and the disconnected "pieces" of their problems seem looming and unidentifiable. In such a situation, the place to begin is to simply understand what is sitting before us. This is often a parallel process between client and clinician: we feel more empowered to address challenges once we obtain clarity about the nature of those challenges, their origins, and how these problems can be solved. Your desire to feel empowered through understanding is reflected even now by your engagement in learning through this book!

Clients also need to experience this sense of empowerment through understanding, and once the clinician has developed a comprehensive case conceptualization and treatment plan, the clinician can share aspects of this conceptualization with the client. The purpose of sharing the case conceptualization is for the clinician and client to come to a shared and mutual understanding of the problem and what is occurring within and around the client (Christon et al., 2015). This is often a milestone moment in building the therapeutic alliance as clients feel included, respected, and more knowledgeable about themselves and what is occurring in their lives. The clinician can utilize this opportunity to provide psychoeducation, invite the client's feedback and insights into the clinician's hypothesis, and establish a richer collaborative, honest, and therapeutic working alliance. Additionally, with the client's consent, agreement, and appropriate release of information, the clinician may also share the conceptualization (or parts thereof) with other important parties, such as the client's partner/spouse, other family members, psychiatrists or other medical professionals, teachers, and/or caregivers.

Beginning trauma clinicians often experience some hesitation or reluctance to share what may feel like an "analysis" of the client with the client him/herself, but this can actually serve as an open door for discussions regarding the client's fears about being judged and illuminate any areas of disconnect in the therapeutic relationship itself. Clients should be given the opportunity to learn more about themselves, contribute to the process, and experience the empowerment that comes with understanding oneself better. The clinician-client dialogue regarding case conceptualization will likely serve as the first of several important therapeutic talks, as discussing treatment progress will subsequently follow this initial, collaborative exchange. Clinicians are encouraged to practice clinical judgment concerning how much and when to share, and the targeted content and timing should be carefully considered for each unique client. Clinicians should be mindful to share information in a way that empowers rather than deflates or overwhelms the client, which sometimes means that information is paced conservatively, processed slowly and thoroughly, and presented in a manner that communicates the clinician's value and support of the client.

Frequently, the comprehensive topics for clinicians to discuss with clients include:

- *Psychoeducation*
  - The clinician may provide information on the nature and impacts of psychological trauma and respond to client questions and concerns.
- *Four-factor conceptualization (predisposing, precipitating/causal, precipitating/maintaining, and protective factors)*
  - The clinician may present a hypothesis regarding the dynamics and influences of the four factors on the current problem(s) and may invite the client to provide feedback or further insight into this.
- *Stages of change considerations*
  - The clinician may share insights and encourage the client to express feelings about being in treatment, discuss barriers to engaging further in treatment, and share wishes/desires/worries about the treatment process.
- *Results from formal/informal assessments*
  - The clinician may explain the assessment results to the client, including benefits and limitations of the assessment instrument, and discuss considerations for how these results can be integrated in treatment. The clinician can attend to client questions or concerns surrounding assessment information.

- *Diagnosis and/or other identified areas of treatment focus*
  - If applicable, the clinician may provide the client with his or her diagnosis, explain what a mental health diagnosis means and does not mean, and invite the client the process thoughts and feelings about the diagnosis.
- *Treatment plan and therapeutic goals*
  - The clinician may share a general description of the treatment plan, which includes the identified goals, and can encourage the client to provide feedback on these goals. The clinician may also explain the course of therapeutic services, what might be involved, the anticipated length of treatment, and answer any questions the client has about the process overall.

Tri-Phasic Model of Treatment: Conceptualizing the Structure for Trauma Work

At this point, the clinician has synthesized the client's case conceptualization by viewing the full picture of the client, developed a comprehensive treatment plan, and collaborated with the client about this plan. Now the clinician is ready to begin work towards the identified treatment goals. For many clients, the treatment plan may include goals that are separate from trauma-related concerns, but for trauma-specific problems and the associated trauma-focused goals and objectives, clinicians must develop a conceptual framework of the trauma treatment process itself. While there are multiple ways to structure trauma-focused work, one exceptional format is the **tri-phasic model** (Herman, 1992b), which assists clients in moving safely through the therapeutic process in incremental stages.

This tri-phasic model is not a substitution for a theory in trauma treatment, however; this framework serves as a guide that can be applied generally across a variety of theoretical orientations. The three phases in this model include: (1) safety and stabilization, (2) remembrance and mourning, and (3) reconnection (Baranowsky, Gentry, & Schultz, 2005; Herman, 1992b). Each phase of this model emphasizes a unique aspect of client growth while simultaneously promoting the therapeutic process of trauma work, and these incremental phases are very helpful in the development of hierarchical goals and objectives in a trauma-focused treatment plan. The unique therapeutic foci of each phase can be easily seen when the activities of the distinct stages are examined more in depth.

- ***Phase 1: Safety and Stabilization*** Clinical tasks include developing a therapeutic environment that is physically, mentally, and emotionally safe, as well as helping the client stabilize through emotional regulation skill building, such as enhanced self-awareness, recognition of triggers of distress, and practice of relaxation techniques and grounding exercises.
- ***Phase 2: Remembrance and Mourning*** (trauma memory processing) Clinical tasks vary based upon the applied trauma-informed theory but may include therapeutic activities such as discussion of/exposure to trauma memories, reconnection of mind and body, emotional expression and catharsis, grief over losses associated with trauma, and skill building.
- ***Phase 3: Reconnection*** Clinical tasks include aiding clients in shifting towards a more positive self-identity as well as facilitating client reengagement in healthy relationships, recreational activities, meaning-making, and preparing for termination of the therapeutic relationship.

While these phases do not necessarily occur in a strict, linear format (in fact, most clients return to phase one to reestablish safety at various times during phase 2), a stage model allows the clinician to gauge the client's progress in trauma recovery. The phases represent incremental and progressive movement in therapeutic goals, much like the process of taking individual steps in order to climb a staircase. One step leads to another, and skipping steps and clinical tasks may prove to slow down the therapeutic process or even put the client at risk for psychological harm. For example, without the safety and stabilization provided in phase 1, an attempt at trauma-memory work may result in putting the client at risk for **retraumatization** (a process in which the client relives the trauma in a manner which increases symptoms and contributes to further trauma reactions). Clinicians must remain continually aware of the current clinical tasks and stages that are being targeted in the treatment process. The next section of this text explores each of these phases more in depth as a framework for engaging in trauma-focused therapeutic work with clients.

Conclusion

In this chapter, we explored strategies for synthesizing a client's case conceptualization, which included the application of the four-factor model and considerations for the client's stages of change. A synthesized case conceptualization contributes to building an effective treatment plan as well as offers a structure for collaborating with clients and sharing information with them. We also introduced the tri-phasic model as a therapeutic platform in trauma work, which will be highlighted in the subsequent chapters.

At its core, synthesis is ultimately a process of gaining an overall sense of something. As clinicians, we aim to gain a sense of the connections surrounding the complex dynamics in our client's situation and presentation, as well as understand how these aspects fit within the trauma treatment process itself. Sometimes this process is highly empowering while at other times, the process can feel intensely challenging. As clinicians, we must become comfortable with the ebb and flow of the vacillating feelings of professional confidence and the sensation of overwhelming ambiguity and uncertainty. This is very often a parallel experience in which clients also fluctuate in feeling empowered by new knowledge and lost in the process. We must normalize this both for ourselves as clinicians and for our clients with the understanding that as we discover more about the self and trauma, the more aware we become of what is left to explore.

KEYWORD ASSESSMENT

Write definitions in your own words, describe the concept's role in trauma work, list any questions, or make notes of important aspects that you want to remember.

Stages of Change

Treatment Plan

Treatment Goals

SMARTER Approach for Goal Setting

Treatment Objectives

Triphasic Model

Retraumatization

EXPERIENTIAL ACTIVITIES: INTERACTING WITH THE CHAPTER CONTENT

Expand Self-Awareness

1) Review all of the components of conceptualization that might be shared with a client in therapy. Identify four distinct feelings that you have when you imagine sharing the various elements of conceptualization and collaborating with a client. Reflect and complete this phrase for each emotion that comes up: I feel _____ about _____ (specific aspect of the conceptualization/collaboration process) because _____.

Expand Knowledge

2) Consider a problem that you have had or are currently experiencing in your life. Apply the four-factor model to your chosen problem and determine your predisposing, precipitating/causal, perpetuating/maintaining, and protective factors. Illustrate a picture that reflects the dynamics of how these factors work together and influence your experience of the problem.

Expand Skills

3) Using the SMARTER goals approach in conjunction with a synthesized case conceptualization and tri-phasic hierarchy for goals, develop a treatment plan with at least four goals for Cinderella.

SUPERVISORY DISCUSSION: SHARING PERSONAL INSIGHTS AND IDENTIFYING AREAS FOR GROWTH

1) Describe the insights you gained from the four-factor model and your situation. When you consider Cinderella's case, discuss which of the four factors seem especially relevant for her and describe how you would integrate each of these factors into her treatment.

2) Describe the various stages of change. What would it be like for you to work with clients in each of these stages? How will you manage the challenges of each of these client stages?

3) Discuss why a hierarchical structure for treatment goals is important in trauma work. As you look at the treatment plan that you created for Cinderella, identify at least three potential consequences that might result from *not* sequencing goals according to priority.

4) At this point, you have laid the foundation for the main concepts and principles of trauma work, and now you are about to begin learning the operationalization of these concepts in trauma-focused treatment. What are your thoughts and feelings about your growth as a trauma clinician so far and what do you hope to gain in this next phase of learning?

The Tri-Phasic Model

A Trauma-Focused Treatment Process

Chapter 10

Phase 1: Safety and Stabilization in Trauma Work

Imagine you are in a session sitting just across from your client, and a pronounced moment of pause passes between you. At this point, you, the trauma clinician, have a strong understanding of trauma, recognize the trauma-related symptoms in your client, and have considered and integrated the personal and cultural factors that may impact the process. You have recently assessed your client and you have a clear sense of the trauma-related presenting problems and have developed a treatment plan consisting of goals aligned with specific, positive outcomes. As you look at each other, you both think the same overwhelming thought: "Now what?" You've learned nuanced and dynamic elements for conceptualization; now it's time to begin putting trauma work into practical application. In this chapter, we begin the operationalization of concepts through the clinical tasks associated with trauma work's first phase: safety and stabilization.

Overview of Phase 1: Developing Safety and Stabilization for the Client

Despite the nuances of the diverse mental health disciplines, we are united in our ethical obligation to "first, do no harm" and provide safe, therapeutic services. The importance of the phase 1 tasks of safety and stabilization cannot be overemphasized. In fact, these features of clinical practice are not only crucial for the successful completion of treatment but are also the building blocks for clients' optimal functioning and healthy relationships.

A few Christmases ago, I wanted to make chocolate pudding for a family gathering. The recipe called for an egg to be added to piping hot chocolate sauce, which was already cooking on the stove. The recipe cautioned that the egg should not be cracked directly into the chocolate sauce so as to avoid making scrambled eggs in the pudding. (Certainly, no one wants scrambled eggs in their chocolate pudding!) Instead, the recipe directed that egg should be placed in a bowl and then some of the hot chocolate sauce should be slowly and gradually added in with the egg in order to temper the egg and bring its heat up slowly. In trauma work, the same principle applies. Our clients need gradual progression in the treatment process, and an overzealous, rushed approach can lead to unintended, hazardous outcomes. Even a well-crafted and evidence-based intervention could pose potential risk for harm to the client if the implementation is ill timed or if the client is not prepared for the potential emotional intensity of the treatment process.

Unfortunately, many beginning clinicians feel tempted to move too quickly into the memory exposure stage of treatment out of an urgency to ease the client's pain and restore proper order to his or her daily living. In fact, clinicians may experience significant pressure to rush the process from clients themselves and perhaps even from other stakeholders, or individuals and organizations who have a shared stake in the client's recovery (such as family members, the client's employer, and insurance companies). Many clients and their associated systems (financial, employment, and familial) enter the treatment process with the expectation that trauma treatment works like other quick-recovery medical procedures, in which the attending physician assumes all the responsibility in the process and the patient is in and out after a quick fix. Clients and their stakeholders are sometimes discouraged and frustrated when the clinician dispels this myth, and they may even display resistance towards a slower, more titrated approach. However, clinicians can model behaviors that are intentionally slow-paced and reflective, which provides clients the opportunity to practice similar techniques aimed at increasing self-awareness and understanding (Corey, 2017). Proper pacing alongside careful attention to client safety and stabilization underpins all positive trauma treatment outcomes.

In the beginning phase of trauma treatment, the clinician's primary objective is to develop and/or enhance the client's safety and stabilization. In this therapeutic context, **safety** focuses on clients' external factors (and perceptions of these factors), such as their physical environment and interactions with other people, while **stabilization** focuses on clients' ability to recognize their internal experiences and adjust as needed to regulate their emotional responses. Clients vary in terms of how long they need to build up these necessary skills, and consequently, this phase of treatment may progress rapidly for some clients, while others may spend months and sometimes years working on goals associated with safety and stabilization. Effective pacing of the therapeutic process requires clinicians to resist the rush to begin trauma memory work interventions and carefully attend to aspects of safety and stabilization as critical and foundational goals that must be thoroughly established first.

Safety: Providing the Therapeutic Conditions for Clients to Heal

An important aspect of the therapeutic alliance is the concept of safety. To understand the role of safety in trauma work, consider the parallels between clinical practices and the everyday habit of safe driving. To ensure safe driving, we strive to consistently use our seatbelts, abstain from texting while driving, avoid alcohol before driving, and assess for car-related issues, such as maintaining the brakes, headlights, and tire pressure. All of these efforts are directed towards reducing the risk of an avoidable car accident. In a similar way, trauma clinicians employ knowledgeable and intentional effort in working to reduce the psychological, emotional, and physical risks for our clients as they embark on the journey of trauma work.

There are two dimensions to safety: perception (the client's experience of feeling safe and believing themselves to be safe) and reality (objective markers that clients are truly safe). Developing the perception of safety can take time, particularly for survivors of abuse, due to conditioned fear responses that may have become easily triggered. Although the clinician cannot fully control the overall safety in the lives of clients, attending to therapeutic safety issues is not only an ethical obligation but also a way for clinicians to model a trustworthy, caring relationship. In regard to both the perception and the reality of client safety, the clinician must intentionally address the following areas of safety. These goals are summarized here and then explained in further detail.

The clinician's role in the development and enhancement of client safety entails:

■ Modifying the physical environment of the clinical space
■ Developing trust between clinician and client
■ Offering predictability of therapeutic actions
■ Facilitating client empowerment

Safety Within the Therapeutic Environment

Whether services are provided in a school, hospital, private practice, or some other mental health setting, physical safety includes a trauma-sensitive environment. A trauma-sensitive setting considers the hypervigilance felt by many clients with trauma histories and seeks to reduce as many environmental triggers as possible. Physical features in the clinical office that are trauma-sensitive include reducing the potential for distracting or startling noises, appropriately distancing the furniture between clinician and client (close, but not too close), avoiding the use of strong smells (such as perfumes), and maintaining awareness that some clients, especially military or law enforcement personnel with PTSD, may be uncomfortable being seated with their backs to the door. Privacy should also be a top priority as clients enter and exit sessions, especially when there is a chance that clients coming and going may know each other. Calming décor and other physical features in the setting enhance feelings of comfort and therapeutic safety for clients. Of course, the reality of physical safety is crucial for both clients and the clinician; safeguards, such as security personnel, well-lit parking lots, and other features should be utilized as appropriate to each specific clinical setting.

Safety Through the Development of Trust

The development of trust between client and clinician can sometimes be a complex process, but very often, trust emerges from basic clinical tasks and awareness. In the budding therapeutic alliance during the beginning stages of treatment, trust is built, most simply, when the client understands what to expect from the clinician, and the clinician meets these expectations as consistently as possible. All therapeutic relationships should begin with a thorough informed consent (even from clients who are minors) followed by a detailed explanation of the clinician's role, which serves as an aid in the development of client expectations for the clinician. Clinicians should be as consistent as possible in meeting the expectations outlined in the informed consent and always follow through with any commitments that are verbally expressed to the clients. During this initial informed-consent explanation, the clinician must also address what the client can expect of the therapeutic process, including the inherent risks of trauma treatments and the reality that some symptoms may become worse before improving as trauma memories are recalled and processed.

In trauma work, informed consent is ongoing, and the clinician must always be willing to provide the client with an explanation for what will happen in treatment (particularly in phase 2, when trauma memory work occurs) and remain attentive to the client's feelings about the process. This principle was taught to me most memorably during my work with a 15-year-old boy who had an extensive history of emotional neglect and attachment disruptions. As part of ongoing informed consent, I explained to my client (using developmentally appropriate language) that as part of the treatment process we would eventually begin working through his trauma history and memories that caused him so much distress. Almost instantly after I said this, my client wheeled around to face me, gave me a look that I will never forget, and shouted, "No!" I realized in that powerful moment that my client was not ready to move into phase 2 of trauma work and that the mere suggestion of delving into such sensitive material violated his psychological safety and compromised our therapeutic relationship. I took my client's cues and remained firmly planted in the safety and stabilization phase of treatment.

Safety Through Predictability

Another manner by which clinicians meet client expectations is through the practicalities of session structure. Predictability is a key aspect of therapeutic safety and can be accomplished through behaviors such as starting and ending sessions on time. I've often heard from students who I supervise that they tend to give their clients extra time beyond the session allotment to show how much they care about them. However, extending sessions may inadvertently have the opposite effect because, not only can it cause the clinician to be late for the next client, but it also can blur boundaries and create instability for the current client by raising uncertainty about when future sessions will end and questions about *why* the clinician is making an exception for him or her. Individuals who have experienced abuse and neglect could be particularly vulnerable to even minor unpredictable behaviors of the clinician, and one of the greatest therapeutic needs of this population centers on the stability and consistency of a strong therapeutic relationship. The clinician's commitment to consistent behaviors and clear boundaries helps to reduce uncertainty and promote trust in the therapeutic alliance.

Safety Through Client Empowerment

Trauma often generates feelings of helplessness and crippling disempowerment. In all types of traumatic situations, the individual experiences a loss of control over his or her circumstances, and in cases of interpersonal trauma, perpetrators exacerbate this feeling through the abuse of power. A sense of powerlessness (along with the inherent power imbalance between clinicians and clients) may be therapeutically attended to by empowering clients to maintain as much control over the therapeutic process as possible (such as collaborative goal setting and treatment strategy selections) and by encouraging clients to freely provide feedback on what they need during treatment (Crumpton, 2017; Quiros, Kay, & Montijo, 2012). Many clients who were victims of abuse and violence felt stifled in any right to make choices, and they often carry a sense of invalidation and feel as though their voices have been silenced. Empowering clients to share feedback about their counseling experience offers a therapeutic opportunity to provide a client with a restorative experience in which one's voice is regained and heard.

Clinicians can also empower clients by highlighting the client's resiliency and potential for growth (Marlowe & Adamson, 2011). The truth is that despite how harrowing a client's past has been, he or she has survived and demonstrated bravery by seeking help. "Working with trauma is as much about remembering how we survived as it is about what is broken" (van der Kolk, 2015, p. 213). Clients are often so focused on the areas in which they lost control during the trauma event that they easily overlook moments, perhaps even brief ones, in which they demonstrated empowerment over their own life and situation. At first, many clients describe "the end" of their trauma narrative as the point at which the fallout of the trauma occurred. As an empowering reframe, the clinician can remind the client that this is actually not the end of the story. The current "end" of the story is in the here-and-now: a moment in which the client is recognizing his or her wounds and needs and is taking courageous action to overcome the power of the past. When clinicians take opportunities to highlight areas of client empowerment, these therapeutic steps foster the client's sense that he or she is regaining personal empowerment. The client's growing sense of empowerment significantly contributes to therapeutic safety and helps clients recognize and move through the difficult emotions that often accompany trauma work, such as fears and self-doubt.

Stabilization: Facilitating the Client's Growth in Regulation and Emotional Tolerance

When a person encounters a traumatic situation, at the most fundamental level, the power of the trauma emerges from the sense that one has been overcome or engulfed by the most painful types of emotions, such as fear, horror, dread, disgust, or despair. Simply put, a situation is traumatic because the circumstances have extended far beyond the person's ability to cope with it. As a result, clients often feel crushed and overpowered by their own emotions. Therefore, clinicians should approach trauma treatment with the understanding that the client is arriving in a highly vulnerable state in which the client's internal resources for coping and regulation are too depleted, exhausted, or insufficient to bring the individual back up to baseline functioning.

As a metaphorical parallel, imagine a stacked tower of blocks like in the popular game *Jenga*®. When a person's internal and external resources are strong, a few blocks removed from the tower can be tolerated and things remain relatively stable. However, for clients who are swept up in the currents of trauma, their "*Jenga*® tower" of coping feels as though too many blocks have been removed and it is dangerously close to toppling over. In the safety and stabilization phase of trauma work, the primary goal of the clinician is to help the client restore some of those lost keystone blocks to the tower, metaphorically speaking, and enhance stabilization before pushing the client to reengage in emotionally challenging work.

With this in mind, specific considerations should be taken to assess the client's ability to tolerate painful emotions and cope with increased levels of distress before moving on to any form of trauma memory work (Korn, 2009). While clinicians should continuously aim to maintain the client's feelings of safety and also sustain a nonjudgmental approach to avoid unnecessarily triggering the client's defenses, a safe environment alone is not sufficient to support clients through the emotional intensity of recovery work. Stabilization work is necessary to decrease the client's varying levels of emotional distress and increase the client's capacity to tolerate high emotional states, and these stabilization goals are summarized here.

A clinician's role in the development and enhancement of client stabilization includes:

- Facilitating the client's emotional identification and expression
- Enhancing client regulation
- Attending to client self-awareness and coping skills

Stabilization Through Identification and Expression of Emotions

Emotions (also referred to as "affect") influence our ability to be attuned to others, solve problems, and focus our attention (Cole, Martin, & Dennis, 2004). Positive emotions, such as joy, hope, and confidence, keep us engaged with the outside world, while negative emotions, such as fear, shame, and despair, restrict our interactions. Research indicates that trauma not only potentially leads to negative emotions, such as anxiety, shame, rage, guilt, fear, and depressed mood, but it may also cause amygdala dysfunction in some individuals, which can lead to an inability to correctly read the emotions of others and restrict their own emotional expression (Bilgi et al., 2017). These direct and indirect consequences of trauma can impair relational functioning, only exacerbating further emotional distress. However, with therapeutic interventions, even clients with restricted emotional expressional expression can dramatically improve their functioning. Several years ago, I worked with an elderly client who had a history of severe abuse and neglect, but she showed no emotional range (also known as "flat affect"). After several months of counseling, we celebrated her first time showing strong emotion, which was when she gave "the finger" to a person who cut her off in traffic. While this may not sound monumental, the client's experience of allowing herself to feel and express anger was a pivotal point in her recovery process.

Stabilization Through Emotional Regulation

Explored in depth in Chapter 6, **emotional regulation**, which is the ability to return to a state of equilibrium during an experience of intense feelings, develops early in childhood through secure caregiver attachment, but one's ability to emotionally regulate can be inhibited by insecure attachment and/or overwhelming experiences (Bowlby, 1969). My water aerobics instructor led us in an exercise in which we were intentionally put off balance in the pool. She explained that it was important for our bodies to know how to adjust and self-regulate when we felt off kilter. In the same way, healthy infant connection with caregivers provides the necessary template for self-regulation during distress through modeling emotional coping, attending to the infant's physical and emotional needs, and providing soothing interaction to facilitate a return to equilibrium (Espeleta et al., 2018; Hambrick et al., 2019).

Without this regulatory template, **emotional dysregulation** may occur, in which intense emotions become unmanaged reactions. Trauma can disrupt emotional development, impact an individual's ability to cope with strong feelings, and increase propensity for emotional dysregulation (Hancock & Bryant, 2018). Childhood neglect, even without any occurrences of physical or sexual abuse, increases one's propensity for emotional dysregulation as a consequence of the repeated emotional conditions of stress, hunger, sleeplessness, and other unmet needs, all of which triggers an instinctual and profound fear response in infants and young children. For this reason, clients with a history of insecure attachment, childhood abuse, neglect, and other traumatic events may need to remain in the stabilization phase of treatment for several months (or sometimes even years) to develop or enrich emotional regulation.

Without a strong platform of emotional regulation, the surfacing of past trauma memories may contribute to dysregulated emotional states. When emotional distress is triggered, the client may move towards hyperarousal (fight/flight) or hypoarousal (freeze/dissociation), or possibly vacillate between these two nervous system responses (Siegel, 2015). In fact, the rapid cycling of these emotional states can intensify the same feelings of being out of control (helplessness) and increase feelings of threat to survival (fear, hopelessness), which mirrors the emotional sensations that occur during a traumatic experience. Because of this, clients may find it especially difficult to effectively utilize quick relief strategies, such as commonly utilized standard relaxation techniques. John Gottman (1993) used the term **emotional flooding** to refer to the cascade of intense emotions that triggers these hyper- and hypoarousal states, which ultimately leads to emotional dysregulation.

Psychiatrist Daniel Siegel describes the sudden and powerful process of moving into a dysregulated state as "flipping your lid" (Siegel & Bryson, 2012). "Flipping your lid" occurs when emotional flooding triggers the survival response, and as a result, rational thinking, communication, and higher cognitive functions "go offline" in the brain and become inaccessible. In a hidden-camera reality TV show, unknowing contestants were put in challenging and stressful situations, such as lengthy exchanges with an overbearing and hassling customer service agent. The purpose of the situation was to trigger the unsuspecting individuals into losing their cool, but contestants won a prize if they were able to remain emotionally regulated within the allotted time. The show was somewhat stressful to watch, but brought up intriguing considerations regarding how some people are able stay calm under duress while others are not. The show also highlighted the potential for individuals to recognize when their blood was beginning to boil and utilize self-soothing tools to prevent emotional dysregulation.

Trauma work in Practice: Emotional Dysregulation in Session

A central goal for clinician development in trauma work includes the ability to recognize when a client is becoming emotionally dysregulated and needs stabilization. To identify extreme emotional states, there are several verbal and non-verbal indicators that can aid clinicians. A client who exhibits a hyperarousal response may become angry, loud, and aggressive, while a client who displays a hypoarousal response may seem disengaged, lethargic, and numb. The following is a clinical example of a client becoming dysregulated through a hypoarousal reaction during our session.

Mackenzie sat on the edge of my brown leather office sofa as she described her recent high school graduation and the hilarious antics that she and her friends had later that night. Her eyes sparkled as she described the details of their teenage-girl bonding, and she enjoyed being able to share this joyful occasion with me. As she finished her story, I remembered from a past session that she was worried that her uncle might attend the graduation, so I asked if he had been there. Without giving me a response, Mackenzie's muscles stiffened, and her eyes seemed to wander away from me in a glazed and distant manner. She was unresponsive to my questions and appeared "frozen." By abruptly changing the subject to her abusive uncle, I had unintentionally triggered a flood of memories and feelings, and I knew not to probe further about the uncle at that moment until she was able to return to a more regulated state.

Trauma clinicians must help clients identify ways to return to equilibrium once they begin to experience hyper- or hypoarousal and eventually expand their tolerance for difficult emotions, thereby decreasing their propensity to become dysregulated. In the above example, the first thing I did as the clinician was to resist getting lost in my own thoughts of self-loathing for mistakenly upsetting my client. The ability to maintain our own emotional control and regulation is crucial, especially when a client is dysregulated. I spoke to Mackenzie in a calm, assuring tone and provided her with a therapeutic sandtray as a grounding tool that she had found soothing in past sessions. I asked her to describe what she was feeling in her body, and she said she felt "numb" and "like the air had gone out of her." Then, she and I engaged in some activation exercises, such as stretching and walking around the room. Since hypoarousal is often accompanied by a lowered heartbeat, activation activities are designed to increase the client's heartbeat. Once I noticed her arousal level had increased from dissociated to engaged, I repaired our relationship (healthy attachment involves modeling how to overcome relational ruptures) and reestablished safety by apologizing for my abrupt subject change and explained to her that I would give her more warning before discussing sensitive subjects such as her uncle.

The Impact of Emotional Dysregulation

If you have ever tried to tell a highly dysregulated person who is in a reactive state to calm down, you've probably noticed that this is usually ineffective and can even escalate the situation. This is much like trying to teach someone how to swim while he or she is drowning—it is usually unhelpful, insensitive, and unproductive. Moments of being out of control in emotional dysregulation can feel frightening and embarrassing. Clients sometimes attempt to regain control over their emotions by utilizing unhealthy coping mechanisms in a desperate attempt to numb painful feelings and to return to a calmer state (Briere et al., 2010). In fact, attempts to master emotional dysregulation could underpin many unhealthy behaviors and avoidance strategies, which include self-harm, alcohol and drug use, dissociation, and sexual promiscuity (Espeleta et al., 2018; Linehan, 1993; Stinson, Robbins, & Crow, 2011). Emotional dysregulation can lead to these and other impulsive behaviors, such as angry outbursts or intimacy issues (such as being too clingy or too distant), and this often results in further relationship instability and poor relational connection (Hooper, Spann, Tiyahri, & Kimberly, 2017). Individuals may have little insight into why they react disproportionally to situations, like the golfer who routinely throws his club despite correction from other players. People experience low insight into their patterns of personal dysregulation because emotional regulation is primarily developed during early childhood interactions and attachment, a period that is usually not accessible by conscious memory (Raju, Corrigan, Davidson, & Johnson, 2012).

The high intensity of disproportionate reactions requires clinicians to constantly manage their own countertransference in order to remain emotionally regulated themselves. Being aware of the potential for emotional flooding helps clinicians manage the temptation to also become dysregulated and overreact to the client's behavior or reactive statements. Clinicians must mindfully choose not to take momentary client outbursts personally, and they must use their own regulation strategies as a model for the client and take the posture of a positive emotional beacon in guiding the client to a more regulated emotional state.

Emotional Regulation Training

One of the key tasks of phase 1 trauma work is to help clients emotionally regulate in ways that promote health and wellness. As clients increase their emotional awareness and learn to read internal cues from their nervous systems, they will be able to slow down and better regulate their responses. During hyperarousal states, clients generally benefit from slower breathing and soothing activities that are calming to them individually, and conversely, clients in hypoarousal states need activities that increase energy levels, which can be achieved through laughter and physical or recreation activities (Raju et al., 2012). Aerobic exercise is also effective at moderating both hyper- and hypoarousal states and improving mood (Crombie, Brellenthin, Hillard, & Koltyn, 2018). Gratz and Roemer (2004) proposed a clinical treatment approach to emotional regulation, including: (1) acceptance of intense emotions (as opposed to trying to stop the outburst or prohibit the emotions, which often increases avoidance behaviors) and (2) targeted work to reduce unhealthy coping and increase goal-directed behaviors across emotional states. The next section focuses on several stabilization skills that clients can use, including self-awareness, recognition of triggers, relaxation techniques, and grounding to tolerate a range of emotions and improve healthy coping.

Self-Awareness as a Stabilization Skill

Self-awareness is the personal recognition and acknowledgment of one's internal feelings, thoughts, reactions, tendencies, methods of meaning-making, and the personal connections created between life experiences. Many clients arrive for counseling with highly limited self-awareness and insight, which often makes increased self-awareness an early and foundational goal for trauma work. Self-awareness is a critical element for a number of therapeutic tasks, including enhanced emotional stabilization. Through actively expanding self-awareness, attention is turned inward as an individual reflects upon internal thoughts, feelings, preferences, attitudes and other aspects of self (Morin, 2011). When the client is able to identify and recognize the internal signs of hyperarousal and hypoarousal, he or she is more capable of acknowledging the current state of distress and the need to take action to return to equilibrium. This process slows impulsive, reactive behaviors and improves the potential for purposeful, self-soothing actions.

Trauma Work in Practice: The Power of Self-Awareness in Stabilizing Emotional Dysregulation

Imagine the powerful hyperarousal state of a young man who became very agitated and angry when his wife arrived late to their date night. The man was fuming and refused to engage in conversation as his wife sat down to the table. However, this man utilized self-awareness to recognize his disproportionate reaction to the situation, and he subsequently made efforts to stabilize himself. Through the use of self-awareness, he acknowledged his anger and feelings of betrayal then he utilized deep breathing exercises to slow down his accelerated heart rate. Once physiologically calmer, he explained to his wife that her tardiness left him feeling devalued, which was a trigger for him. His wife was better able to understand her husband's strong reaction and was then very willing to reaffirm how important he was to her and explain the reality (traffic) for her delayed arrival. By the time dessert arrived, both members of the couple had emotionally regulated, which all began through the man's efforts to engage in self-awareness.

On the other end of the spectrum, imagine the hypoarousal state of a teenage girl who was just cut in the varsity soccer tryouts. Upon leaving school, she felt very lethargic, had no desire to socialize, and was unable to focus on her homework. By taking some time to engage in reflection and self-awareness, the girl recognized these sensations as a temporary hypoarousal reaction to her recent rejection, and consequently, she made intentional efforts towards self-care by taking the weekend to engage in activities that increased her energy, such as laughing at comedy shows on Netflix and walking her dog at the park. Again, self-awareness was the tool that normalized challenging feelings and reactions, and it provided a guide for restoring stability and balanced regulation.

Self-Awareness and Subjective Units of Distress

Self-awareness is a powerful skill that clients can learn or improve upon to monitor levels of emotional dysregulation. The Subjective Units of Distress Scale (SUDs) is a commonly utilized resource that is designed to help individuals become more aware of and describe their level of emotional distress (Wolpe & Lazarus, 1966). This scale involves a self-assigned score that ranges from 0 (no distress) to 10 (highest possible distress). I often encourage clients to practice self-awareness by telling me their current SUDs score in session, and then, outside of session, clients are challenged to journal about their changing SUDs scores throughout the week and describe what each score feels like in their body. A client may report that he is at a SUD level of 7, which he describes as moderate feelings of anxiety evidenced through increased heart rate, sweaty palms, decreased appetite, and some flashbacks but no suicidal thoughts. Clients will also express distress differently, and a SUD level of a 4 for one client will likely be very different than a 4 for another client. As another option, clients might draw a representative image that illustrates the signs and characteristics of each number on their SUDs scale. No matter the manner by which a client creates his or her scale, the critical goal of the task is to increase self-awareness by reflecting on the various levels of distress. This activity builds as clients begin to identify situational patterns in which his or her various levels are triggered, and then, specific coping and regulating strategies can be developed and tailored.

The nature of trauma induces an extreme state of emotional deregulation, so the client's practice of skills associated with emotional awareness and recognition of his or her various dysregulation levels (SUDs scores) not only aids the client in the current recovery process but also provides valuable tools for facing life's challenges. For example, Juan sought counseling with me for help regarding his frequent conflicts with his boss. As Juan learned to identify his levels of emotional distress during our sessions, he was also able to recognize at work when his SUDs were increasing above a 6, which signaled to him that he needed to take a break in order to return to a more relaxed, receptive state before attempting to further communicate with his boss.

In addition to SUDs scores, there are other measurements, such as using a heart rate monitor (for example, a fitness watch) in session, that can provide clients with feedback on their levels of dysregulation. Devices like heart rate monitors can indicate transitions between dysregulated states, as very low heart rates may reflect hypoarousal while very high rates may indicate hyperarousal states. The range for a normal resting heart rate depends on the client's age and other individual variables, so clinicians must be knowledgeable of considerations regarding any physiological assessment method. Measures like these provide real-time feedback for current levels of distress as well as offer methods for observing the physiological changes that may result from deep-breathing exercises and other interventions that increase self-awareness.

Recognition of Triggers as a Stabilization Skill

Triggers are the conscious and unconscious "express lane" neurological highways that connect traumatic memories with sensory information (sights, sounds, smells, types of touch, etc.), and these triggers are associated with very strong emotions, such as fear. Over time, clients can begin to recognize triggers as nothing more than false activations of the stress response system (false alarms). When clinicians promote the understanding that triggers are associated with past memories and are not a sign of current danger, clients often experience relief and the initial feelings of panic decreases as clients are assured of current safety, which allows them to more easily return to a state of equilibrium. Clinicians can reframe triggers as simply "stuck" feelings and memories that will be reprocessed later in treatment, which offers the client hope that the overwhelming power of triggers will likely eventually decrease as treatment progresses (Perryman et al., 2019). In the meantime, clients can learn to manage their triggers through recognition and psychoeducation that promotes the sense of safety.

Many clients experience a sense of shame associated with their trauma, but feelings of shame can be especially triggering for clients with a history of insecure attachment and/or abuse. Clinicians must be mindful to avoid unintentionally triggering clients through statements that could be construed as shaming or judgmental and, instead, communicate unconditional positive regard to help clients feel emotionally safe (Armstrong, 2015). For example, Lucy often complained during our sessions about how few well-paying jobs there were for her as an art major. When I asked her if she had considered other majors that might lead to higher-paying jobs, she became very defensive. Although I asked the question in an empathetic manner, Lucy's mother was highly critical of her and her interests, and consequently, my question was perceived by Lucy as passive aggressive and condescending rather than inquisitive. I noticed Lucy's sudden change in connection with me, and we discussed what feelings came up when I asked that question and how her mother's criticism has affected her. By raising her awareness of the trigger, Lucy was able to recognize how past experiences influence her reactions, and eventually, she was able to remain regulated and better differentiate between whether or not someone was truly demonstrating criticism towards her.

Despite our best efforts, it is impossible for clinicians to perfectly avoid triggering our clients, but we can reframe these situations as opportunities for therapeutic work in the here and now, as in the case of Lucy. By expanding self-awareness of personal triggers, clients can begin to apply multiperspective skills in order to recognize and accept various situations as distinct from their trauma experiences and, thus, respond differently and in new ways. As treatment progresses and the therapeutic alliance strengthens, clinicians are increasingly able to identify a client's specific triggers and also positively utilize the unknown minefield of unintentional triggers.

Relaxation Techniques as a Stabilization Skill

Self-awareness is invaluable in trauma work in numerous ways, including its role in a client's ability to relax. In fact, an important aspect of self-awareness is recognizing what produces peaceful and safe feelings in addition to what triggers negative reactions. Van der Kolk (2006) suggests that effective integration of trauma memories occurs more readily when clients remain in a receptive state in which their bodies are calm and relaxed during the process. While there are numerous relaxation techniques, such as diaphragmic breathing, progressive muscle relaxation, and visual imagery, not every technique is effective with each client. Clients should have a "toolbox" of relaxation exercises that they have identified as personally effective for them and which can be used in a variety of settings.

Frisby (2019) found that students experience **emotional contagion**, or a duplication of someone's emotional state, with instructors who developed rapport and were perceived as supportive by the class. As the instructor displayed feelings of enthusiasm and enjoyment about the course content, the students experienced increases in these same emotions. The emotional contagion phenomenon also occurs at home in the family system, between partners in a relationship, and in group settings. The transference of emotional mood and energy is a key principle for clinicians in trauma work, and clinicians must be mindful that they are providing a calm and hopeful affect for their clients. While clinicians give off emotional energy, trauma professionals are exposed to the powerful emotional contagions of clients as well, and a central piece of positive, professional boundaries and self-care is reflecting on what emotions belong to the client and what emotions belong to self.

Grounding as a Stabilization Skill

Trauma can sometimes distort one's sense of time and orientation, and the neurobiological mechanics of trauma memories often blur the lines between past danger and current safety. **Grounding** is a clinical technique designed to pull the individual out of the reliving experience of a traumatic memory and reorient the individual to the safety of the present moment, thereby serving as a crucial method for reducing the risk of retraumatization during trauma work (Black, 2006). Grounding a client in the awareness of current safety also aids in the maintenance of emotional regulation. When clients are able to stay grounded in the present moment, the need to activate a hyper- or hypoarousal survival response decreases as the client has fewer moments of trauma reexperience. Clinicians can foster grounding through exercises that require clients to actively focus on their present surroundings, thereby connecting their internal awareness with their external reality. As a helpful guideline for clinicians, clients should engage in grounding exercises before, during, and after exposure to triggered memories of trauma.

Grounding techniques are important to employ when a client seems overly caught up in a memory, becomes overwhelmed by emotional flooding, or experiences moderate dissociation. During times like these, the clinician utilizes grounding to bring the client "back into the room" and into present awareness. Grounding activities can take many unique forms, but universally, the goal of a grounding exercise is to move the client back into the cognitive, thinking side of the brain and to become physically aware of herself or himself and the current surroundings. To accomplish this, a clinician may ask a client to name some items around the room, feel the floor beneath their feet or the arms of their chair, touch something hot or cold, or recite the current day and time. The use of scents, such as scented oils or candles (use cautiously as some may trigger allergies), can be one of the most effective grounding techniques as the sense of smell has a neurobiological benefit. The olfactory nerve is located very close to the amygdala and, therefore, a pleasant scent can quickly terminate a false alarm through a positive scent-memory association (Sugiyama et al., 2015). There are also several scripts online that clinicians can narrate to promote grounding for clients. A personal favorite grounding exercise is a gentle pillow toss with clients. I have found this to be very easy and effective way to help clients ground to the present since the activity requires the client to engage parts of the brain that attend to depth perception and spatial awareness. Other grounding techniques may be simple and more subtle, such as asking if the client would like a glass of water and providing it for them. All of these grounding strategies share the common goal of aiming to interrupt an unhelpful process that the client is currently experiencing in session, and clinicians must use careful decision-making to gauge when a client needs an emotional or psychological break.

Another way to achieve grounding can be through **mindfulness**. Mindfulness is a skill that helps individuals intentionally focus their attention on the present moment in a reflective manner, which can be particularly useful for managing the intrusive thoughts of trauma (Wei, Tsai, Lannin, Du, & Tucker, 2015). Mindfulness is effective for improving emotional regulation, reducing impulsive behaviors, alleviating stress, stabilizing mood, and even preventing relapse of substance abuse (Gawrysiak et al., 2017). Mindful-based cognitive therapy has not only demonstrated symptom reduction for mental health symptoms, such as depression, but it has shown to be effective for improving somatic problems, such as pain management and inflammatory bowel disease (Schoultz, Macaden, & Hubbard, 2016).

Trauma Work in Practice: Grounding Techniques to Ensure Safety

Years ago, my client Ilene, was sharing about an event that had happened that week, and she suddenly burst into hysterical sobs. In the moment, my first reaction was to feel panic as I was worried about Ilene's safety and ability to drive home as our session was nearing the end of time. I knew that Ilene's primary need in that moment was to return to the safety of the moment and to regulate her emotions, so I decided to employ some grounding techniques before our session ended. In an empathetic but direct tone, I acknowledged the power of the feelings that Illene was experiencing but also explained how the intensity of her distress meant she needed to take a break from those emotions and reorient to the present moment. I asked Ilene if we could stand together and stretch, touch a variety of soft and calming objects in the room, and engage in some deep breathing while practicing mindfulness. Ilene agreed that she needed to calm at that time, and she and I completed these activities together for several minutes. The reflections I made during this experience focused on the calming and regulating changes that I was observing in Ilene physiologically, and I did not return to reflecting the emotions associated with her previous dysregulation as this would have likely restarted her dysregulation. After I made sure Illene had fully stabilized by assessing that she was alert, emotionally regulated, and safe to drive, I encouraged her to use her hands-free link to call a friend to discuss their fun weekend plans on her drive home in order to prevent her thoughts from slipping back into focus on the distressing event. The next week we processed the experience of both her dysregulation as well as her experience of regulation in session, and we discussed how she might utilize these self-awareness, grounding, and regulation skills outside of session.

In addition to the grounding techniques discussed, a final grounding strategy that may be utilized for client stabilization comes through the clinical skill of **immediacy**. Using immediacy, the clinician shares his or her observations of what is happening with the client in the *here and now* (Ivey, Ivey, & Zalaquett, 2014). For example, a clinician may say to the client, "I can see by your expression that you are feeling a great deal of distress as we discuss your marriage. You've stopped looking at me, and you are very quiet and withdrawn." Attending to emotional reactions that occur during sessions can provide additional awareness of the client's internal world and any past experiences connected to that expression.

In a clinical experience of immediacy, one of my clients routinely arrived late to our sessions, and he usually provided a number of excuses for his tardiness. One day, I noted how anxious he looked as he took a seat in my office after arriving 15 minutes late. "Frank, you seem to be very shaken by the fact that you are late. Can you stay with those feelings for a moment and tell me more about what you are experiencing right now?" By attending to those feelings, he described the overwhelming fears that taunted him from the moment he woke up as he tried to get ready for our sessions. Additional memories then surfaced of his father fighting with his mother in the mornings before he caught the bus for school. Immediacy helps both the clinician and the client become aware of current emotional states so they can be used for exploration as opposed to avoided through defensive reactions.

Conclusion

As the therapeutic process moves into the active stages of trauma work, an emphasis is always placed, first, on enhancing and developing the client's safety and stabilization. This phase of treatment establishes the critical building blocks upon which effective trauma treatment is conducted. Safety, which includes clinician attention to conditions in the therapeutic environment, the development of trust, practices of predictability, and enrichment of client empowerment, provides the necessary components for clients to begin engaging in the process. Safety is accompanied by a focus on client stabilization, and these critical elements involve work towards the client's identification and expression of emotion, ability to regulate, and effective use of self-awareness. The time and focus on the client's mastery of these initial but imperative goals may range from brief to extensive, but a solid foundation in this area of treatment is absolutely essential before any movement forward in trauma work.

While safety and stabilization are critical elements of treatment for clients, they are also crucial aspects in clinician development. As clinicians, we must consistently monitor our own levels of emotional distress, both in and out of session. The self-awareness of our own emotional states is a powerful way to manage countertransference and ensure that personal reactions do not impose on our ability to provide empathetic and objective responses to clients. By identifying our own triggers and utilizing stabilization skills, we can improve the care we provide to our clients as well as enrich and maintain our own mental health and well-being.

KEYWORD ASSESSMENT

Write definitions in your own words, describe the concept's role in trauma work, list any questions, or make notes of important aspects that you want to remember.

Safety

Stabilization

Emotional Regulation

Emotional Flooding

Triggers

Emotional Contagion

Grounding

Mindfulness

Immediacy

EXPERIENTIAL ACTIVITIES: INTERACTING WITH THE CHAPTER CONTENT

Expand Self-Awareness

1) Review the importance of the feelings of empowerment in trauma work. Enhance your own sense of empowerment by selecting a fictional, archetypal, historical, or imagined figure that represents you as a trauma clinician. Write a brief story plot in which you (your chosen figure) must somehow overcome a challenge or quest (metaphorically representing trauma work).

Expand Knowledge

2) Draw your own SUDs scale by identifying each marker on the scale and describing your unique signs and characteristics for each number on your scale. Create a personal scale for both hyper and hypoarousal.

Expand Skills

3) Research additional relaxation, grounding, and mindfulness techniques. Practice at least one of these techniques for yourself and then practice guiding someone else in these techniques through a role-play.

SUPERVISORY DISCUSSION: SHARING PERSONAL INSIGHTS AND IDENTIFYING AREAS FOR GROWTH

1) Share your experience of creating a metaphorical parallel through a story plot. What did you discover about your self-perceptions as a trauma clinician and your feelings of empowerment? What inner or external resources did you call upon to overcome your metaphorical challenge or quest? Discuss how these aspects might translate into your real-life practice.

2) Discuss the insights you gained from creating your SUDs scale. How can you manage various levels of personal dysregulation as you work with clients who may be dysregulated?

3) As you consider the metaphor of the *Jenga*® game, discuss its parallels with vulnerability in stabilization and the trauma treatment process. How can you help clients have an accepting attitude towards their intense emotions?

4) Reflect on your understanding of the safety and stabilization skills outlined in the chapter. Discuss a professional plan for yourself in which you identify specific goals for how you could bolster your clinical skills and resources within each of these domains.

Chapter 11

Phase 2: Remembrance and Mourning in Trauma Work

I've watched many movies over the years, but I still vividly recall the first time I saw one adventure movie in particular. At the climax of this film, the hero faces an impossible task: two hopelessly distant ledges span a great abyss, and standing on one ledge, the hero must successfully make it across the expanse below and reach the other ledge in order to continue onward in his quest. However, this task is not as it seems, and the feat does not simply involve finding a way to cross over. The true challenge of the task is for the hero to face his fear and trust what he cannot see. In a powerful moment of courage and faith, the hero chooses to take a single, brave step out directly over the engulfing void below. Intuitively, the act of stepping out over an abyss feels foolishly futile, and as I watched the movie, I remember gasping at the terrifying agony of the hero's decision to trust that, somehow, he was going to survive this implausible venture. I held my breath and felt the tremendous relief right alongside the hero when his step of faith did, indeed, find concrete footing. As the hero looks down to see what prevented him from falling, he discovers that the abyss below was actually an optical illusion, and the path for his journey had always been there, unwavering and secure all along. Even though he wasn't aware of it, the hero had never been in true peril when he took his step of faith.

As we enter phase 2 of trauma work, clients and clinicians both feel as though they have reached "the step of faith challenge." The task of facing the emotional monsters and haunting ghosts brought on by trauma can sometimes feel counterintuitive, overwhelming, and hopelessly frightening. Here at this crossroad, we find ourselves at a juncture in which we must choose to trust the process, recognize that the power of traumatic memories is, in many ways, an illusion in the present moment, and have faith that this journey is indeed secured by many supports as we take the brave step out and onward. While trauma memory work can feel overwhelming at first, this part of the journey offers the client the opportunity to grow from fear to courage, from silenced to empowered, and from wounded to strengthened.

At this point in the treatment process, several major therapeutic goals have been reached: the therapeutic relationship and safety measures have been established, the client has developed strong coping and stabilization skills, and the client and clinician have mutually agreed upon specific goals in trauma recovery. As phase 1 successfully reaches completion, phase 2 of trauma work can begin, and treatment now focuses on processing the psychological and emotional impact of the trauma memories through remembrance and mourning. The client is now ready to move away from avoidance behaviors and gain control over the fear, shame, and intense emotions that have held the client captive to the past.

Understanding the dynamics and considerations for this stage of trauma work is complex yet crucial. In the first part of this chapter, we discuss trauma treatment principles, which are broad guidelines that clinicians can apply to all client cases in order to maintain a comprehensive perspective of this phase of the recovery process. Following this section, various trauma-specific treatment models are presented, and these theoretical frameworks provide the clinician with specific treatment goals and theoretically-congruent clinical strategies. The chapter concludes with a discussion on several common trauma-specific interventions, which are utilized in several of the models highlighted. In summary, trauma treatment principles offer a guiding *perspective* for the clinician, trauma-specific treatment models inform the *orientation to the goals and process* for phase 2, and trauma-specific treatment interventions offer the clinical tools for *how* these therapeutic tasks will be addressed and accomplished.

Trauma Treatment Principles: Applying Universal Guidelines

Regardless of the selected theory or the type of trauma addressed, clinicians can implement trauma treatment principles that carry universally applicable guidelines for this phase of treatment. In many ways, these principles serve as an orienting compass upon which the clinician can rely while navigating this especially dynamic phase of trauma work. As clinicians help clients move through the clinical tasks of trauma remembrance and mourning, the clinician's guiding principles of trauma treatment include the provision of treatment rationale, continual attunement to treatment priorities, and considerations for the grief that often accompanies trauma. With these three principles in mind, clinicians maintain a comprehensive perspective for the work of phase 2.

Rationales and Explanations of the Process

Preparation for phase 2 of treatment begins with psychoeducation about the therapeutic value and purpose of processing the losses, cognitive changes, and difficult memories associated with trauma. While clinicians do not need to go into lengthy detail, providing a rationale for the theoretical models and selected techniques enables clients to play an active role in their treatment and to understand the process better. By nature, a traumatic event is characterized by feelings of terror and crippling disempowerment, so clinicians must ensure that clients do not experience therapy in the same way. The therapeutic process, especially during this sensitive phase of the process in which memories are confronted, should not be unpredictable, scary, or outside of the client's understanding or control. This means that clinicians must take the time to offer explanations to the client. In order to fully give consent for treatment, clients need to understand the *why and how* of the process. Not only does recovery work require processing traumatic memories, but this stage also involves grieving the losses, both tangible and intangible, connected with trauma. For clients, the intentional choice to dive into the painful memories and grief of trauma can feel counterintuitive, especially considering how much energy the client has spent in effort to avoid such feelings.

When I provide the rationale for trauma processing to my clients, I often explain by using the metaphor of a wound (in fact, the word "trauma" comes from the Greek word for "wound"). When a wound begins to heal, a scab often develops, and any attempt to remove a scab that has hardened as a protective covering over a wound is often painful. Without the protection of the scab, the wound feels raw and reexposed to the outside elements. However, there are some wounds that need to be cleaned out and there may be splinters that require removal in order for the tissue to heal properly. In contrast to figuratively "ripping off the scab," together the client and clinician can gently and carefully work through the hardened defenses that protect clients from painful memories and the associated feelings of shame, fear, and powerlessness, and the wound of trauma can be cleansed. Splintered, fragmented memories can then be replaced with a cohesive trauma narrative. This recovery process is neither quick nor easy and does not eradicate the trauma from the client's memory or life story. Scars from trauma often remain. However, proper wound care results in healing of the damaged tissue so that it no longer poses a health concern for the present or future. The faint scars that remain testify to the individual's survival and resilience.

Ongoing Assessment of Treatment Priorities

Once the client understands the purpose for trauma memory processing, including both the potential benefits and risks, treatment priorities are considered based on the information gleaned during the assessment. Clinicians must carefully reflect on which goals and needs appear to be most pressing for the client at that juncture of the process. Gentry, Baranowsky, and Rhoton (2017) postulate the top four priorities for successful trauma work: (1) a strong therapeutic alliance, (2) an ability to emotionally self-regulate, (3) cognitive restructuring of dysfunctional thinking patterns, and (4) exposure or narrative work to integrate fragmented memories. As the client moves into this next stage of treatment, the first two treatment goals, therapeutic alliance and self-regulation, should have been sufficiently established during phase 1. The third and fourth treatment priorities, cognitive restructuring and exposure work, are the hallmark tasks of phase 2, but frequently, a periodic return to the other two tasks is required. Cognitive restructuring and exposure help clients to identify false assumptions from traumatic experiences and reprocess "stuck" memories into cohesive narratives, and these theory-based interventions are discussed more in depth later in the chapter.

Unfortunately, the clinician's sense of urgency to move further and deeper into these trauma-targeted goals can blur the focus of what is most needed at that time in the therapeutic process, and clinicians can confuse their desires for client readiness. In order to keep treatment priorities devoid of countertransference and congruent with client readiness, the clinician must continually reflect on the question, "What does my client need the most *right now*?" Clinicians can mentally revisit the four categories of treatment priorities (therapeutic alliance, emotional regulation, cognitive restructuring, and trauma exposure work) to hypothesize on the changing answers to this important question as the therapeutic process continually unfolds. In this way, the clinician remains oriented to the needs of the client and confident of which goal is being currently addressed in session.

Grief and Loss in Trauma

Trauma's companion is loss. The potential losses that may stem from trauma include the loss of life, health, relationships, home, identity, sense of integrated self, innocence, job, finances, concentration, trust, and faith. Grief is an internal response to both tangible and intangible losses and often includes emotions such as anger, resentment, confusion, emptiness, betrayal, and sadness (Shear, 2015). The process of grieving losses is central part of trauma work and healing, and while losses are painful to acknowledge, these aspects should not be considered topics to be avoided. "We cannot go around the pain that is the wilderness of our grief. Instead, we must journey all [the way] through it, sometimes shuffling along the less strenuous side paths, sometimes plowing directly into the dark center" (Wolfelt, 2003, p. 11).

Acknowledging and processing the grief that ensues from trauma is not an easy process for clients nor clinicians. In order to communicate attunement, understanding, and acceptance of a client's grief, clinicians must resist the urge to fill moments of silence with words or contrite messages to "fix" the problem of loss or explain why it occurred. We cannot rescue clients from their pain, but we can be with them through their pain. Remaining present and engaged even in silence is a powerful way to communicate empathy.

Human nature instinctually drives us to avoid pain. Consequently, there is a natural tendency to either avoid individuals who are grieving or subconsciously push them to get better quickly and move on. When we feel the urge to push others to feel better or "get over it," this is often more about our needs rather than the needs of the person in pain, and this tendency is typically reflective of our desire to avoid painful or uncomfortable emotions. Grief cannot be rushed nor fixed, and attempts to avoid or gloss over grief often fail as grief demands our attention. Pipher (2019) explains, "Facing our grief requires openness and courage. We must explore it with curiosity and patience and allow it to stay in our hearts [and our therapy] until it is ready to leave" (p. 276).

Complicated and Disenfranchised Grief

While most people progress naturally through the grief process, **complicated grief** occurs when an individual seems to get stuck in their emotional distress and/or experience significant and enduring impairment in functioning (Shear, 2015). When the loss is due to bereavement (grief associated with the death of a loved one) and the grieving process is *severe* and *prolonged*, the client may meet criteria for the *DSM-5* diagnosis of persistent complex bereavement disorder (APA, 2013). Losses apart from bereavement, particularly loss resultant of trauma, can also complicate the grieving process.

Disenfranchised grief is a specific type of grief that can complicate trauma recovery as this type of grief involves *intangible* losses that often do not receive social support. According to Doka's theory of disenfranchised grief (1989, 2002), situations of disenfranchised grief may include a relationship that is not recognized (such as a mistress), a loss that is not recognized (such as a loss of a dream), a griever that is not recognized (such as an elderly person), a stigmatized death (such as suicide), or an expression of grief that differs from expectations of the potential support system (such as a person who is grieving but does not show emotions) (DeGroot & Vik, 2017; Keck, 2018). The clinician's therapeutic efforts to honor and facilitate grief through support and compassion for the pain provides important validation and understanding for the client. In this way, "[g]rief is witnessed when it is openly acknowledged, publicly mourned, or socially supported" (Keck, 2018, p. 21).

While grief represents the overall process of acknowledging, remembering, and honoring a loss in conjunction with all the associated feelings, **mourning** can be considered the outer expression of grief through activities such as crying, talking about the deceased person or the loss, and ceremonial activities that promote remembrance and social support (Wolfelt, 2003). Grief work often involves aspects of mourning, and clinicians can help clients identify ways in which they can externalize their inner feelings of loss. Although each client's grief is unique, Worden (2008) identified four general tasks for mourning: 1) accepting the reality of the loss, 2) processing the pain of grief, 3) adjusting to the world without the deceased or material loss, and 4) finding an enduring connection (Dubi, Powell, & Gentry, 2017; Worden, 2008). Clinicians can incorporate a variety of therapeutic mourning activities, such as an integration of the client's cultural practices of mourning or the externalization of grief represented through created artwork or scrapbooks that reflect the losses associated with trauma.

Trauma Work in Practice: Grief and Trauma Recovery

Daniel arrived for mental health services as part of an outpatient referral network for military veterans. As a 29-year-old army solider, Daniel was medically discharged after he sustained significant injuries to the left side of his body during a deployment to the Middle East. His primary care physician encouraged Daniel to seek mental health services due to his difficulty sleeping. When he arrived for counseling, Daniel shared with his clinician, Paula, that he was having some anxiety but doubted whether services were needed since he did not have PTSD "like his other buddies." After completing the intake and assessments, Paula developed a strong case conceptualization for Daniel, and she determined that while he did not meet the full criteria for PTSD, Daniel did present with some trauma-related symptoms and his treatment plan included trauma work integration. Paula and Daniel's alliance grew, and Daniel's resistance towards the process softened as Paula provided him with psychoeducation about trauma and the benefits of mental health work.

After a successful completion of phase 1 of trauma work, Daniel felt prepared to enter phase 2. He assured Paula that his memories of the military event that resulted in his injuries did not cause distress for him, and he reported that he was not experiencing problems with flashbacks or hypervigilance. However, Paula recognized that Daniel's trauma-related needs went beyond a singular event, and she helped Daniel begin reflection on the intangible losses associated with the injury. This was an aspect Daniel had not yet considered, and he was shocked to discover the intensity of his grief surrounding the loss of his envisioned future, the loss of his career aspirations in the military, the loss of many of his athletic and physical activities, and the loss of his former relationships with his family and friends as they grappled with their own grief surrounding Daniel's new disabilities. Paula recognized that Daniel's unacknowledged grief and inhibited mourning were, in fact, more powerful for him than the traumatic event itself. For Daniel, phase 2 of treatment did not require much trauma memory work but rather took a focus that offered Daniel opportunities to recognize and honor his grief and losses. As Daniel acknowledged and processed through his grief, his adjustment problems and trauma-related symptoms naturally diminished.

In phase 2, the universally applicable trauma treatment principles transcend all clients and all models. These guiding beacons remind clinicians to be prepared to offer rationales and explanations for this stage of the process, as this phase is often anxiety-provoking for clients; remain oriented to the evolving priorities of treatment; and integrate aspects of grief, loss, and mourning into the therapeutic process. These principles aid clinicians in developing and maintaining a comprehensive perspective for trauma-informed care for this point in trauma work.

Trauma-Specific Treatment Models: Utilizing a Theory

A foundational aspect of clinical decision making in trauma work is the selection and utilization of a trauma treatment model or models. These models inform many of the goals and therapeutic tasks, especially in phase 2, and the clinician's guiding theory provides a specific hypothesis for the etiology and resolution of trauma symptoms. Trauma-specific models are also accompanied by interventions and clinical strategies that are congruent with the premise of the theory, and clinicians should be very mindful to implement interventions that are theoretically consistent rather than incorporate a smorgasbord of interventions. The selection of a trauma-specific theory is a critical milestone for clinicians, and while having a general knowledge of a variety of theories (as is presented here) is very helpful to be able to understand the diversity of treatment perspectives and orientations, many clinicians select two or three models in which to become highly knowledgeable, skilled, and competent in clinical application with clients. Ethical and competent practice is always a consideration; therefore, new interventions and approaches should always be conducted under the supervision of experienced clinicians, and attention to research-informed and empirical support should ultimately drive treatment choices.

In trauma work, theoretical models are implemented with the clinical intention of reducing a client's trauma-related symptoms and achieving the client's treatment goals. Evidence-based treatment (EBT) represents a distinction of treatment models that have demonstrated sufficient evidence, based on scientific evaluation, in producing positive outcomes for a specific diagnosis, such as a reduction of trauma symptoms for individuals diagnosed with PTSD. In conjunction with evidence-based treatment, clinicians must also aim to engage in evidence-based practice (EBP), which represents the broader integration of assessment-driven and outcomes-oriented approach in trauma work. In a seminal document, the APA's Presidential Task Force on Evidence-Based Practice (2006) defined **evidence-based practice** as "the integration of the best available research with clinical expertise in the context of patient characteristics, culture, and preferences" (p. 147). Together, these three elements (best available evidence through research, clinical expertise, and client characteristics) help clinicians to develop the most beneficial and therapeutic approach to mental health care, including trauma treatment. This framework of guiding, informative sources for evidence-based practice aids practitioners in monitoring treatment suitability, remaining within professional scope, and tailoring treatment for the unique client.

Knowledge and the application of evidence-based and research-supported trauma treatment modalities is a part of ethical practice, professional integrity, and represents the highest standard of care for clients who are hurting. The following section provides a brief overview of several treatment models that have gained the distinction as "evidence-based" on many rating platforms. These models include prolonged exposure, trauma-focused cognitive behavioral therapy, cognitive processing therapy, eye movement desensitization reprocessing, narrative exposure therapy, and dialectical behavioral therapy.

Prolonged Exposure

Prolonged exposure therapy, or PE (Foa & Rothbaum, 1998) is based on the premise that exposure to fear-causing stimuli (trauma memories) over time can result in decreased emotional and aversive response to the memories. In order to extinguish the fear response from the stimuli, PE utilizes the interventions of *imaginal exposure*, which occurs through a detailed retelling of the trauma narrative in session, and this intervention is often followed by *in vivo exposure*, in which the client confronts trauma triggers in real-life situations (Harlé, Spadoni, Norman, & Simmons, 2019). Memories become desensitized over time, and inhibitory learning occurs as the client disconfirms the idea that the feared stimulus is harmful and realizes that he or she can experience emotional responses to the stimulus and still be safe (Craske, Treanor, Conway, Zbozinek, & Verviliet, 2014). While working through and confronting a hierarchy of avoidance behaviors, clients utilize the SUDs scale to monitor distress levels and relaxation exercises to stay within the window of tolerance, which is discussed more in depth later in the chapter.

Trauma-Focused Cognitive Behavioral Therapy

Trauma-focused cognitive behavioral therapy, or TF-CBT (Cohen, Mannarino, & Deblinger, 2006) is a short-term treatment conducted primarily with children and adolescents. Traditional cognitive behavioral interventions, such as the client's identification of unhelpful thoughts, are integrated into a trauma-sensitive and goal-focused treatment protocol. In addition, conjoint sessions are conducted with children and parents or caregivers to improve family communication and enhance parenting skills (Lewey et al., 2018). TF-CBT is a phase-based model with the following components: psychoeducation, skill building (such as relaxation), affect regulation and cognitive coping, trauma narrative work and the processing of trauma experiences, in vivo desensitization to triggers, and the enhancement of safety and future development.

Cognitive Processing Therapy

Cognitive processing therapy, or CPT (Resick & Schnicke, 1992) is a combination of cognitive restructuring and exposure therapies aimed to challenge faulty beliefs related to the trauma and decrease emotional sensitivity to triggers. The ultimate goal of CPT is to change the story that clients tell themselves about the trauma. CPT is a structured approach conducted usually within 12 sessions. The manualized steps of CPT include psychoeducation, exposure work (usually accomplished through written accounts of memories) aimed to process the meaning that the client has applied to the trauma, and identification of the automatic thoughts surrounding trauma-specific areas (such as shame and trust) and stuck points (thoughts or beliefs that keep PTSD symptoms going). The model also aims to challenge distorted thinking and, in the final phase of treatment, identify and incorporate new views of traumatic event (Chard, Ricksecker, Healy, Karlin, & Resick, 2012).

Eye Movement Desensitization Reprocessing

Eye movement desensitization reprocessing, or EMDR (Shapiro, 1989) is a trauma treatment based on the Adaptive Information Processing, or AIP theory Shapiro, 2018), which postulates that emotional difficulties and defensive reactions to triggers may originate from memories that are dysfunctionally stored in the brain. EMDR interventions focus on reprocessing these memories to reduce their emotional volatility and alleviate trauma-related symptoms. Reprocessing occurs through the client's *dual awareness stimulation*, which involves activating both hemispheres of the brain simultaneously. To accomplish this, the use of alternating eye movements, auditory beeping, or taping while processing target memories enables clients to effectively reorganize the traumatic memory (Balboa, Cavallo, & Fernandez, 2019). The process aims to integrate fragmented memories and clear out negative cognitions as well as reinforce positive cognitions, such as "I am lovable" and "I can heal and be successful." Although EMDR was originally developed for trauma-related disorders, its utility has been expanded to treat other mental health issues, such as depression and anxiety (Krupnik, 2019)

Narrative Exposure Therapy

Narrative exposure therapy (NET), which includes a combination of CBT, exposure-based, and testimonial therapies, was originally developed by Schauer, Neuner, and Elbert (2005) as a model to address the cumulative impact of traumatic stress on refugees and other victims of war and organized violence (Peltonen & Kangaslampi, 2019). NET involves *chronologically* retelling one's life story, focusing particularly on traumatic events, with the intended goal of integrating the client's experiences into a coherent life narrative. The NET approach utilizes the development of timelines and biographical narration to link "cold memories" (factual details of the traumas) and "hot memories" (emotions and sensations associated with the traumas). "This anchors the event(s) in time and reduces the sense of current threat" (Robjant & Fazel, 2010, p. 1032). Constructing a "testimonial" life story can be a powerful healing tool, especially when done in the context of a community of survivors who have all experienced multiple traumas. The therapy concludes with the clinician presentation of the client's written biography, which serves to officially acknowledge and document his or her testimony.

Dialectical Behavioral Therapy

Dialectical behavioral therapy, or DBT) (Linehan, 1993) integrates CBT components with work on radical self-acceptance as a method for targeting trauma symptoms and improving interpersonal functioning. DBT has been successfully used to treat individuals diagnosed with both PTSD and personality disorders (particularly, borderline personality disorder) by building deficient interpersonal skills, increasing emotional regulation capacity, emphasizing personal responsibility, and prioritizing the reduction of self-harming and suicidal behaviors (Kliem, Kroger, & Kosfelder, 2010). The treatment modules in DBT include mindfulness (acceptance as opposed to avoidance), emotional regulation, distress tolerance, and interpersonal effectiveness (skill building such as boundary work and assertiveness). DBT clients have a consultation team and participate in weekly individual therapy, group sessions, and phone support (Wilks, Korslund, Harned, & Linehan, 2016).

Trauma-Specific Interventions: Integrating Clinical Strategies

Trauma-specific treatment models orient the clinician to the goals and protocol for trauma work, especially in phase 2. However, many of the theories discussed share commonalities in their emphasis on cognitive restructuring, trauma narrative development, and trauma memory work (exposure), and various models utilize similar interventions to accomplish these clinical tasks. Again, clinicians must be consistent in applying theoretically congruent interventions, but when clinicians understand the variety of theoretically based interventions, they are also often better able to make informed choices to select a model for treatment. Even if the clinician's trauma treatment model does not warrant use of these specific interventions, a broad understanding of the common clinical interventions often utilized in phase 2 aids clinicians in remaining current in the field and in literature.

Cognitive Restructuring

When an individual survives a traumatic experience, fundamental changes to belief systems are virtually inevitable, as the person integrates the reality of the trauma with his or her understanding of the world. Sometimes, however, these changes in beliefs can be profoundly negative and problematic. The shattered assumptions theory (Janoff-Bulman, 1992) postulates that trauma can challenge three main categories of beliefs: the self as worthy, the world as good, and the world as meaningful. For many clients who seek trauma recovery, clinical attention must be placed on the inaccurate or unhelpful assumptions or self-defeating beliefs that have emerged in association with the trauma. To address this trauma-specific aspect of treatment, clinicians may implement the strategy of **cognitive restructuring**, which is the therapeutic process of identifying and challenging distorted thoughts and beliefs and replacing them with rational and helpful thoughts that promote healing and wellness (Corey, 2017). With a marked emphasis on the role of thoughts and beliefs, cognitive restructuring is frequently integrated within the treatment models that fall under the umbrella of cognitive behavioral therapies. When clinicians integrate this focus in treatment, they do so with that understanding that "cognitive interventions help individuals actively learn to identify historical thinking biases, substitute accurate here-and-now interpretations for biased cognitions, and/or change emotional responsivity to cognitions" (Kredlow, Eichenbaum, & Otto, 2018, p. 269).

During cognitive restructuring, the first therapeutic task is for the client to become increasingly aware of his or her own thoughts and beliefs. Cognitive awareness aids in reducing **cognitive distortions** or dysfunctional patterns of thinking that lead to distressing feelings and problematic behaviors (Caselli et al., 2018). Identifying and challenging cognitive distortions is an important focus in trauma work because the misinterpretation of traumatic events, such as self-blame for a sexual assault, can increase the risk problematic thinking patterns, contribute to posttraumatic symptoms (such as attention deficits), and increase negative affect (Booth et al., 2019). Table 11.1 is a list of several common types of cognitive distortions alongside examples of possible corresponding beliefs emerging from traumatic experiences.

The fallout of trauma creates an intense drive to protect oneself, and the trickle-down effect of these subconscious defense efforts often translates into the development of cognitive distortions, which are ultimately intended to protect oneself from possible danger. While cognitive restructuring may be applicable to many types of mental health issues, cognitive restructuring in trauma work focuses specifically on the thoughts and beliefs associated with the trauma event itself and the ensuing impacts. Cognitive distortions have the potential to be so profound that they may increase risk for suicidal ideation, and therefore, cognitive distortions are important targets for post-trauma intervention (Fazakas-DeHoog, Rnic, & Dozois, 2017).

Cognitive restructuring can occur even by making simple alterations to the terminology being used about the trauma. It may seem very minor, but this adjustment can dramatically shift a client's perspective on trauma. For example, my client Martha presented with guilt and shame over the "relationship" she had with her cousin during her youth; however, Martha was 13 years old and her cousin was 32 years old at the time. As we worked through treatment, Martha began

TABLE 11.1 Common Cognitive Distortions

Cognitive Distortion	Example
Overgeneralization	All men are abusive.
All-or-nothing thinking	Nothing good will happen to me in the future.
Disqualifying the positive	Even though my family and I survived the tornado, life is not worth living.
Magnification or minimization	I just found out that I have stage 4 cancer, but I think the doctor is overreacting.
"Should" statements	I should have fought off my attacker.
Labeling or mislabeling	My accident proves that I am reckless.
Filtering	Since my dad cheated on my mom, I will probably marry someone who will cheat on me.
Jumping to conclusions	I saw the way that woman looked at me, and she clearly thinks I am a loser.

to recognize the distortion she held, which centered on her perception that the experience was what she referred to as a "consensual relationship". Martha began to reframe the event as one in which she was "molested" by her cousin, and the language we used in session mirrored these cognitive adjustments. As a result, Martha's guilt and shame about the relationship transformed into feelings of appropriate anger towards her cousin, and she was able to experience compassion for her younger self. Cognitive restructuring targets many distortions related to trauma-specific issues of safety, control, power, and self-worth.

Trauma Narrative Development

A **trauma narrative** represents the client's process of retelling the sequence of events associated with the trauma in a cohesive, chronological way in order to gain mastery and understanding of the trauma. In phase 2, the development of the trauma narrative often involves helping clients weave together the pieces of their memories into a full "story." Trauma narrative work may utilize verbal and/or written processing as clients describe their experiences, and this clinical strategy is used in various treatment models, such as narrative exposure therapy and trauma-focused cognitive behavioral therapy.

The therapeutic process of developing a cohesive trauma narrative goes beyond a simple retelling of the experience and often includes facilitating the client's experience of meaning-making, which is the reflective practice of discovering insights into challenging life circumstances and gaining greater understanding of the suffering. "Meaning-making is a process which looks to increase one's ability to describe how an adverse life event occurred and attributing causality to the event, thereby helping integrate it into one's global meaning system" (Kopacz et al., 2019, p. 78). As clients try to make sense of traumas and begin to recognize that, while the events themselves were out of their control, they are no longer in a position of helplessness, their hope and confidence during recovery may increase (Frankl & Boyne, 2017). Trauma narratives offer clients the opportunity to coherently put together the story of their experience and then begin to understand it in a new and empowered way.

Exposure Work

As clients revisit the pieced-apart memories that come together to form a trauma narrative, this process inherently includes exposure to the distressful aspects of the trauma memories themselves. The avoidance of trauma reminders is one of the hallmark characteristics of PTSD and also one of the symptoms that causes significant disruption in daily functioning for clients. In direct contrast to avoidance, the process of **exposure** involves the client's willingness to face memories and fears, and depending upon the guiding theory of treatment, the clinical intervention of exposure can be conceptualized as a reorganization and renewed understanding of trauma memories. During the exposure process, clients intentionally bring up trauma memories in a structured and planned format with the intended purpose that the fear associated with these memories will decrease over time and a cohesive trauma narrative will emerge.

Very often, exposure is the aspect of trauma work that is the most anxiety-provoking for both the client and clinician alike, as clients must summon the courage to enter "the heart of the cave," but must do so with confidence that they will safely reemerge. The snowballing impact of trauma is profound, and in many ways, enduring trauma-related symptoms reflect unresolved memory organization, distorted perceptions, and/or the brain's ongoing attempt to protect the individual from threat. Exposure is a commonly utilized clinical intervention associated with many trauma-specific models, such as prolonged exposure therapy and EMDR. This section of the chapter reviews key elements of the exposure process, which includes habituation, titration, containment, working within the window of tolerance, and dual awareness. However, before exploring the specific ways exposure is used in treatment, clinicians must have a general understanding of how trauma impacts memory.

Trauma and Memory

Memories are critical, because we use the past to inform our reactions and understanding of the present. The fallout of trauma leaves scars written on one's memories, and these memories themselves often become the focus of treatment in phase 2. In order to understand the therapeutic benefit and rationale of exposure, trauma clinicians need a strong working knowledge of how trauma affects memory. While memory serves a variety of purposes, one important function is its categorization of experiential information as either *normative*, which involves the mundane details of life that our brains discard and forget, or *noteworthy*, which are emotionally charged experiences that our brain intuits as important data to refer back to in the future. Information that comes from common, everyday occurrences easily assimilates into our patterns of thinking as a cohesive narrative, or **explicit memory**, and the information is neatly filed away and stored appropriately in long-term memory. However, a traumatic experience, which is highly charged with distressing emotion, can disrupt the brain's systematic categorization process. An **implicit memory** is a type of memory encoded with powerful emotions, such as fear, and is fragmented with only pieces of information. Very often traumatic experiences are stored in the brain's memory with these characteristics.

Our memories are subject to a high degree of errors and biases (Wagoner, 2017). In fact, a great deal of debate has surrounded the reliability and validity of trauma survivors' memories and accounts of circumstances. As full memories or details within memories emerge during trauma work, Langberg (2003) explains, "The fact that a memory surfaced does not guarantee its truth. The fact that a memory was repressed for years does not mean it is untrue" (p. 121). Thankfully, as clinicians, we do not bear the burden of proof, nor do we necessarily have the ability to determine whether the details of the clients' stories are accurate. We are able, instead, to focus our efforts on providing empathy, building a strong therapeutic alliance, and listening to the clients' stories without judgment. The goal of our work is not to determine the validity of memories nor separate fact from fiction; rather, our focus remains on helping the client integrate memories into their life narrative (Schiraldi, 2009). Regardless of accuracy, memories and the interpretation of past events dramatically impacts our beliefs and worldviews.

When these memory organization concepts are translated into real life, we can easily see its relationship with many trauma symptoms, such as reexperiencing and hypervigilance. When clients describe reexperiencing symptoms of trauma, they often characterize it as a sensation in which the trauma is playing over and over in their minds like a "broken record," continually on repeat. Descriptions like this very accurately reflect the way implicit memories can become "stuck" in short-term memory networks and, consequently, become easily triggered by current defenses (Schiraldi, 2009). As clinicians sensitively approach the exposure process with clients, psychoeducation about memory can be helpful for clients. Equipped with a more informed perspective, clients are then able to engage in the interventions associated with exposure with an empowered understanding of how and why confronting the memories themselves will be beneficial and therapeutic.

Habituation and Exposure Work

Exposure work is always grounded in a theoretical model, and the interventions and approaches to accomplish this goal are diverse. "Exposure takes various forms, including graduated versus intense (or flooding therapy), brief versus prolonged, with and without various cognitive and somatic coping strategies, and imaginal, interoceptive or in vivo (or in real life)" (Craske et al., 2014, p. 1). No matter what type of approach is selected, the underpinning value of exposure is that it is effective through the process of **habituation**, which is the reduction of anxiety and arousal in the presence of a feared stimulus over a period of time (Benito & Walther, 2015).

An example of habituation can be seen in the patterns developed in a family who lives near railroad tracks. When new friends come to visit, guests may have a startled reaction every time the whistle of the train suddenly blows. However, the family who has lived by the tracks for years is accustomed to the train's sounds and no longer reacts in the same manner. The sounds of the train are not gone, but the sense of danger has left. In the same way, through the process of habituation, clients learn to recognize that memories themselves cannot hurt them. Exposure to memories within a supportive, affirming environment can also break the shame and emotional grip the memories have held on clients. Exposure work offers clients an opportunity to discover that they do not need to avoid memories or reminders of the trauma to stay psychologically safe; they learn that they can coexist with memories and can be empowered enough to acknowledge, confront, and even move beyond the ghosts of the past.

Titration and Exposure Work

As previously mentioned (but cannot be overemphasized), the key to ethical trauma work is to help the client experience safety throughout treatment. The potential for retraumatization with exposure necessitates that the clinician judiciously monitors the client's degree of emotional arousal, which then informs the appropriate levels of exposure to trauma stimuli. Effective exposure work is guided by two aspects: 1) the theory-informed approach to the process and methods of exposure, and 2) the client's ability to emotionally and psychologically tolerate the exposure so that the intervention is experienced by the client as positive and helpful rather than overwhelming and frightening. This second aspect is crucial and requires responsibility on the part of the trauma clinician to protect the client from retraumatization by carefully pacing treatment and degree of exposure to. Contrary to the trauma work training presented several decades ago, the goal of this phase does not hinge on the client's experience and expression of strong or intense emotions. In fact, a slower, less intense pace of treatment provides a model for clients regarding how to slow down their reactions to triggers. A slower process also creates space for both cognitive and emotional reflection and processing, and as a result, the client has ample opportunity to acknowledge and integrate the positive inner changes and perceptions that are occurring. By processing and purging of emotions over a period of time, clients feel more in control during the therapeutic process and the potential for emotional hijacking is reduced.

Titration is the clinical term for the mindful therapeutic approach that aims to limit exposure to trauma memories to small, incremental amounts. This cautious "dosing" of exposure allows clinicians to continually assess the client's emotional state by observing his or her reactions and offer sufficient grounding as needed before the next "dose" of exposure (Black, 2006). Baranowsky et al. (2005) use the metaphor of braking and accelerating to describe the process of cautiously moving forward into the trauma memories and then backing off exposure as needed.

For example, clinicians may ask clients open-ended questions or prompts to accelerate exposure (such as, "Tell me more about how you felt to experience that."), while close-ended, grounding questions can apply the brakes and return the client to the present session (such as, "Would you like a glass of water?"). Titration is a crucial safety feature of exposure work, and clinicians must be aware of how their therapeutic choices and reflections influence the pacing of exposure and emotional intensity for the client.

Containment and Exposure Work

Unfortunately, it is not always possible to control when exposure will occur (such as when the client experiences a flashback or engages into aspects of the trauma narrative without a therapeutic structure or prompting), and clients may need to deal with trauma memories that spontaneously intrude into clients' thoughts at inconvenient times. For situations like these, **containment**, which is a mindful choice to mentally compartmentalize a thought, emotion, or memory, can be helpful, and there are many containment exercises that can assist in titrating exposure. Particularly emphasized by the EMDR model, an example of a containment exercise involves the clinician's prompting the client to visualize an imaginary place to safely "store" memories when needing a break from exposure work. While the client may imagine psychological "containers," these containers can also be literal and integrated into trauma work in a variety of ways. I often have clients decorate a wooden box with images that represent comfort and serenity, and the client may also store positive and comforting pictures and phrases inside the container, which can serve as safekeeping for the client's psychological material. Clients are able to open the box during times of exposure (such as during session) and then choose to close it as a representation of mindfully taking intentional breaks from processing memories and focusing on coping exercises. The clinician must implement clinical judgment to assess when a client is becoming overwhelmed or needs to take a break from exploring a thought or feeling, and the clinician can sensitively remind the client of his or her "container" and take a moment for the client to metaphorically place the thought in the container for safekeeping and psychological separation.

Window of Tolerance and Exposure Work

Safe and effective exposure work involves a maintaining a balance between alert and calm states. The space between hyperarousal and hypoarousal generally represents the psychological and physiological state in which the client is both emotionally regulated and cognitively engaged in the therapeutic process, and this therapeutic "space" is known as the **window of tolerance** (Ogden, Minton, & Pain, 2006). Within this window, the client is able to access implicit memories and experience some degree of emotional arousal, but the intensity is manageable and does not exceed the client's ability to tolerate the emotions. When trauma memory work is being targeted, clinicians aim to facilitate a therapeutic climate in which the client's defenses are low and the upper brain, which houses the skills of reasoning, communication, and potential for new learning, is engaged. Courtois and Ford (2016) explain, "Treatment is geared towards expanding the window [of tolerance]. The client is encouraged to incrementally approach and feel rather than avoid or shut down painful or difficult emotions" (p. 148). The clinician's role is to encourage clients to use the stabilization skills they learned in phase 1 of treatment, such as diaphragmatic breathing and safety imagery, at the first sign of movement towards the edge of the window. If a client does move outside the window of tolerance, which is evidenced by signs of hyper- or hypoarousal, clinicians can provide compassionate support, extend psychoeducation and normalization of the client's emotional intensity, and offer several grounding and relaxation exercises to assist the client's return to safety and to a stabilized and regulated state.

Dual Awareness and Exposure Work

Another aid in exposure work utilizes the strategy of **dual awareness**, which carries implications for both clients and clinicians. For clients, dual awareness involves the process of accessing memories from the past while simultaneously remaining attuned to the present safety. As clients remain aware of their present safety, their defensive reactions are less likely to be activated, and dysregulation problems, such as emotional flooding and dissociation, are managed and mitigated. The concept of dual awareness can be explained to clients and framed as a self-awareness tool for grounding. When clients understand the role and purpose of dual awareness, they are also able to dialogue with the clinician about their abilities to effectively remain in the present moment while simultaneously accessing trauma memories, which bolsters the client's sense of safety in the process.

Dual awareness also serves an important function for clinicians, as it allows us to fully attend to our clients' stories and their reactions to the therapeutic process while remaining aware of our own internal responses of countertransference in order to stay cognitively and emotionally present in the session. In other words, a clinician's dual awareness is characterized by vigilance of what is happening in our clients and what is happening in ourselves. For client and clinician alike, dual awareness is an important and ongoing process during this stage of confronting traumatic memories and losses.

Cautions for Trauma Clinicians: Considering Important Aspects of Phase 2

Whether the applied trauma-specific treatment modality directly integrates exposure work or addresses traumatic memories and symptoms through another means, clinicians must be mindful that there is always the risk for retraumatization. Trauma memory work is therapeutically beneficial when a client is able to process trauma-related thoughts and feelings from a therapeutic distance and at a manageable pace. However, trauma memory work can be harmful when a client "relives" the trauma in session. Cognitive and exposure techniques that seek to desensitize emotional reactions can do just the opposite and become the catalyst for emotional flooding and destabilization (especially with prolonged exposure), so clinicians must be careful attention to client safety and treatment protocol and supervised practice is essential. While clients frequently experience an initial increase in symptoms with any treatment approach (such as an increase in intrusive thoughts in the few days following an EMDR processing session), a significant increase in symptoms or decrease in client's overall functioning should be addressed immediately with a temporary cessation of intervention and return to safety and stabilization.

As clinicians safely and manageably structure the client's experience of confronting traumatic memories, they must also keep in mind that trauma memory work is a sensitive balancing act in which the client experiences a tolerable amount of distress as pieces of the memory are confronted, and then the client is once again stabilized as a sense of empowerment is restored. Schwartz (2000) explains, "A delicate balance between disruption and stabilization must be continually renegotiated or the traumatized patient and the therapist will be perpetually overwhelmed or stalemated" (p. xix). The manner through which this balancing act is engaged is based on the selected trauma-focused theory, and clinicians should carefully select an appropriate theoretical model to guide treatment based on each client's individual needs.

Beginning clinicians sometimes feel pressured to address and work through *all* aspects of a client's trauma history, and for many clients, this is an unrealistic expectation. Some clients may be ready to focus on and process only one trauma event in therapy, even though there may be multiple traumatic events in a client's history. At other times, clients may be able to process only specific aspects of the trauma, and other elements may simply be too overwhelming for the client to work on at that point in his or her life. Trauma work is very often a *process* that spans years with major breaks in therapeutic work. Clinicians should consider this dynamic and be cautioned not to urge clients to engage in parts of their trauma history that they may not have a desire or ability to explore at that point in their lives.

Clinicians must also keep in mind that each client varies in terms of the degree to which he or she is able to tolerate memory processing, and *not all clients need to retell painful details of their trauma*. In fact, there are many therapeutic interventions that show promising evidence for effectiveness in treatment that do not necessarily include overt memory processing. Treatment approaches that emphasize body work include somatic experiencing, or SE (Levine, 1997) and sensorimotor psychotherapy, or SP (Ogden et al., 2006). In these models, treatment goals aim to increase the client's awareness of physical sensations and learn self-regulation of reactions to specific body sensations. Additionally, systems-focused approaches, such as Schwartz's internal family systems (IFS) model, can be particularly useful for client problems with dissociation. Creative approaches, such as dance, music, drama, and art (discussed further in the next chapter), can be integrated into treatment to process non-verbal memories and improve mind/body connection (Baker, Metcalf, Varker, & O'Donnell, 2017). Animal-assisted treatments, such as equine therapy, can also be very effective in treating PTSD (Wharton, Whitworth, MacCauley, & Malone, 2019). Other interventions that have gained attention in trauma work include acupuncture, yoga, neurofeedback, and virtual reality therapy.

As a final consideration, trauma clinicians are encouraged to continuously apply assessment during this stage of treatment. This ongoing assessment involves utilizing clinical judgment, objective instruments, and the client's subjective feedback to evaluate how treatment is progressing. Youngstrom (2012) suggests adjusting or changing the treatment course (theoretical models/interventions) if no significant progress is made by the second month of treatment. Of course, this timeframe will vary based on setting and length of time allowed with the client as well as other client factors, such as the client's stage of change and the influence of other stressors. Clinicians may also consider adjusting the therapeutic model or slowing down the pace of treatment when clients show signs of resistance. According to Mitchell (2007), resistance is the client's signal to the clinician as an indication that changes need to be made regarding the clinician's behaviors or approach. These client signals may indicate that changes need to be made in treatment modality, the problem/diagnostic focus needs adjustment, the interventions are experienced as incongruent for the client, the pace of the process is off kilter, or energy needs to be redirected towards the therapeutic relationship. All of the solutions and adjustments for these therapeutic problems stand in stark contrast to the clinician's urge to push the client event harder towards treatment goals. As we remain flexible and open to feedback, our ability to accommodate our clients' needs increases and we are better able to navigate the winding path of treatment.

Conclusion

Phase 2 of trauma work focuses on the therapeutic goals of remembrance and mourning, which ultimately leads to a reduction of trauma-related symptoms. While this stage of the process is often conceptualized as the hallmark of trauma work, the skills and concepts of the safety and stabilization phase still remain vitally present and applicable during memory work. This chapter discussed the universal concepts of trauma treatment principles, the various types of trauma-specific treatment models, several common trauma-specific clinical interventions, and cautionary considerations for clinicians during this phase of the therapeutic process.

Very often, trauma-related symptoms are rooted in the overwhelming feelings of pain and fear associated with traumatic memories. When a client is able to reorganize these memories, experience catharsis and resolve for these powerful emotions, and become empowered rather than crippled by the past, the harmful impacts of trauma are diminished, and healing begins to emerge. For clients, this process reflects a monumental act of courage and vulnerability, and for clinicians, the willingness to travel with another person into trauma's deepest caves is nothing short of heroic. The journey is not always easy, and we, as clinicians, may feel our own apprehensions about engaging in this work. However, courage doesn't exist without the presence of doubt or trepidation, and when we acknowledge our own fears, we are better able to aid our clients as they confront theirs.

KEYWORD ASSESSMENT

Write definitions in your own words, describe the concept's role in trauma work, list any questions, or make notes of important aspects that you want to remember.

Complicated Grief

Disenfranchised Grief

Mourning

Evidence-Based Practice

Cognitive Restructuring

Cognitive Distortions

Trauma Narrative

Exposure

Explicit Memory

Implicit Memory

Habituation

Titration

Containment

Window of Tolerance

Dual Awareness

EXPERIENTIAL ACTIVITIES: INTERACTING WITH THE CHAPTER CONTENT

Expand Self-Awareness

1) Review the list of cognitive distortions and identify your tendencies towards any of these patterns. Consider how stress influences your thoughts, and reflect on how your tendencies towards certain distortions function for you (as a defense, protection, preparation for a negative experience, etc.).

Expand Knowledge

2) Reflect on what you believe to be the main change agents in trauma recovery (cognitive restructuring, mind/body connection, cohesive narrative, etc.), and then create a list that identifies these specific and key ingredients for psychological healing from trauma. Now compare your list of beliefs and values with the various trauma treatment models presented in this chapter. Research at least two of these models to learn more about them and then determine how congruently or incongruently these models align with your personal theoretical orientation. Allow this process to illuminate which trauma-specific models resonate the most with you.

Expand Skills

3) Review the concept of containment and how this might be helpful for you as the clinician as you personally manage exposure to traumatic content from your clients. Create your own imagined, visually drawn, symbolically depicted through a chosen object, or literal container that you can use for your work as a trauma clinician.

SUPERVISORY DISCUSSION: SHARING PERSONAL INSIGHTS AND IDENTIFYING AREAS FOR GROWTH

1) Discuss what you learned about yourself and your patterns in cognitive distortions. How do you think your tendencies towards certain types of cognitive distortions could impact your work with your clients? How can you increase your awareness of this dynamic and positively manage it?

2) Share the insights you gained regarding your beliefs about the change agents in trauma recovery. Which theoretical models interest you or resonate with you the most? Discuss a practical plan for how you plan to gain the needed training and supervision to integrate these models into your trauma-focused practice.

3) Share about your experience of creating your clinician container. What was this process like for you? How do you think you might use this in your professional work? Discuss how the concept of dual awareness connects with the strategy of containment.

4) This chapter highlighted trauma memory work and exposure, which are often emotionally charged and anxiety-provoking aspects of trauma treatment. What thoughts and feelings come up for you as you imagine facilitating this process? What aspects bring up the most anxiety or concern and what aspects do you feel the most positive about?

Chapter 12

Phase 2 Enhancement: Creative Treatment Approaches in Trauma Work

Towards the end of my graduate studies, my classmates and I were assigned a capstone project in which we were to write about our core beliefs regarding the role of the clinician in trauma work. I remember puzzling over this assignment. How could I best communicate something so deep, so personal, and in many ways, so abstract and experiential? I easily could have written an academic statement about unconditional positive regard, patience and pacing, and the power of the therapeutic relationship, but this felt so insufficient to truly reflect my *experience* as a trauma clinician. For me, this is a sensation I simply can't put into words alone. However, I have found that metaphors can often illuminate and beautifully convey an affective and abstract experience when verbal descriptions prove lacking. As a remedy for this dilemma, I asked my professor if I could submit a metaphorical short story in lieu of a traditional academic paper as a way to better illustrate the essence of the powerful, existential experience I feel when I join with my clients in trauma work. I crafted my story with the goal of depicting my role as the clinician and illustrating my experience of the overall process of trauma work. The following is an excerpt from my story:

> I clamored and fumbled my way through the crowd on the road, desperately trying to reach the place where a little child crouched on the ground with her head in her hands. She was bruised and bloodied, alone and frightened. I tried to speak to her, but she jerked away from me, hissed at the extension of my hand, and shook with grief and fury. I lowered myself down next to her, and we sat in the mud made by her tears. We sat in silence together for a very long time as we listened to the broken song of the sparrow being carried on the wind.

> At last, the girl looked at me anew, and we stood together with trembling, feeble legs to take our first tentative steps in the journey onward as fellow sojourners. It was time to go Home. The dust of the road covered our feet as we took those initial, uncertain steps, but the sudden whisk of a fragrant, sweet breeze surrounded us and picked us up like feathers, causing us to dance and spin to a new song on the wind. Instead of the broken song of sorrow, we began to hear the melody of Hope. And so, we traveled, bandaged hand in bandaged hand, down the road until we reached Home.

By writing a metaphorical story, I significantly diverged from the traditional way of describing trauma work in a class paper. However, I believe that this creative format still offered a significant amount of important information about the therapeutic process while also presenting ample opportunities for reflection. This story may not represent exactly what my professor expected when he created the assignment, but the overall goal and intention of the academic task was still met.

In trauma work, a similar phenomenon can occur. We may think we have an idea for how treatment will look, only to discover that the way in which our clients approach the process is sometimes more creative, abstract, unique, and "off script" than the portrayal found in our textbooks. Traditionally, most people envision the context of trauma work as one in which the client and clinician sit in an office and dialogue with one another for the entirety of the session. However, this traditional format is not the only manner through which trauma-focused goals can be achieved, and alternative, creative modalities sometimes prove to be more effective and powerful than talk-based work alone.

In this chapter, phase 2 of trauma work is reframed as an opportunity for the inclusion and integration of creative interventions and expression. The therapeutic benefits and rationale for creative interventions, which often center on the role of metaphorical expression, are discussed and explored from a trauma-focused lens. Specific creative modalities, such as play therapy, sandtray therapy, and art therapy, are introduced as effective mediums for trauma work, and considerations for clinical application are also addressed.

Evidence-Based Treatment and Creative Interventions: Building Bridges for Clients

Knowledge and skill in evidence-based trauma treatment are critical competencies for all trauma clinicians. However, these models still carry limitations and considerations. While the treatment goals, sequences, and theoretical principles of evidence-based treatment remain a constant guide, at times, trauma clinicians must adjust to accommodate client issues and needs that present as a consideration for treatment. These unique client issues may involve cognitive and developmental considerations, comorbid diagnoses and issues, complex presentation of trauma, difficulties in verbal communication, resistance and ambivalence to the process, and diverse cultural values. These issues can often have a profound impact on the success of even an evidence-based trauma treatment model, and clinicians are tasked with adjusting the process to meet these important client needs (Cook, Dinnen, Simiola, Thompson, & Schnurr, 2014). By definition, evidence-based trauma treatments are effective, but other modalities and mediums of treatment delivery that have not yet gained evidence-based status but are research-informed may be highly beneficial for some clients. While some creative approaches can stand alone, very often, many creative approaches can be woven into the framework of evidence-based principles and best-practice considerations in trauma work.

For clients who present with considerations outside the suitability of a traditional, talk-based format, creative interventions often provide a tremendously helpful resource as an adjunct or alternative modality in trauma treatment. **Creative interventions** are research-informed approaches that provide clients with unique and artful mediums of expression to expand insight and awareness, offer enhanced psychological safety, and increase engagement in the trauma treatment process. The delivery of trauma treatment through creative mediums may include the use of toys and play materials, sand, music, movement, and art media, and these materials become conduits for non-verbal communication and possess many qualities that are especially relevant in trauma work.

Very often, creative interventions provide the bridge for clients to reengage in the trauma work process and to do so in a manner that feels authentically representative of themselves and their experiences.

Metaphor as a Medium for Communication: Integrating Therapeutic Benefits

There are many therapeutic benefits of creative interventions, but chief among them is the powerful inclusion of metaphors. In therapeutic work, **metaphors** are used by paralleling two seemingly different things in a way that illuminates and enriches the understanding of a person's experience or perspective (Tay, 2012). For example, one client might explain that she feels depressed, but when prompted to create a metaphor for this experience, she might say, "I feel as though I've been dropped down into a cold, dark, isolated pit with no way to escape." Depression and a pit are not overtly similar, and yet, when a person links them together metaphorically, one's unique experience of depression is communicated and understood with much deeper meaning and power. Finlay (2015) explains, "Metaphors offer a way of seeing a reality indirectly and in a different way that, in turn, allows new meanings to come into being" (p. 338). The therapeutic power of metaphors is especially relevant in trauma work, as metaphors offer a platform for enhanced expression, psychological distance and safety, and the projection and externalization of trauma content.

Metaphors Are Expressive

Metaphors have the power to serve as mediums for expressing highly abstract and often deeply embedded issues and emotions (Goldberg & Stephenson, 2016). The old adage says, "a picture is worth a thousand words," and the same is true in trauma treatment. Metaphorical drawings, scenes in the sand, collages, sculptures, and symbolic figurines serve as the conduits through which clients can communicate in a new way about personal experiences and perspective. Trauma often leaves behind a labyrinth of thoughts and emotions, and metaphorical images created through art and creative expression become translators for messages that are often too complex or painful to communicate through words alone.

For instance, imagine the victim of domestic violence who struggles to describe just how "mean" her boyfriend is to her. The clinician is attuned to this challenging struggle and offers the client an opportunity to select a symbolic figure of herself and of her boyfriend from an assortment of miniatures or images. She chooses a snarling three-headed dog that has broken free from its chain as a metaphorical representation of her boyfriend and she selects a scarecrow as the representation of herself. In contrast to metaphors used only in language, physical images (like figurines, photos, or visual art) provide an opportunity to expand the metaphor even further, which, in turn, provides an opportunity to facilitate deeper reflection and communication. To accomplish this, the clinician invites the client to discuss the metaphorical parallels by asking the client why she selected these particular figures as representations of herself and her boyfriend. As the client carefully looks at the figure, she explains, "Bobby seems totally out of control and cut loose, and everywhere I turn or any way I approach him, it seems as though he is ready to attack me. He's so territorial—like a rabid animal in his rage." When prompted to share about how the scarecrow represents her, the client shares, "I chose the scarecrow because it's stupid—it tries to scare things off, like the dog, but everyone knows it's fake and it doesn't actually keep anything bad away. This scarecrow has a smile on its face, but really, it's just hollow inside—it has no heart, backbone, or brain. It can't even stand up on its own. That's me: a fake bag full of straw that just looks like a person." Through this client example, consider how much more is communicated through these metaphorical images than by words alone.

Metaphors Provide Psychological Distance and Safety

Metaphors also provide the client with **psychological distance** from the trauma (Schoeneberg, Forth, & Seto, 2011). Clients often arrive to treatment with ambivalence towards the process and are fearful that they might become overwhelmed by confronting aspects of trauma. Creative interventions attend to this dynamic by offering a nonthreatening way to process highly sensitive material (Perryman et al., 2019). Many clients may feel much safer to begin at a distance by creating a piece of art that symbolically represents an aspect of the trauma rather than to verbally and overtly discuss it, which is consistent with a titrated approach in treatment. The clinician's open posture towards the client's preference of expression (verbal or non-verbal) offers a sense of choice and empowerment for the client by enriching the client's sense of control in the treatment process and by putting the client in the lead for pacing the content. By allowing the client to approach challenging feelings and memories through a medium that innately offers psychological distance and space, the client's sense of safety during trauma memory work is vastly enhanced (Desmond, Kindsvatter, Stahl, & Smith, 2015).

Metaphors Are Projective

At its core, a work of creative art is an external expression or **projection** of an internal perspective or experience. An outward projection of an internal experience gives the client a bird's-eye view of the trauma versus "being back in it once again" from a first-person perspective. Clients are able to literally see, touch, and take in representations of their trauma experience and to do so as a safe observer, which acts in stark contrast to the disempowering and frightening experience of being thrown into a flashback. The projection of a metaphorical symbol empowers the client by external-izing feelings, experiences, or aspects of the trauma, and the client is offered a novel way to explore personal experiences from different vantage points (Finlay, 2015). In this way, the client becomes his or her own mirror and can gain new insight and awareness in ways that are limited through verbal discussion alone. The opportunity to physically interact with metaphorical symbols of the trauma from an empowered perspective gives clients the platform to experientially, rather than just verbally, process the trauma and engage in titrated exposure. Clinicians facilitate this process by providing the opportunity for creative expression, being attuned to the client's metaphorical meanings, affirming the client's experience, expanding the metaphor for deeper reflection, and utilizing the metaphor as a platform for further work in trauma treatment (Tay, 2012).

Neurological Basis for Creative Interventions: Engaging the Whole Brain

Certainly, the communicative powers of metaphor speak for themselves, but the utility of creative interventions in trauma work is also grounded in neuroscience. Perryman et al. (2019) explains that when we verbally communicate, we utilize the left hemisphere of our brain; however, the brain's right hemisphere is the warehouse for personal experiences and intense emotions. The nature of trauma creates a fractured sensation—a piecemeal experience, with emotions, thoughts, and events feeling disjointed and convoluted. In traditional talk therapy, the client must heavily utilize the left hemisphere of the brain to dialogue. However, most of the trauma information and sensations are stored in the right hemisphere, which can often perpetuate the feeling of fracture as the client grapples to integrate a psychologically tangled experience into linear verbal expression. Because of the way the brain organizes a traumatic experience, verbal trauma narratives can be highly challenging for clients, as memories are often encoded as sensory and affective recollections and, therefore, lack a storyline (Kern & Perryman, 2016). When a client says, "I just can't talk about it," this statement may not represent client avoidance or resistance but, rather, may be reflective of the neurological organization of the trauma, in which the client truly cannot articulate the experience. While this is a limitation for talk-based trauma treatments, creative mediums engage both the left and right hemispheres of the brain in a way that facilitates reconnection and integration (Perryman et al., 2019). In this way, the trauma narrative becomes more coherent, and clients are often able to access repressed memories or aspects of the trauma that have previously been outside conscious awareness (Finlay, 2015).

Many evidence-based models emphasize cognitions, problem solving, and coping, which are all critical elements in trauma recovery. However, this strictly cognitive approach is designed for clients who arrive for treatment with a reasonable amount of regulation and who are able to access higher areas of the brain for rational and abstract thinking and learning. Unfortunately, significant dysregulation is a frequent and profound aspect in the fallout of trauma, and these higher-order cognitive tasks are often neurologically far out of reach and therapeutically unreasonable, especially in cases of traumatized children (Desmond et al., 2015). For these clients, the "talking cure" is destined to fail, and a neurosequential approach that targets more lower-brain methods of regulation and communication, such as those found in play and non-verbal expression, is often a much more appropriate place to begin (Gaskill & Perry, 2017). Creative interventions provide clients with opportunities to start with what they need: regulating experiences through physical movement, opportunities for non-verbal communication, and relational attunement in the therapeutic relationship. The body of research continues to grow in support of nontraditional forms of trauma treatment that highlight sensory integration through mind-body activities (Kaiser, Gillette, & Spinazzola, 2010; Metcalf et al., 2016).

Another quality of creative interventions that cannot be underestimated is the fundamental element of fun. While this may seem simplistic, there are profound neurological rationales for the intentional use of fun and play in trauma treatment. When something is novel, intriguing, and engaging, the brain's reward center is activated and stress decreases, which in and of itself is a powerful experience for a client who may spend a significant amount of time in the fight/flight/freeze activation modes (Hass-Cohen, Findlay, Carr, & Vanderlan, 2014). By engaging the client through enjoyable activities, the client's stress is lowered, creating a more neurologically conducive state for learning, practicing new skills, and integrating experiences deeper and further. The therapeutic function of fun can be paired with the "window of tolerance" concept discussed in the previous chapter.

In addition to the neurological basis for clinical utility, creative interventions also present other important rationales for use in trauma work. One of the primary goals in trauma work often includes the bolstering of the client's resiliency, and creative interventions offer opportunities to enhance the client's capacity for creativity, appreciation for beauty, and integration of imagination, all of which are characteristics shown to foster resiliency (Hass-Cohen, Bokoch, Findlay, & Banford Witting, 2018). Creative interventions are highly relevant for developmental considerations, especially for children and adolescents, as language delays are often a common impact of trauma. Creative expressions may also be more culturally congruent and sensitive, and clients have the opportunity to infuse cultural elements into a creative product. Overall, the inclusion of creative interventions in trauma work is an effective and resourceful way of honoring and integrating the whole person of the client.

Creative Interventions in Trauma Treatment: Applying Play, Sand, and Art Therapy

While the therapeutic rationales for the inclusion of creative interventions are numerous and compelling, clinicians must be mindful that creative interventions do not represent a stand-alone method for trauma treatment. Trauma treatment always requires a guiding theoretical model, and creative interventions subsequently work within this model with a clear and purposeful goal that aligns with both guiding theoretical tenets and the client's unique treatment plan. Metaphorically speaking, a creative intervention is a lot like water—as fluid, it can fit into many places, but a structured container is needed in order to effectively manage it. This means that the appropriate use of any creative intervention requires a theoretical framework. Creative approaches can also be used as adjuncts to larger treatment models, like TF-CBT or EMDR, and clinicians must always have a clear rationale for use and intended outcome.

Creative interventions in trauma treatment universally share the therapeutic qualities and benefits described, but the mediums and modalities of these various creative resources are diverse and distinctive. Clinicians may incorporate modalities such as play therapy, sandtray therapy, or art therapy, and while there are parallels between these approaches, there are also important distinctions. Each of these trauma treatment delivery formats offers unique therapeutic benefits and considerations, and clinicians should be knowledgeable of these aspects and the populations best suited for these modalities.

Play Therapy

Implemented primarily as a treatment modality for children under the age of 12, **play therapy** has its roots in the psychoanalytic work of Klein (1975/1932) and Anna Freud (1946) and was further expanded and influenced by Axline (1947), who infused a humanistic, person-centered approach. Play therapy rests on the notion that, for children, the process of "playing out" the personal, internal world is "the most natural dynamic and self-healing process in which they can engage" (Landreth, 2012, p. 9). "Playing out" an experience means that the child is allowed to communicate through his or her play, which involves verbal and non-verbal expression and metaphorical symbolism in the toys. Play therapy is highly experiential, and the child often metaphorically enacts a narrative, providing a powerful platform for healing.

In play therapy, play is considered the language for communication, and toys are representative of the child's words (Landreth, 2012). Play therapists are trained to understand this "language" and value the meaning of children's play as the primary avenue for expression, catharsis, and healing. Through attunement and connection, the play therapist receives and responds to this dynamic process in ways that sensitively integrate the developmental and trauma considerations.

Play therapy harnesses the therapeutic powers of play, which Schaefer and Drewes (2014) synthesized into four primary therapeutic categories:

1) *Play fosters emotional wellness*
    Play therapy can enhance positive emotions, provide the setting for counterconditioning of fears, and offer opportunities for stress inoculation and management.

2) *Play enhances relationships and connection*

Play therapy offers the experiential power of the therapeutic relationship, attends to attachment, and provides opportunities to practice social skills in the here and now.

3) *Play increases personal strengths*

Play therapy provides opportunities to practice and apply skills in problem solving and self-regulation and promotes moral and psychosocial development.

4) *Play facilitates communication*

Play therapy offers developmentally congruent methods for a child's natural mode of self-expression, offers a modality that accesses the unconscious, and provides opportunities for direct and indirect teaching.

As a simple way of explaining the process of play therapy to adult caregivers who bring their child for services, I often say, "If someone were to ask you what you and I did in here today, you will likely say, 'We talked,' but what you and I talked about was very important and our conversation probably felt very different from most of the conversations that you have with others. Similarly, if you ask your child what he did in our play therapy session, he will likely say, 'We played.' But, in the same way that our talk today feels like a different kind of conversation than day-to-day discussion, your child's play in session is also very important and experienced by your child in a way that feels different. His play promotes his personal expression, self-understanding, growth, and healing, and my job is to be with him in that process and to facilitate it further for him."

Paralleling traditional talk-therapy treatment models, play therapy is also applied through various theoretical orientations, including child-centered, Adlerian, Jungian, filial, cognitive-behavioral, ecosystemic, Gestalt, and attachment-focused frameworks. There are more than 100 studies that support play therapy's effectiveness, but among all the theoretical models investigated, child-centered play therapy is, by far, the most widely researched and applied approach in play therapy (Ray, 2015). Play therapy has been shown to be effective for multiple types of clinical issues, including trauma, across a diversity of populations (Lin & Bratton, 2015). Research continues to support the use of play therapy, and play therapy treatments such as Theraplay, Adlerian play therapy, child parent relationship therapy, filial family therapy, and child-centered play therapy are recognized as promising and evidence-based modalities in some national registries.

Similar to the way in which basic listening skills transcend all theoretical models, play therapy also incorporates basic play therapy skills that are applicable across all theoretical orientations, including facilitative statements such as reflection of feeling ("You're really sad that your mom left."), tracking play behaviors ("You picked that one up."), reflecting the content of play ("The bunny doesn't want to stay with the others, so he ran over there."), esteem building ("You kept trying and you figured it out."), facilitating creativity ("In here, that can be whatever you want it to be."), returning responsibility ("You wish I'd do that for you; that is something you are able to do if you'd like."), and therapeutic limit setting ("You are really mad right now. I am not for hitting. You hit the bop bag and pretend it's me."). The role of the play therapist is to provide a safe and caring relationship in which the child feels understood and accepted, and basic play therapy skills enhance and facilitate the therapeutic relationship and process. Once a child begins to develop a safe connection with the clinician in which he or she feels understood, the "playing out" of the child's internal world is often very natural and fluid, and play therapy represents a seamless and congruent medium for the child's growth and healing.

Trauma Work in Practice: Play Therapy and Emotional Catharsis in Trauma

When six-year-old Michael became my client, he was battling a life-threatening illness. Michael's illness left him looking and feeling much different than his peers, and his medical treatment required numerous procedures that were highly painful and invasive. Michael's situation broke the hearts of every adult around him, and with the intention to compensate for so much of his lost childhood, the adults offered him pity and lax rules in an effort to "just keep him happy." These adults were acutely aware of his medical trauma. Michael's pain was overwhelming for them, and anytime Michael showed a flicker of unhappiness, the adults jumped to baby him, entice or entertain him, or distract him in some way. Unfortunately, this response left Michael feeling emotionally isolated, as though his negative feelings were too much for the adults he so desperately needed to lean on.

When Michael began play therapy with me, the stress, trauma, and systemic patterns were greatly impacting him. Michael was displaying extreme tantrums, bullying his classmates, refusing to comply with instructions, and seemed emotionally remote and distant in his relationships. During my first child-centered play therapy session with Michael, he entered the playroom, took a long look around at all the toys, and then eyed me very suspiciously, suspecting that I was yet another adult attempting to pacify him and "make him happy." With defiant eyes locked on me, he began to knock every toy off the shelf and declared that he refused to play with any of it. I calmly reflected Michael's behaviors and feelings back to him in a tone that communicated that I understood, respected his feelings, and wanted him to feel empowered in his choices: "You are knocking all of those off. You really want me to know that you don't want to play with any of those right now. You are in charge of what you want to do in here."

This pattern continued for a few sessions, and slowly, Michael began to realize that this situation and relationship were different and that I had no expectations for how he should feel or act during our time together. In this safe, accepting space and relationship, Michael was finally able to begin expressing the full magnitude of his anger and feelings surrounding his trauma. Michael began to play with the toys, and he focused a great deal on the puppets in the playroom. For many sessions, Michael took a bunny puppet over to the sandbox, and repeatedly, he very aggressively and harshly smashed and crammed sand up inside the hand hole of the puppet. He pounded and pounded the sand inside the bunny until it was overflowing, and between his gritted teeth, he would forcefully say, "This will make you feel better, bunny! Stop squirming and be still!" This play was intense and challenging for me to bear witness to, but as his play therapist, I knew how very important it was for Michael that I stay with him in his emotional pain and allow him to express it in way that could be fully understood. Based on this and other details of his play, I reflected, "They are saying it will make the bunny feel better, but the bunny is hurting so much and is so scared. The bunny wishes it would stop. The bunny is so mad that they won't listen to him to stop." The emotional catharsis of this experience was transformative for Michael, and as he was able to continue to share his deepest feelings in session through his play, his behavior outside the playroom improved significantly.

Consider the numerous therapeutic limitations of a talk-based approach in Michael's case as well as the impacts that a directive, talk-only format might have had on the therapeutic relationship. Play therapy offered Michael an authentic and relational *experience*, not just discussion *about* an experience, and thus facilitated Michael's feelings of empowerment and choice and offered him a context to process very sensitive content in a safe and developmentally appropriate way. Through play therapy, Michael was able to express himself openly, freely, and fully, and he was truly heard.

Sandtray Therapy

Sandtray therapy began with the work of Lowenfeld (1979), who incorporated sand, water, and miniatures as materials in the therapeutic process. The symbolic nature of the miniatures was expanded by Kalff (1980), who infused Jungian principles with the sandtray method. Since that time, sandtray has been used as an independent modality, implemented within various theoretical frameworks, and utilized as a creative intervention adjunct with talk-based models (Kosanke, Puls, Feather, & Smith, 2016). When sandtray is used with children, it is commonly referred to as *sandplay* and more closely mirrors the process of play therapy as the child actively plays with the miniatures in the sand. In contrast, sandtray work with older adolescents and adults typically involves the use of sandtray prompts, and these prompts represent goal-oriented and clinician-determined content for the client to symbolically create in the tray. In this type of sandtray work, the client selects and arranges stationary figures in the sand to create a symbolic scene or projected world. The experience often concludes in an opportunity for the client to reflect and process his or her sandtray with the clinician. Sandtrays can be fluidly integrated as part of a conjoined intervention in trauma work with prompts that target various aspects of trauma treatment goals and objectives.

The materials for sandtray are critical for the therapeutic quality of the process and are discussed in Homeyer and Sweeney's (2017) comprehensive text. The sand in all sandtrays allows the client to kinetically connect with the creation process and also serves as a powerful and elemental symbol of earth, transition, and life. The sand is often offered in wet or dry form, which adds a diversity of dynamics to the sandtray creation process. Containers for the sand are recommended to be approximately 30 inches by 20 inches in width and length and 3 inches in depth. Sandtray containers are considered especially facilitative when the bottom of the tray is blue, which is psychically representative of water. Together, the sand and blue base of the tray create the sensation of earth and water, which sets the template for powerful intrapsychic work.

In addition to the sand in the sandtray, clients are also provided with a large assortment of diverse miniatures from which to choose. These figures are often exposed on shelves and organized in general categories, such as people (i.e., doctor, baby, solider, bride, groom, or knight), animals (i.e., dinosaur, sloth, wolf, spider, snake, turtle, or mouse), vehicles (i.e., tractor, spaceship, ambulance, or boat), buildings (i.e., house, hospital, church, castle, lighthouse, jail, or school), landscape (i.e., bridge, treasure chest, wishing well, cave, or trees), cultural elements (i.e., angels, Star of David, national flags), household items (i.e., cell phone, money, trash can, toilet), and fantasy (i.e., wizard, dragon, alien, fairy godmother, comic book/cartoon characters, or witch) (Homeyer & Sweeney, 2017). The more expansive and diverse the assortment of miniatures can be, the more opportunities the client has for therapeutic symbols and expression.

The purpose of sandtray miniatures is to provide the client with archetypical or symbolic representations of abstract experiences, sensations, feelings, thoughts, relationships, and aspects of self. In this way, sandtray taps into the power of projection, offering a number of powerful therapeutic benefits in trauma work. As previously discussed in this text, trauma is often accompanied by tremendous interpersonal challenges which can pose as barriers or challenges to the development and maintenance of the therapeutic alliance. During sandtray work, the client has the opportunity to project relational transference onto the miniatures rather than direct these projections towards the clinician (Kosanke et al., 2016). In contrast to the potentially damaging and unconscious elements of transference in the therapeutic process itself, sandtray utilizes and channels projection in a way that becomes insightful, useful, and safe for the client.

Sandtray also offers ample opportunity to express and externalize the fragmenting effect of trauma. Many clients with trauma experience a feeling of "splits" in self, possess splintered memories, or feel caught in a complex web of entangled feelings. Through the power of symbolic projection, sandtray provides a rich context in which these elements of contrast and diversity can be more easily and vividly explored. Because sandtray is a physical creation of an intrapsychic projection, the client transitions from the passive position of being "held captive" by the impacts of trauma to the empowered role of actively creating and constructing his or her own world (Moon, 2006).

Homeyer and Sweeney (2017) recommend a general framework for sandtray prompts and processing. First, the clinician prepares materials and explains the sandtray process and rationale to the client. The clinician then invites the client to create a sandtray with a prompt, which can be very open and nondirective (such as "create your world in the sand") or highly focused and targeted (such as "create a scene in the sand that reflects how you experience your trauma symptoms"). The clinician silently observes and takes note of the client's selection and creation process. Very often the process by which a client creates a scene, such as a client's difficulties in choosing a figure or the client's holding and touching certain miniatures for extended periods of time, offers as many opportunities for later reflection as the created scene itself. Once the client signals that his or her tray is complete, the clinician begins the verbal processing portion of the experience by asking for a title of the tray scene or world. Processing goes further as the clinician then invites the client to share more about the tray, including reflection regarding what is happening in each scene or portion of the tray. Lastly, the clinician invites the client to discuss specific figures or miniatures in the tray. Throughout this process, the clinician reflects back the client's own interpretation of the sandtray, makes observations, and offers opportunities to expand the metaphor.

Trauma Work in Practice: Sandtray and the Trauma Process

Sharon, a 32-year-old client, came to treatment very motivated to work through her trauma history. Sharon had experienced multiple incidences of sexual abuse and rape during her childhood and adolescence, and consequently, she was plagued by trauma symptoms of avoidance, hypervigilance, somatic problems, nightmares, and failed romantic relationships in adulthood. As an insightful client, Sharon could link her current problems with her past traumas and desperately wanted a new lease on life, but as ready for change as she seemed, Sharon's progress in therapy seemed to hit a wall as she and her clinician moved into phase 2 of trauma work. Sharon's anxiety about working through her trauma memories abruptly spiked, and she suddenly felt tremendous ambivalence about trauma-focused work and was unsure about remaining in counseling at all.

Sharon's clinician, Julia, recognized Sharon's need for safety, titration, and psychological distance from her trauma memories, and she knew the place to begin was simply with addressing the source of Sharon's ambivalence. Julia provided Sharon with a brief explanation of sandtray and how it might be helpful for her, and then she invited Sharon to "create a scene that represents your feelings about moving forward in trauma work." Sharon took her time building her sandtray, and once complete, the sandtray contained a single scene: a monkey with its hand covering its mouth sat in the center of the tray, half of its body submerged down in the sand as though it was sinking. Around the monkey encircled a series of ominous figures, such as a faceless ghost, a praying mantis with outstretched limbs, a worm figure with jagged teeth, skeleton hands, and a single, bloodshot eyeball. The figures loomed in all around the monkey in a tight circle, and the entire set of miniatures was enclosed in a small, fenced-in area with no opening to either enter or exit.

After taking a long look at her scene, Sharon explained to Julia that she chose to entitle her tray "Don't Speak." Julia invited Sharon to share about what is happening in the scene and with the figures. Sharon tearfully began to explain that for decades the secret of her sexual abuse has smothered her, and she feels like the monkey in the center of the tray whose mouth is covered and who is surrounded by encroaching and frightful figures. She described the figures surrounding her ("the monkey") to be representations of the different aspects of her trauma in regard to sensations she physically felt and things that she saw. Sharon explained that as much as she tries to avoid these painful images and reminders, they seem to always be right in front of her and constantly encircling her. These trauma reminders, represented by the figures, are "pushing the monkey down deeper and deeper, and the monkey is slowly sinking into the sand." Sharon stated that the goal of all the figures seems to be to "keep her quiet," and she is terrified that if she lets out even a whisper of her secrets, they will penetrate further and finally push her all the way down under the sand, and she will never be able to return to the surface. Sharon explained that this was the reason for titling her tray "Don't Speak"—all of the symbolic trauma figures are constantly telling her not to talk about what happened.

Julia listened, reflected, observed, and expanded Sharon's process and experience, and as a result, Julia understood that Sharon held a powerful core belief about herself and her trauma ("I will not survive confronting my trauma") which was heavily influencing the treatment process. This brought to light new goals for trauma work in safety and stabilization, which had previously been overlooked because of Sharon's zealousness to progress through treatment. Julia returned to phase 1 of treatment with Sharon and offered specific focus on her fears related to confronting and processing her memories related to the trauma. Sharon and Julia effectively identified and challenged her cognitive distortions, developed a reframe and new way of thinking about the process, and eventually, she was able to safely and successfully complete her trauma work. In metaphorical connection with her tray, Sharon was finally able to "remove her hand from her mouth" and find her voice again.

Art Therapy

While art and self-expression have been linked in the human experience for thousands of years, the pioneering work of Naumburg (1950) formalized art as a therapeutic modality in the 20th century. Similar to play and sandtray therapy, **art therapy** harnesses the power of non-verbal and metaphorical expression through a kinesthetic, creative, and externalizing process that utilizes painting, sculpting, drawing, or collaging (Schouten, de Niet, Knipscheer, Kleber, & Hutsche-maekers, 2015). While there are many therapeutic overlaps, art therapy differs from play and sandtray therapy in that it results in a lasting creation that can be observed and revisited more readily, and this medium can be utilized for clients across the lifespan. Play and sandtray therapy utilize materials, such as toys and miniatures, on which the client projects symbolic meaning, but in contrast, art therapy presents a literal and metaphorical blank canvas upon which the client can visually express self and personal experiences in ways that feel most congruent. In art therapy, projection is raw and uninfluenced by other objects, and the final art creation is a product that is truly crafted by the client alone.

Supported by an abundance of research, art therapy offers a number of unique therapeutic attributes in trauma work (Hass-Cohen et al., 2018). A central aim of trauma work highlights the decrease of trauma-related symptoms in conjunction with exposure to trauma reminders. The use of art techniques in exposure work provides the client with a physical medium through which each aspect of the memory is explored piece by piece (Schouten et al., 2015). As the client creates exposure-focused art, the client focuses on individual details of the trauma experience but does so by working on only one aspect of the art creation at a time, thereby structuring the trauma exposure in a naturally titrated way (Desmond et al., 2015).

As an additional benefit, **externalizing memories** (taking a mental image and projecting it out physically through art) can provide the client with the psychological sensation of feeling as though the haunting image or flashback is out of oneself, and implicit memories become explicit (Gantt & Tinnin, 2009). Whenever flashbacks attempt to resurface, clients can recognize this experience as the brain working to organize memories, and artwork of separate images can provide an avenue through which the client can view the memory images collectively and take charge in organizing them into a coherent narrative. Art becomes the way in which the client can document his or her journey through trauma work, and the client can return to old artwork and reflect on changes, new insights, and new meaning that are discovered along the way.

Art prompts may be very open-ended or very focused, and these prompts can be easily aligned with other trauma-focused models. For example, an open prompt may be something as simple as "draw a picture of the problem" or "collage your strengths." Alternatively, a more focused, trauma-specific prompt for phase 2 work might include "paint your feelings of grief and loss that stem from trauma." Similar to sandtray, art therapy processing allows the client to verbally discuss as much or as little as he or she would like, and the clinician's role is to bear witness to the process, reflect, observe, and invite the client to notice aspects of his or her own creation that enhance meaning and insight.

Trauma Work in Practice: Art Therapy and Case Conceptualization

Monica was a 19-year-old client, who arrived for outpatient mental health services following her two-week stay in psychiatric hospitalization for self-harm and suicidal ideation. Monica's case report came to her new clinician, David, with a lengthy history of complex trauma beginning in early childhood, including time spent in multiple foster homes and experiences of ongoing abuse. Based on Monica's recent state and her painful and extensive trauma history, David knew that trauma work would need to be conducted slowly and carefully. David took his time during the initial information-gathering sessions in order to develop a strong case conceptualization for Monica, and as an element of this process, he offered Monica a simple prompt which was to paint a picture of herself. Monica had previously described herself as artistic and imaginative, so she seemed to relish the idea of engaging in an art-based activity for the session. However, Monica's demeanor transformed from excited to somber, serious, and focused as she painted herself.

David provided a quiet but connected presence with Monica as she painted, and he observed subtle changes in Monica's face and body posture as she created different aspects of her painting. Once complete, Monica's painting of herself revealed a series of images of separate body parts rather than one whole-being person. Monica painted only one of her eyes, which was wide-open and frightened, her thighs, which were bent and traced with scar marks from past and recent self-harm, and a view of her back from the waist up, revealing only her hair and shoulders. Monica shared with David that she simply could not paint herself fully and that these are the only parts of herself that she feels aware of: "one eye for all that it has seen," her thighs for "the relief cutting brings" to her, and her hair, which represents the only aspect of herself that she "prizes and takes cares of."

As David and Monica processed her painting, David became aware of important considerations for Monica, which were not discussed in her file. Through this artwork, David noted Monica's lack of whole-person integration, disconnect from parts of herself, splits in her recollections and awareness ("only one eye that is seeing"), and her physical and affective changes during her creation process. These qualities alerted David to important treatment foci, which included further assessment and monitoring for dissociative tendencies and possible personality splits. The artwork that Monica produced provided David with critical insight and treatment considerations that might have been overlooked or gone unacknowledged otherwise.

Considerations for Creative Interventions: Incorporating an Additional Specialty

The incorporation of creative interventions in trauma work is powerful and meaningful for many clients. In addition to the numerous therapeutic benefits, creative interventions also offer a comfortable and easily accessible avenue to integrate the client's cultural heritage, personal beliefs, and worldview into treatment. However, creative interventions may be contraindicated with some clients, who may feel uncomfortable with the creative arts process, experience anxiety about their creativity being evaluated, or who have a comorbid diagnosis that is ill-fitting for non-verbal, abstract, and semi-unstructured interventions.

Clinicians must also be mindful that the application of a creative intervention in trauma work represents a unique and different skill set than the verbal processing skills used in talk-based therapy. While many clinical concepts transfer to creative therapies, these modalities involve truly a unique clinical skill set. Clinicians are encouraged to conceptualize trauma work as well as creative modalities as specialty areas of mental health practice. Joining these treatments together means that the clinician should aim to specialize in both trauma work *and* a creative intervention modality, such as play, sandtray, or art therapy. Consequently, clinicians need additional education, training, and supervision in the creative modality of choice. The opportunities for integrating creativity in trauma work are vast and extensive, and many more modalities exist beyond those presented here, including animal-assisted therapy, dance and movement therapy, drama therapy, adventure therapy, yoga therapy, music therapy, and expressive writing and poetry therapy. Many of these therapeutic modalities offer an accompanying certification with guidelines and standards of practice, and clinicians should be knowledgeable of their scope of competence in the application of any of these treatment interventions. Appendix B provides a table of the professional organizations associated with specific creative treatment modalities.

Conclusion

Creative formats in trauma work can aid clients in unique and highly therapeutic ways. This chapter highlighted the therapeutic power of creative modalities, such as play, sandtray, and art therapy, and introduced these formats as especially facilitative for trauma-focused work. Creative modalities offer new ways to target the therapeutic tasks associated with the remembrance and mourning phase of treatment, and these approaches can also be easily incorporated into the other phases of the tri-phasic model of trauma work. When applying any intervention, trauma clinicians must apply ethical clinical decision-making by utilizing research-informed rationale for each intervention and by maintaining a clear theoretical orientation and goal-directed approach.

Creative expression is an experiential process, and while research for its use and benefits is compelling, a narrative description of these modalities cannot provide a clinician with a true sense of the *experience* of what it is like to creatively and metaphorically communicate aspects of one-self. As clinicians, we gain perspective of the power of an intervention when we take the risk to engage in the process of creative expression ourselves. As a parallel, it's one thing to imagine the taste of a meal by simply reading a recipe; it's quite another thing to personally try out the dish. When we learn how to communicate metaphorically for ourselves, we are able to offer enhanced attunement to the meaning within our clients' metaphors. Metaphors teach us how to listen with more than just our ears and see more than with our eyes alone.

KEYWORD ASSESSMENT

Write definitions in your own words, describe the concept's role in trauma work, list any questions, or make notes of important aspects that you want to remember.

Creative Interventions

Metaphor

Psychological Distance

Projection

Play Therapy

Sandtray Therapy

Art Therapy

Externalizing Memories

EXPERIENTIAL ACTIVITIES: INTERACTING WITH THE CHAPTER CONTENT

Expand Self-Awareness

1) Select or write your own quote, story, or poem that best expresses your beliefs about the role of the trauma clinician and the experience of providing trauma work.

Expand Knowledge

2) Using Appendix B as a resource, investigate one of the professional organizations associated with a specific type of creative modality. Learn about the education and training requirements and continuing education opportunities, and read at least one peer-reviewed article on the use of this approach within trauma treatment.

Expand Skills

3) Select and engage in a metaphorical exercise (such as an art or sandtray activity) with a partner and take turns in each role (client and clinician). During the clinician role, practice the skills in which you provide a silent but attentive presence during the creation process, then invite your partner to process through open prompts while listening and reflecting what your partner shares, and finally expand the metaphor by offering observations. At the close of the activity, share with your partner what this process was like for you in each of the roles.

SUPERVISORY DISCUSSION: SHARING PERSONAL INSIGHTS AND IDENTIFYING AREAS FOR GROWTH

1) Share your story, quote, or poem and describe what this experience was like for you. Reflect on how you chose or wrote this particular narrative. What aspects of yourself did you tap into in order to create or select it? Reflect on the ways metaphorical expression differs from a literal discussion of your experience in trauma work.

2) Discuss what you learned from your investigations into a particular type of creative modality for trauma work. What unique therapeutic qualities does the approach bring to trauma treatment? Identify any emerging professional goals that you are now considering because of this learning.

3) Share your experience and the insights you gained from participating in a creative intervention in the role-play. From the perspective of the client, what did you discover about the therapeutic qualities of creative expression? As the clinician, what do you believe were some of your facilitative strengths as well as your areas for growth?

4) Describe the various areas of clinical judgment that are required when implementing any type of creative modality in trauma work. This may include considerations for the client's developmental stage, culture, diagnoses, personality, and so on. How will you be able to determine whether a creative approach is a facilitative inclusion in treatment or is contraindicated for a client?

Phase 3: Reconnection in Trauma Work

Tanya burst into my office with excitement. She had hardly made it to the sofa when she began to tell me about the "incident" from this past weekend. "I was at the grocery store looking at birthday cards for my girlfriend when this lady, who was also looking at cards, came up to me and said, 'It's so important to pick out just the right Mother's Day card.' And, do you know what? Thanks to you, I didn't have the old urge to punch that lady right in the face!" After a chuckle and a time to acknowledge the power of that moment for Tanya, I reminded my client that her progress was due to the hard work *she* had done over these past seven months. I also smiled as I reflected on how this strong and tenacious survivor of childhood abuse, who had been hurt at the hands of her mother and her mother's boyfriend, had transformed from a person so emotionally volatile and easily triggered to an individual who could remain self-composed and positively work through trauma triggers, such as an imposing Mother's Day card comment. As Tanya shared, she was able to identify her mastery and empowerment over her thoughts, feelings, and reactions to what was once a profoundly triggering type of encounter, and during our time together that day, we celebrated and reflected on Tanya's growth and change over the course of her journey through trauma work.

My therapeutic alliance with Tanya had progressed slowly but meaningfully over the course of her treatment. Tanya's abusive history left her with lingering scars of trauma as well as significant attachment problems, which ignited powerful transference and concerns about trust in our therapeutic relationship. Phase 1 (safety and stabilization) of trauma work with Tanya required tremendous time, patience, and focused efforts on the development of trust and regulation, but the achievement of these goals offered a powerful platform and firm foundation upon which Tanya could begin to confront some of her trauma memories during phase 2 of the therapeutic process. Over the course of six months, this stage of treatment was periodically paused as I responded to Tanya's cues that we needed to return to aspects of phase 1 before going further into memory processing. In the two months leading up to this particular session, Tanya's memory work had become increasingly positive, empowering, and significantly less distressing for her. The day that Tanya shared the story about the Mother's Day card comment, I knew this moment reflected Tanya's growing awareness of her "new way of being" in the world—a way of being in which she was no longer overcome by her trauma symptoms and reactions. This session marked the day that Tanya and I entered phase 3 of trauma work.

As discussed previously and as reflected in Tanya's case, the tri-phasic model is not always linear (meaning that not all clients experience an even progression through phases 1–2–3), and movement back and forth between phases 1 and 2 as needed is a normative part of the therapeutic process. Clients often worry that a transition back into an earlier phase may indicate a personal failure or imply a negative prognosis, but clinicians can reframe this experience for clients by explaining that a return to a previous phase is not a setback but, rather, reflects the client's expansion in the building of skills, enhanced tolerance for trauma work, increased self-awareness of and attention to personal needs, and deeper growth and recovery. While the transition into phase 3 does not necessarily mean that the client is fully "cured" from trauma's impact, there are several objective indicators that can be used to evaluate a client's readiness to begin phase 3 work. These include a decrease in trauma symptoms based on assessment, achievement of clinical goals, and the client's self-report of a desire and readiness to move towards termination.

In this final phase of trauma treatment, clients apply the skills they have learned thus far in therapy to their daily lives while continuing to build the resources and support they will need after treatment has ended. The hallmark themes of phase 3 center on the client's efforts to actively rebuild a life after overcoming trauma and to prepare for future challenges that will be faced without the support of the therapeutic alliance. At this junction in the therapeutic process, the client experiences increasing control over his or her reactions to trauma-related memories and, as a result, now feels more empowered, more capable of making life decisions, and more confident in the ability to manage challenging situations that may arise in the future. Simply stated, for phase 3 of trauma work, "The ultimate goal is to prepare clients to live fulfilled, productive lives without a counselor" (Gingrich, 2013, p. 139).

Once trauma memories have become "disempowered" and losses have been grieved, clients can begin to reconnect with themselves, with others, and with their community, and focus their energy on purposeful living. Depending on the needs and goals of the client, phase 3 often involves three primary therapeutic tasks: enhancing the client's previously established skills for future living, reflecting on the client's personal changes and therapeutic gains, and preparing for termination. Similar to the other phases of trauma work, clinicians should tailor this phase to the unique client, which means that this phase may progress rapidly for some clients while, for others, this stage of therapeutic work may be lengthy and extensive.

The reconnection tasks in phase 3 of trauma work include the following.

Task 1: Enhancement of the client's previously established skills:

- Bolster social reconnection and expand healthy interpersonal patterns
- Increase capacity for self-regulation

Task 2: Reflection on the client's personal changes and therapeutic gains:

- Identify personal strengths and areas of resiliency
- Explore posttraumatic growth
- Recognize transformations in identity
- Celebrate progress and therapeutic achievements

Task 3: Preparation for termination:

- Provide a follow-on plan for unexpected or premature termination
- Facilitate closure to the therapeutic relationship and experience

As a client's trauma symptoms decrease and lose power, the client often finds him or herself in a position of restored energy for life's tasks. Many clients spend years with the need to dedicate a significant portion of their mental, emotional, and physical resources to simply managing their trauma symptoms, but once these symptoms dissipate, clients often feel as though they have "a new lease on life." Phase 3 revisits some of the social and regulation skills that the client has already addressed in early phases of treatment, but this time, these skills are explored without the burden of intense trauma symptoms. Phase 3 also provides the client with the opportunity to reflect on personal growth and closure as one chapter of their story comes to an end and another begins.

In this chapter, an overview of each of the reconnection tasks are discussed, which includes the goals associated with the client's enhanced application of previously developed skills, reflection on the existential changes and growth that naturally coincides with trauma recovery, and the termination process. Cautions and considerations for clinicians as they help facilitate this final stage of treatment are also discussed. While trauma often dominates a client's thoughts and feelings about what has happened in the past, the therapeutic work of phase 3 sets its sights away from the past and onto the client's transition into a positive and hopeful future.

Task 1 of Reconnection: Enhancing Previously Established Skills for Future Living

As treatment evolves into phase 3, the foundational work that was developed during earlier stages returns as a major focus, but this time, skills are approached from a different orientation. Instead of aiming to develop these skills, clients revisit interpersonal and regulation skills as areas for enhanced utilization in daily living. In phase 3, the discussions surrounding interpersonal and regulation skills shift from the context of trauma and move into the context of optimal lifestyle functioning.

Social Connection and Interpersonal Intimacy

By nature, humans are relational beings. The quality of our relationships, to a large degree, determines the quality of our lives. One of the most significant challenges for trauma survivors (particularly for those with complex trauma) centers on the development and maintenance of healthy, interpersonal relationships. As humans, we are naturally built for relationships and connection, but trauma reorients us to a defensive posture of protection. Close, reciprocal relationships involve communication, collaboration, and tolerance for vulnerability. Unfortunately, all of these relational qualities and skills can be damaged by traumatic experiences, which often results in a defensive rather than open interpersonal posture within the traumatized individual.

Fear drives avoidant behaviors in an attempt to reduce the likelihood of an encounter with trauma triggers and to prevent further relational pain. In an effort to minimize the potential for dysregulation, these interpersonal patterns often result in social isolation and/or attempts to overcontrol one's environment and other people. Social difficulties snowball, compound, and often become more entrenched, which inevitably affects friendships, parenting, work relationships, sexuality, marriage/partnerships, and other forms of intimacy. However, a history of trauma does not doom one to a lifetime of relational difficulties. The brain can be rewired from a drive for protection back to connection.

Clinical attention to the social aftermath of trauma involves many of the tasks already completed in phases 1 and 2 of treatment as well as the acquisition of additional interpersonal skills.

The components of treatment from phases 1 and 2 that contribute towards connection include self-awareness, grieving losses, emotional regulation skills, processing memories, and, in some cases, the development of "earned secure attachment" through the therapeutic relationship. For many clients, the social skills developed during phase 1 and 2 become the foundation upon which their relational goals for the future can be addressed. With trauma symptoms now reduced, phase 3 provides the client with the opportunity to revisit these interpersonal skills with a forward-thinking, long-term perspective.

Phase 3 relational connectivity goals include:

- Increase the client's differentiation of self
- Establish and maintain appropriate boundaries
- Form new relationships and expand one's social support network
- Address sexual issues (as applicable)
- Consider and define forgiveness
- Confront past relational hurt and pain (as applicable)

Differentiation of Self

In order to positively connect with others, a delicate balance is needed between the sense of *togetherness* (the ability to remain emotionally connected) and *individuality* (the ability to be autonomous). This balance is reflected in the family systems concept of **differentiation of self**, or (DOS (Bowen, 1978; MacKay, 2017), which is characterized by an emotional maturity to distinguish oneself from others by not surrendering personal thoughts, feelings, and values within close relationships. Individuals with lower DOS often hope to quickly ease the discomfort and anxious feelings that arise in relational conflict, and as a consequence, they frequently demonstrate high emotional reactivity to others and/or respond in a manner that minimizes the importance of their personal values in order to "keep" the relationship. On the other hand, individuals with high DOS "manage the intense discomfort of the other person disagreeing with them, without distancing or moving to accommodate the other's views at the expense of their own clear thinking" (MacKay, 2017, p. 641). In trauma work, increased, positive differentiation of self can be improved through assertiveness training, emotional regulation, relational rupture and repair work between clinician and client, and through the practice of setting and maintaining boundaries.

Boundaries

In their seminal book *Boundaries*, Cloud and Townsend (2017) compare **boundaries** to property lines that serve as permeable borders between us and others, designed to allow "good" things to pass through and keep "bad" things out. In regard to boundaries, two possible extremes exist: 1) a lack or absence of boundaries (no property border), which allows both the "good" and "bad" to pass through, or 2) excessively rigid boundaries (impermeable walls), which restrict the passage of both the "good" and "bad." In the wake of trauma, clients often experience difficulty in defining the appropriate permeability of their boundaries, and they frequently experience one of these two extremes across a variety of interpersonal relationships.

Trauma, particularly interpersonal trauma, can drastically impact boundary development. As Cloud and Townsend (2017) point out, "Victims of physical and sexual abuse often have a poor sense of boundaries. Early in life they were taught that their property did not really begin at their skin" (p. 36). Trauma survivors very often experienced absent or limited choices during the trauma, and the mental and emotional task of restoring a sense of personal empowerment and the reality of choices can be challenging. For clients who experience diffuse boundaries, the interpersonal skill work often involves understanding the meaning and use of the word "no" and taking ownership for one's decisions. Boundary setting often involves saying "no" and creating personal priorities, such as the client's decision to decline a dinner invitation with someone with whom the client feels uncomfortable or to refuse a request to take on a volunteer position when there is already too much work on the client's plate. On the other hand, some clients lean towards the other end of the spectrum by adhering to overprotection through rigid boundaries, which inevitably inhibits relational connection. For these clients, boundary work often involves the practice of taking interpersonal risks, such as the client's decision to attend a book club meeting with people he or she doesn't know well or the choice to sit with co-workers at lunch rather than remaining isolated in his or her office.

While each extreme presents with different challenges, a common theme for both ends of the spectrum centers on the client's challenge to apply relational discernment. In order to develop healthy boundaries, **relational discernment** requires the client to practice an appropriate level of trust in conjunction with the reality of imperfections in others. Relational discernment also requires the client to distinguish between the normative imperfections in others and critical "red flags" that may be present in the relationship, which could indicate unhealthy interactions or danger. The client's ability to accurately assess the potential danger in a relationship is crucial for preventing retraumatization of the past and for preventing new trauma experiences.

Development of New Relationships

Setting boundaries may involve making changes to current relationships, ending toxic relationships, and/or forming new relationships. New connections may include relationships with peers in recovery-related settings (such as support groups), friendships, and romantic partners. Clinicians can help clients navigate the intimidating landscape of meeting new people by providing support and encouragement for any of the client's fears or insecurities as well as offer guidance on safe places to begin (such as referrals to support groups or ideas for recreational activities to meet other people with similar interests). The expansion of a social network will look very different for each client. Factors such as the client's personality, age, culture, ethnicity, religion, sexual orientation, and recovery progress should all be taken into consideration when developing a social plan. Clinicians can highlight the benefits and importance of social connection and encourage clients to try new things and meet new people, but clinicians must remain mindful not to push clients too hard or too fast as they venture out socially. Very often, the experience of an interpersonal relationship without the burden of trauma symptoms feels novel, uncertain, and, at times, intimidating for clients. While this is a positive change, clinicians can offer empathy and support for clients as they reengage in the social world in new but often personally uncharted ways.

Healthy Sexuality

For clients with a history of trauma, especially sexual trauma, intimacy and sexuality can be painful and difficult. Trauma's impact on relational intimacy may incite fears of abandonment, rejection, vulnerability, loss of control, conflict, and violence. Clients may struggle with effectively communicating, asserting their needs, staying present in the moment, experiencing feelings of shame, and enjoying physical touch and sexual arousal. Sex is a very sensual experience, and the sights, sounds, tastes, smells, and touch of sex can be highly triggering, especially for survivors of sexual abuse. This creates a high potential for flashbacks, dissociation, and dysregulation.

Clients can, however, work through these issues and experience pleasure and fulfillment in their sexuality. Some clients may heal from traditional trauma treatment interventions, including reduction of cognitive distortions, grounding, relaxation, and trauma memory processing. Other clients may benefit from additional resources, such as the seminal book *The Courage to Heal* (Bass & Davis, 2008), psychoeducation to help differentiate healthy intimacy and sex from abuse and coercion, and incorporation of intimate partners into sessions that utilize treatment approaches such as cognitive-behavioral conjoint therapy and emotionally focused therapy (EFT) for couples (Gingrich, 2013). Finally, some clients may need referrals to professionals who specialize in sex therapy.

Forgiveness

The concept of forgiveness can be very challenging for clients as they attempt to move forward from their trauma. They may harbor unforgiveness towards perpetrators, family members, God, and even themselves. Forgiveness is a willful act of letting go and refusing to be entangled in the bitterness, hatred, and resentment that shackle an individual to the past. Using a general understanding of forgiveness and its role in trauma recovery, clinicians must also approach this topic with the sensitivity that the concept of forgiveness is subjective, and each unique client will view forgiveness through his or her own cultural and spiritual lens.

In some cases, clients may feel an urgency to forgive or experience pressure to forgive from members of their family or religious community. However, when clients feel compelled or pressured to forgive before they have had the opportunity to work through powerful emotions, such as grief, anger, and betrayal, the outcome may result in increased suppression of these important feelings and a deepening sense of shame as the client wonders, "Why can't I just forgive?" For these reasons, the topic of forgiveness is most appropriately included in phase 3 of trauma work as a final element to process. In this therapeutically sequential order, clients have had time to recognize, honor, and process all the associated feelings and can approach the concept of forgiveness on their terms and in their way.

During this aspect of trauma work, the role of the clinician is often to help differentiate the concept of *extending forgiveness* from *allowing excuses* for abusive behavior. Clinicians can also help facilitate the client's sense of freedom to forgive only when and if he or she chooses and feels ready to do so. Often, clients need to hear that a choice to forgive does not necessarily mean or require that the client must reenter a relationship with the person that he or she is forgiving. Forgiveness is an internal process while reconciliation is an external, interpersonal experience, but these two relational tasks are not mutually exclusive. For some clients, the restoration of the relationship is not necessary for one to truly forgive and vice versa.

Confrontation

Once traumatic memories have been processed and the client feels increasingly empowered, a frequent outcome of this process involves the client's resurgence of anger towards the perpetrator of the trauma. With restored confidence through the liberation from trauma symptoms, clients may desire to confront the individual(s) who wounded them. During times like these, clinicians must discuss the potentially weighty pros and cons of this decision with the client while also refusing to give the client advice or directly make the decision for him or her. The choice whether or not to confront a perpetrator is an opportunity for clients to feel a sense of control and empowerment as they explore potential outcomes and, hopefully, make an informed (not impulsive) decision. As clinicians, our role is to provide support and help clients view this decision from multiple perspectives and potential outcomes.

A client's need to confront a perpetrator can also be achieved therapeutically and not literally. Very often, clients can make a more informed choice about a literal confrontation after they have had an imagined, therapeutic experience in the presence of the clinician. Many times, these therapeutic experiences alone satisfy the client's needs and attend to his or her sense of closure, and the client no longer feels the urgency to engage in a literal confrontation. To accomplish this, clinicians may implement the Gestalt "empty chair" technique in which the client role-plays the confrontation using a chair with an imagined image of the offender (Schimmel & Jacobs, 2013). Alternatively, the client may write a "letter of impact" in which the client writes out, in detail, the various ways in which the trauma (and offender) has impacted him or her. Impact letters can be sent or destroyed, depending on the wishes of the client.

As the client prepares to end treatment and reengage in relationships, the social reconnection work of phase 3 involves addressing many of these interpersonal goals: increased differentiation of self, the development of healthy boundaries, an expansion of social supports, increased positive sexuality, engagement in forgiveness, and closure regarding confrontation. The development and maintenance of positive, healthy, and supportive relationships is a key aspect in trauma work, as this serves as one of the most powerful means of prevention of setbacks after termination. In the final stage of trauma work, this aspect of the client's life should not go overlooked or unaddressed.

Trauma Work in Practice: A Client's Interpersonal Focus Within Trauma Treatment

When I began trauma work with Dominique, virtually every meaningful relationship in his life had dissolved. He sought counseling services after his volatile divorce from his wife, who was able to claim full custody of his two children due to Dominique's tendencies towards controlling behavior and anger. With very few friends, Dominique was becoming increasingly isolated, and his custody attorney recommended that he seek mental health services. While the relationship difficulties represented the presenting problem that led him to my office, I soon learned of Dominique's long history of trauma. Dominique grew up in a neighborhood characterized by poverty and crime, and gang activity had plagued his community. By the time he was 17, Dominique had experienced two drive-by shootings, he had been jumped by gang members on four different occasions (one of which included a stabbing), and every man he knew over the age of 25 had been killed, incarcerated, unable to find employment, or addicted to drugs. As a result of the generational, community, and personal trauma, Dominique held very little trust for others, especially other males, and he attempted to protect himself as well as his former wife and children through excessive control. I provided Dominique with psychoeducation about trauma and how his problems connected with his diagnosis of PTSD, and while Dominique accepted these aspects of himself, he explained that his goal for treatment continued to center on improving his interpersonal patterns by decreasing his controlling behavior and anger outbursts.

During my time with Dominique, the bulk of our therapeutic work targeted the goals associated with phase 1 in which Dominique attended to his needs for safety and regulation. As we entered phase 2 of treatment, Dominique made it clear to me that he wanted to engage in only limited trauma work, and he chose to focus only on the trauma of the drive-by shootings. Dominique chose this particular trauma because his extreme hypervigilance at home created enormous stress and tension for him, which often exacerbated his outward expressions of anger and impatience with his family members. During the time I worked with him, Dominique was simply not ready to address his other traumas—he only wanted to address aspects of his life (relationship patterns) that appeared to directly link with his goal of regaining partial custody of his children. After a successful completion of phase 2, which was marked by Dominique's significant reduction of trauma triggers and symptoms while at home, we began phase 3 of treatment. Trauma had impacted Dominique greatly in the area of interpersonal relationships, and the therapeutic work associated with his relational goals proved to be as lengthy and expansive as phase 1. However, with the motivation and determination to see his children more often, Dominique persevered through treatment and changed many of his relationship patterns, which included refining relational discernment, readjusting extreme boundaries, developing communication skills, and accepting the imperfections of self as a foundation for accepting others. After two years of hard work in counseling and a year of legal review, Dominique was able to regain partial custody of his children and be the father that he always hoped he was capable of being.

Self-Regulation Skills for Future Stress

In order to maximize the potential for close relationships and to reduce exaggerated responses to triggers, phase 3 continues the overall treatment goal of enhancing skills by attending to the client's capacity for self-regulation. Effective self-regulation requires the client's self-awareness of his or her various arousal levels, and this important self-awareness is subsequently conjoined with an implementation of positive coping strategies that function as management resources for arousal. The ability to regulate personal arousal can be particularly difficult for clients when they are in a conflict with another person who is also showing signs emotional dysregulation. Clients must learn to monitor their own emotional arousal through use of the SUDs scale in daily and future living and be able to recognize personal signs of physical arousal on their own without the assistance of the clinician. As clients learn that a slight elevation in arousal is not necessarily indicative of danger, they will be better able to prevent extreme arousal, such as panic attacks, and utilize their previously developed skills of grounding, mindfulness, and other regulation techniques to stay within their window of stress tolerance.

While these goals and skills are highly emphasized in other phases of treatment, clients and clinicians revisit regulation in phase 3 with the adjusted perspective of anticipating potential future, rather than present, triggers and challenges. For example, clients often experience setbacks on anniversary dates, as they developmentally grow and understand the trauma with a matured perspective, during certain seasons of the year, or when exposed to new trauma reminders they haven't yet encountered, such as seeing a perpetrator again during a court hearing. Clinicians can normalize the experience of client setbacks that may challenge emotional regulation while also facilitating the development of a prevention plan to minimize the power of potentially negative impacts. After termination, clients must be able to engage in their own process of self-awareness and regulation, and phase 3 of trauma work attends to bolstering the client's independent skills for any future challenges.

Task 2 of Reconnection: Reflecting on Personal Changes and Therapeutic Gains

The goals associated with task 1 of reconnection focus on bolstering the client's previously established skills as he or she prepares to terminate and engage in life without the support of the therapeutic relationship. Once the client has successfully mastered these skills and feels empowered for future independent work in relationships and self-regulation, the therapeutic focus turns to the final reflective tasks that contribute to positive closure and termination of the trauma work journey. These opportunities for reflection offer the client an important time to consider his or her emerging areas of strength and resiliency, recognize the transformation in self-identity, celebrate personal gains, and positively move through termination.

Reflection on Strengths and Resiliency

The journey of trauma work is often immensely challenging, and yet, the milestone of phase 3 indicates that the client has persevered through the process and has overcome enormous difficulties. Here, at the mountain's peak, these moments of incredible personal strength and resiliency should be recognized and honored. For many clients, the same internal resources that propelled the client through the trauma work process will continue to function as an invaluable reserve to call upon when future difficulties are faced. Clients must be able to identify these specific, powerful strengths within themselves in order to tap into these resources in the future as they navigate across the waves of life.

Walsh defined **resilience** as "the ability to withstand and rebound from serious life challenges" (Walsh, 2016, p. 4). Resilience may include self-advocacy, identifying resources for support, enlisting the help of others, and engaging in healthy means of coping to manage the impact of trauma (Kurtz, Pagano, Buttram, & Ungar, 2019; Obrist, Pfeiffer, & Henley, 2010). While resiliency can be a personality trait linked to optimism and other characteristics, a posture of resilience is also something that can be cultivated and expanded both inside and outside of therapy.

Reflection on Posttraumatic Growth

While resiliency is viewed as the ability to "bounce back" to baseline functioning after an adverse experience, **posttraumatic growth** (PTG) can be considered a "bounce forward" to a higher level of functioning and potentially deeper life experience after a trauma. The term "PTG" was introduced by Tedeschi and Calhoun (1996) to describe the transformative process that occurs when an individual engages in the internal struggle to recalibrate in the wake of trauma and grapple with his or her own shattered, previous assumptions, and eventually, this process of reflection leads to significant and positive psychological changes. In other words, the experience of a traumatic event alone does not stimulate growth, but the struggle to understand and adjust previously held beliefs has the potential to produce positive outcomes that improve overall quality of life (Janoff-Bulman, 1992; Tedeschi & Calhoun, 2004). The Posttraumatic Growth Inventory, or PTGI (Tedeschi & Calhoun, 1996) measures these positive outcomes based on five primary domains of PTG: (1) greater appreciation of life and changed sense of priorities, (2) more intimate relationships with others, (3) a greater sense of personal strength, (4) recognitions of new possibilities or paths for one's life, and (5) spiritual development. Examples of PTG include a woman with terminal cancer who began to travel and spend more time with family, a couple who had been estranged and then grew closer after a house fire, a man who had been anxious and fearful since his abusive childhood who ventured out to start his own business, and a teenager who found a new faith in God while living in a refugee camp. For these people, their change in perspective and positive growth emerged *out of* their trauma recovery experience, and they now consider themselves to be stronger, wiser, and more joyful people because of the lessons they took to heart along their journey. Trauma survivors who experience posttraumatic growth perceive their positive outcomes and changes to be *because of*, not *in spite of*, their trauma. Posttraumatic growth transforms the destruction of trauma into something of beauty and meaning.

Tedeschi and Calhoun (2004) utilize the metaphor of an earthquake to illustrate the positive outcomes of posttraumatic growth. The authors explain that following the devastation of an earthquake, new buildings are constructed with enhanced strength in order for the building to withstand the impacts of any future disaster. In the same way that extra support and strength is integrated into new building construction, trauma survivors are also "rebuilt" with new gains as they experience posttraumatic growth. While no one desires for horrific events, such as an earthquake, to occur in order to produce growth for themselves or their community, the impact of traumatic stress can eventually lead to an emotional connection to the meaning-making process, which potentially serves as a catalyst for personal change and influences PTG development (Schubert et al., 2016).

The gains derived from post-trauma experiences do not necessarily balance out the distress or losses associated with the trauma, and clinicians should be careful not minimize the pain caused by these events when highlighting positive outcomes. For example, a man who lost his leg fighting in a war may have gained an appreciation for life and learned not to sweat the small stuff, but he may still have significant grief due to his decrease in mobility. In fact, it is possible to experience both posttraumatic growth and posttraumatic stress simultaneously (Wu, Xu, & Sui, 2016). Clinicians can point out areas of growth with careful consideration of how they phrase their reflections to clients. Statements that begin with phrases such as "at least" or "the silver lining is—" often lack empathy and overlook or minimize pain and loss. For example, a mother who has lost a baby while pregnant may experience the statement "*At least* you grew closer to your husband during this experience and can always try again for another baby" to be very hurtful and insensitive. Alternatively, statements that begin with the words "'despite" or "even with" often reflect areas of posttraumatic growth. In the same conversation with the grieving woman, a statement that attends to posttraumatic growth may sound like, "*Despite* (or *even with*) the incredible pain of your loss, you have found a way to become closer to your husband and keep your hope for the future." Trauma changes our clients' lives, and our role as clinicians is to allow clients to reflect on both the positive and negative aspects of their post-trauma experience.

Reflection on Identity Transformation

Phase 3 is also a time to recognize the client's transformation in identity. As the client makes meaning out of his or her traumas, takes control over personal reactions to trauma triggers, and reauthors his or her life narrative, a mental shift occurs in which the client no longer views him- or herself as a victim but begins to perceive self in a new way. Clients often begin trauma work with the self-identity of a victim, but often this perspective evolves into a survivor identity and, eventually, into an identity that is completely differentiated from the trauma. The end of the evolution in self-perception is one in which the client takes on a more holistic view of self as an individual who has the capacity to thrive and who is no longer defined by trauma (Kick & McNitt, 2016). While the perception of oneself as a survivor rather than a victim is certainly a positive shift, a "survivor" self-perception still centers around the event of the trauma. When clients are able to grow beyond the identity of a survivor, they are able to view themselves as someone who is independent of events that happened in their lives—the trauma is a part of their story, but it no longer labels or defines their self-identity.

This self-identity transformation is pivotal because self-appraisal of personal capabilities will influence how the client thinks, feels, and functions during taxing circumstances. "Perceived self-efficacy is concerned with judgements of how well one can execute courses of action required to deal with prospective situations" (Bandura, 1982, p. 122). An increase in confidence to manage life situations leads to empowerment, optimism, and hope. Trauma survivors and empowered individuals are able to repurpose their pain and focus on changing the things that are under their control, such as taking new risks by going back to school or committing to a relationship. Empowerment and self-identity changes also often spark the desire to reach out to help others by sharing personal experiences and lessons gleaned along the way.

Trauma Work in Practice: A Client's Transformation in Self-Identity

Becca grew up in a positive, loving family, but despite the vigilance and protection from her parents, Becca encountered several situations of sexual trauma and abuse during her childhood and adolescence. With strong supports and resources in place, Becca did not experience significant trauma symptoms at the time of the abuse incidents, and, therefore, she never sought counseling or treatment. However, as an adult, Becca's trauma-related problems began to escalate when she became sexually active as sexual triggers provoked pronounced avoidance symptoms and dissociative tendencies. When Becca began her trauma work, she struggled to even accept the reality of her PTSD diagnosis. Until that time, she had never connected her problems with the external trauma event but rather perceived her sexual avoidance as simply a personal deficit of being a "prude." For Becca, accepting herself as a victim of sexual trauma was a monumental task. However, this initial change in Becca's self-perception allowed her to move forward in the evolution of self-identity transformation. She engaged in trauma work, and over the course of a year, Becca began to see herself as a survivor, rather than a victim, as she gained mastery over trauma-related problems, which began to fade and lose power. When she experienced trauma triggers, she viewed herself as empowered as she practiced her skills to overcome her previous mental, emotional, and physiological reactions to triggers.

Becca successfully terminated from counseling, but her personal journey of reflection continued. Over time, Becca's view of herself and what happened to her continued to transform, and today, Becca perceives her experiences as powerful moments in time but moments that she has reclaimed for herself. In the metamorphosis of Becca's self-perception, she once saw herself as a "prude," then as a "victim," then a "survivor," and now she sees herself in totality as "Becca." This transformation has been accompanied by powerful posttraumatic growth in which Becca feels deeper empathy, compassion, and patience for others who are experiencing the fallout of trauma. Becca shares her story of hope with other men and women who are also on their journey of recovery, transformation, and redemption of life narratives and self-perception.

Reflection Through Celebration

If you have ever watched professional and college football, you have probably noticed that there is a significant difference between what can happen after a touchdown between these two leagues: the end zone celebration. College athletes are restricted from displaying an overt touchdown celebration, and they must return the ball to the official in order to immediately resume the game. Alternatively, professional football viewers are able to join their favorite player in the celebration of a victory by witnessing often well-choreographed dances and expressions of exuberance. These celebrations publicly display the joy and exhilaration that come from a well-fought battle in which the players pushed through incredible obstacles, faced serious risks, overcame enemies, and fulfilled their goals. Likewise, clinicians can join clients in the celebration of important victories and hard-won goals. Celebration occurs in trauma work when clinicians share their admiration for how far their clients have come, attest to the obstacles they have pushed past, honor the achievements they have made, and reflect on the bravery they have displayed.

Task 3 of Reconnection: Ending the Journey Together Through Termination

Termination is the process of ending therapy and serves as a conclusion for an important therapeutic relationship. A critical aspect of trauma-informed care involves properly managing expectations, and therefore, the time to begin preparing clients for this stage of treatment is at the onset of therapy, often during the informed consent discussion, in order to help clients to consistently view the therapeutic relationship as a finite one. A best practice for clinicians includes periodic discussion with clients about how treatment is progressing so that clients maintain a general understanding of the anticipated length of treatment. Ideally, termination occurs after the following conditions are reached: 1) treatment goals are met, 2) the client consistently experiences a decrease in or elimination of symptoms and an increase in overall functioning, and 3) the client and clinician mutually agree that therapeutic work would is no longer required.

At times, however, there are other circumstances that prompt termination, including limits of third-party reimbursement, clinical issues beyond the scope of practice of the clinician, the client's desire to end services early, the development of a conflict of interest or dual relationship, or the client or clinician's move to another location. Regardless of the reason for termination, and when possible, clinicians can structure the process of termination so that sessions gradually decrease or taper off. Frequently, the last one or two sessions with the client represent "wrap-up" sessions.

When termination is abrupt and the clinician is unable to end the therapeutic relationship with meaningful closure, a termination letter may be warranted. Situations like these may occur when a client suddenly drops out of treatment and does not return phone calls or when the clinician experiences a significant medical or family emergency requiring lengthy time out of the office. This letter can include an after-care plan, guidelines for future contact, and a list of appropriate referrals. As much as possible, clinicians should seek collaboration with clients when developing a transition plan, ensure that clients have the necessary resources and referrals that they may need in the future, and carefully document the termination plan and process.

The end of therapy can be a difficult time for some clients. While feelings of sadness and fear are normative and reflect the value of the therapeutic relationship, some clients may experience strong emotional reactions to termination, such as severe anxiety or rage, as they arrive at an intersection between past trauma-related patterns and the anticipated loss of a strong therapeutic bond. "These idiosyncratic reactions usually serve some functional purpose: to escape anticipated rejection, avoid perceived danger, compensate for helplessness, maintain proximity to a source of perceived power, or attain personal power and control." (Davis, 2008, p. 139). When clients experience intense emotions in the anticipation of termination, clinicians can take several steps to provide care for clients during this transition. First, the clinician's affirmation and acknowledgment of the significance of the relationship can validate the client's feelings, provide empathy for the experience, and offer relational connection by sharing his or her own positive (professional) feelings towards the client. The clinician's professional but relationally focused disclosure may sound something like, "It has been a privilege for me to hear your story and to witness your growth over these past several months." Additionally, clinicians can reflect the feelings of grief associated with termination as an indicator of the significance of the therapeutic relationship and the journey traveled together. Clinicians can reframe the feelings of grief as emotional testaments of the power of the therapeutic relationship and as reflections of just how meaningful the journey together has been.

Lastly, the termination process offers clinicians the opportunity to model healthy coping and positively express grief over a meaningful loss while simultaneously maintaining personal boundaries. For example, clinicians may tell clients that they will miss their time together, but clinicians must be mindful of avoiding unethical compromises, such as going out to lunch with the client the next month. At times, clients may need to be reminded of the limitations of professional boundaries, such as the clinician's ethical obligation to refrain from developing a personal relationship with the client or to receive gifts of monetary value. For clients and clinicians alike, termination is also an opportunity to reinforce healthy self-care activities, such as reflection through journaling, art, exercise, and spirituality, as a positive means to cope with feelings of loss and to maintain therapeutic gains. The journey through trauma work often forges powerful therapeutic bonds and unique relationship connections between the client and clinician. The end to this journey can be emotional, meaningful, and reflective of an incredible partnership that developed along the road of healing and recovery.

Conclusion

The reconnection work of phase 3 during the trauma treatment process represents the capstone tasks of this important journey. Clients have the opportunity to enhance and strengthen their interpersonal and self-regulation skills so that they are best equipped for success following termination, and they are able to reflect on the many profound and existential changes that have bloomed within themselves as they have recovered, healed, and grown beyond trauma. Phase 3 is a meaningful for time for clients to reconnect with others with the deepest and truest parts of the themselves, an experience which is, at last, untangled from the snares of trauma.

For clinicians, the conclusion of trauma work with a client presents itself with another parallel process in which we can also reflect on how we've changed and grown as professionals as well as individuals. While our client's stories are not our own, we often still adopt so many of the positive lessons, inspiring strengths, and moments of beauty that emerge out of the experience. These moments often become the beacon of hope that we cling to as we continue on down the road of trauma work with other clients.

In closing, we leave you with this story. On the Big Island of Hawaii, the locals grieved and watched in terror and helplessness as Mount Kilauea poured lava over their treasured and sacred home. In the wake of the river of fire, the land was left scorched, blackened, and stripped of its beauty and life. Treasured places were lost, and there was much to mourn. In time, however, life began to return to the devastated land. Broken places returned to a version of their former glory, and the ashes of what was lost transformed into nourishment for growth and restoration. As life began to rebuild, the locals looked out to the sea and noticed another change- the lava's flow had created a new island, one that had not been there before. This new island rose up from the depths as it pushed beyond the waves that crashed against it, waves that tried in vain to keep the island buried and hidden from the world. Forged through fire, what had once been a mound of ashen lava emerged, now, as a place of beauty for those who had lost so much, bringing unanticipated growth and birthing a new safe haven for those seeking shelter from the ocean's cold waves. While the impact of trauma is monumental, in the end, the power of healing and growth can be even more lasting.

KEYWORD ASSESSMENT

Write definitions in your own words, describe the concept's role in trauma work, list any questions, or make notes of important aspects that you want to remember.

Resilience

Posttraumatic Growth

Differentiation of Self

Boundaries

Relational Discernment

Termination

EXPERIENTIAL ACTIVITIES: INTERACTING WITH THE CHAPTER CONTENT

Expand Self-Awareness

1) Identity transformation occurs for clients as well as for growing trauma clinicians. Reflecting on yourself as an emerging trauma clinician, create a series of "I am" statements. Use these statements to identify your values, areas of strengths, and feelings about personal and professional identity.

Expand Knowledge

2) Using a character from book or film who has experienced an interpersonal trauma, write a Letter of Impact from the perspective of this fictional person. Imagine that this letter is integrated into the character's trauma treatment, and consider what the character might like to do with the letter after it is written.

Expand Skills

3) Review the case of Dominique from the chapter, and imagine that he is your client. Consider how you might explain to Dominique that many of his interpersonal problems and relationship patterns are influenced by his trauma history and trauma-related symptoms. Also identify how you would specifically address some of the relationship goals outlined in his case through theory and intervention.

SUPERVISORY DISCUSSION: SHARING PERSONAL INSIGHTS AND IDENTIFYING AREAS FOR GROWTH

1) Discuss the insights that you gained about yourself through your "I am" statements. Reflect on how your statements match or mismatch with how you hope to perceive yourself personally and professionally.

2) Describe what it was like for you to complete the Letter of Impact. Discuss what you noticed about the process and how these observations better inform you for important aspects of how you will support your clients who engage in this activity.

3) Discuss the case of Dominique and practice explaining how trauma is related to interpersonal patterns and social skills. Also discuss the specific interventions you would apply to meet Dominique's relationship goals.

4) Share your thoughts, feelings, and reactions about the concept of posttraumatic growth. Return to the chapter's conclusion story about the new island that emerged following a volcano. Reflecting on the metaphorical connections with posttraumatic growth, provide a name for this new island and share the meaning and rationale behind your name choice.

Chapter 14

Beyond the Session: Professional Growth in Trauma Work

As I sat in my cap and gown during my graduation ceremony, I took a long moment to gaze around at my peers, faculty, and mentors, and all the crowd that had gathered to watch us receive our master's degree diplomas. Of course, I was overjoyed on that day, but I was also sobered. As I sat in my seat, listening to the commencement speech, I just couldn't shake the reality that I was graduating and, therefore, I was deemed "prepared" for the tremendous responsibility of mental health work. By all accounts, I was as prepared as one could be: I was graduating from an outstanding program, I had fully mastered every class and learning objective, and I was confident in the quality of the exceptional supervision that I had received. But, while my diploma declared that I was adequately educated and trained, I felt intimidated by the work ahead of me and acutely aware of the gaps in my professional experience. Fast forward a decade later, and once again I sat at my graduation ceremony, this time for a doctoral degree. By this time, my trauma expertise was greatly enhanced, my specialty areas were developed, and my education and training had reached further than I ever dreamed. And, yet again, I found myself completely humbled in the acceptance of my degree. For me, the feeling of professional doubt was unwavering and stubbornly enduring despite my level of education and experience.

During these milestone moments in my life, I celebrated my achievements but also felt a powerful awareness of my limits. In fact, the dual sense of competence and uncertainty has been my professional companion across the years, and I have no doubt that this sensation will continue to find its way to me over and over again. Oddly, a strange phenomenon often occurs with the acquisition of training, education, and experience: it seems that the more we learn, the more aware we become of how little we actually know and how much is left to explore.

At the conclusion of any meaningful undertaking, whether it be a graduation or the completion of this text, the summative moment presents a rich opportunity to reflect on what you've gained, how you've changed, and where you are going next. In this final chapter, we direct our attention to the future and where we go from here in our journey of ongoing development as trauma clinicians. The road towards professional expertise in trauma work is guided by establishing trauma competency, expanding trauma-focused skills in a theoretical framework, and engaging in trauma-focused advocacy, which are each reviewed in our final discussion.

Professional Goal 1: Establishing Competency in Trauma Work

Across all professional disciplines, mental health practice requires a number of **professional competencies**, which identify the knowledge, skills, and professional practices and dispositions that are required in order to effectively and ethically offer therapeutic care. Professional competencies outline objective, professional criteria that indicate that one has achieved the agreed-upon standards of competence for an area of practice or specialty skill, including trauma work. In 2013, 60 leading experts in trauma, who represented various disciplines and theoretical orientations, came together to develop the New Haven Competencies, which outlined the five core competency domains for trauma clinicians (Cook, Newman, & The New Haven Competency Group, 2014). These five core competency domains include:

1) **Scientific knowledge about trauma:** The trauma clinician will demonstrate an understanding of and an ability to communicate about the various etiologies, influences, and presentations of trauma.

2) **Psychosocial trauma-focused assessment:** The trauma clinician will demonstrate an understanding of the various trauma-related assessments and considerations for these assessments, including strengths, limitations, and influences of client culture and context.

3) **Trauma-focused psychosocial intervention:** The trauma clinician will demonstrate an understanding of research-supported trauma interventions, apply a phased treatment approach, and effectively and thoughtfully incorporate significant client considerations into treatment.

4) **Trauma-informed professionalism:** The trauma clinician will demonstrate ethical practice, seek to cooperate with and integrate various relevant systems, and offer trauma-informed advocacy.

5) **Trauma-informed relational and systems issues:** The trauma clinician will demonstrate an understanding of the systemic impact of trauma and attend to these issues as well as interpersonal concerns and aspects of resiliency.

An additional area of trauma-focused competencies highlights the global and essential aspects of trauma work practice, including the clinician's ability to facilitate the therapeutic relationship, attend to a client's safety concerns, tolerate trauma-related content, manage his or her personal values and beliefs, engage in self-care, and evaluate and apply research-informed trauma-focused practices, interventions, and theories (Cook, Newman et al., 2014). While a general overview of these five domains is provided here, each domain lists a number of specific competency criteria that every beginning trauma clinician should be able to demonstrate as a reflection of his or her ability to provide safe and effective trauma work practice.

These competencies serve as an exceptional guide for beginning trauma clinicians as they seek to identify areas in which they need additional growth and learning. Competencies serve as an effective professional assessment tool in which one can evaluate his or her strengths as well as important points for growth and areas for needed professional development in trauma work practice. For example, when Daniel reviewed the specific competency criteria for trauma work, he and his supervisor were able to discuss each specific competency in connection with Daniel's practices and skills. Daniel demonstrated evidence of mastery in most of the listed competencies, but he and his supervisor agreed that Daniel needed continued training and supervision in his ability to effectively initiate assessment by inquiring with all clients, not just those who present with overtly trauma-related concerns, about their history of trauma exposure. Competencies ensure practical and ethical standards for those who offer a specialty area of practice, like trauma work, and competency standards also serve as a tool for assessment and evaluation by providing a set of guiding goals for professional areas of mastery.

Trauma competencies should also always be aligned with one's professional discipline, and clinicians are encouraged to view their parent organization's position on competence in trauma work alongside the professional goals outlined by other groups. Trauma clinicians must keep in mind that a trauma work specialty is *additive* to the foundation of their primary professional identity as a psychologist, counselor, social worker, or marriage and family therapist. One's professional discipline should always remain the guiding identity that defines professional scope, perspective, and treatment orientation to trauma work. In addition to maintaining professional membership and involvement in a discipline's parent organization, such as the American Psychological Association (APA), American Counseling Association (ACA), National Association of Social Workers (NASW), or American Association for Marriage and Family Therapy (AAMFT), trauma clinicians may also consider joining professional groups or organizations that are designed for those specializing in trauma, such as the Association of Traumatic Stress Specialists (ATSS) or the International Society for Traumatic Stress Studies (ISTSS).

Professional Goal 2: Expanding Trauma-Focused Skills in a Theoretical Framework

Trauma-focused skills are identified as specific targets for areas of competency in trauma work, and this text highlights critical trauma-informed and trauma-focused skills that can be applied in practice. While these skills offer direction for the general goals and direction of trauma work, the skills themselves must be constructed and delivered through a theoretical platform, also referred to as **theory-based skills**. As discussed previously, the tri-phasic model does not substitute for a theory but rather serves as a framework for implementing theoretically based skills. Trauma clinicians must continue to explore, become knowledgeable of, and obtain supervised practice in trauma-focused theories.

Evidence-based and empirically supported treatments are the place to begin in the development of richer trauma skills, but clinicians are also cautioned to avoid a strict adherence to any one particular model. Unfortunately, the research endeavors, which aim to validate a treatment's efficacy in order to raise the modality to evidence-based status, have inadvertently created a competitive climate for trauma-focused theories and models. Consequently, divisions and fractures have emerged in the trauma community as to which trauma treatment model is truly "correct." As a result, these divides may distract clinicians towards defending a particular theory rather than to keeping focus on the best practices in trauma treatment and the client's interests.

As beginning trauma clinicians navigate the field and consider the various theories, novice professionals must remember that facilitating trauma recovery does not rest on a single theory alone; the entire therapeutic process, from relationship building to reconnection, is needed to foster lasting change for clients (Forbes et al., 2010). Gentry et al. (2017) suggest that as research continues to develop and new findings are discovered, instead of asking the question, "Which of these trauma treatment models is the best?", clinicians are encouraged to ask, "What are the active agents in this model that make it effective, and how do these facilitative aspects parallel or differ from other models?" The latter question will help clinicians to carefully consider modalities and make informed clinical decisions about which modality is more appropriately suited for a unique client and why. Instead of searching for the "best" trauma model to implement universally, clinicians should focus on developing skills that transcend most evidence-based and empirically supported models. This way, the clinician can adjust to a different theoretical approach (approaches the clinician has been adequately trained and supervised in) in order to best meet the needs of the client. When it comes to selecting a theory for trauma work, the client should always be the guiding beacon in clinical decision making.

Professional Goal 3: Engaging in Advocacy and Prevention

A hallmark characteristic of trauma is a person's profound sense of disempowerment within the situation. For clients, this disempowerment occurs during and, at times, after the trauma event, and a similar sensation of helplessness can occur in others indirectly exposed to the trauma, thus increasing their risk for vicarious traumatization. For clients, loved ones, and clinicians alike, a powerful countermeasure to feelings of disempowerment is the action of advocacy. **Advocacy** is another competency area for trauma specialists, as it reflects the professional obligation to promote positive, systemic change. The aim of advocacy is to be a voice for those who have been hurt or marginalized by trauma, and advocacy often involves psychoeducation to individuals, groups, institutions, and the greater society (Sackett & Jenkins, 2015). The benefits of advocacy for our clients and the broader populations are self-evident, but advocacy efforts also function as an empowering and rewarding activity for trauma clinicians by offering an additional avenue in which clinicians can experience fulfillment in knowing they are making a difference.

On several occasions while treating the numerous abuse victims that continued to cross the threshold of my office, I felt my work was similar to shoveling snow while it was still snowing. However, as I began to expand my influence beyond my clinical practice and utilize my understanding of trauma to assist community groups by offering parenting classes and mentoring programs that aimed to increase awareness and prevention of childhood trauma, I felt as though I was contributing in a small way to stop the snow from falling in the first place. For me, I have discovered that the more energy I extend towards advocacy efforts, the less fatigued I feel in my trauma work practice and the more preventative change I can see.

Advocacy can occur at both the micro and macro levels. Micro levels of advocacy include helping individuals, couples, and families by connecting them with resources, writing letters on their behalf, making court appearances, mentoring youth, and participating in other activities that address individual needs. On a macro level, advocacy includes raising awareness, lobbying for policy change, developing programs, and providing trauma-informed trainings not only for mental health professionals but also for other groups, such as religious entities and business corporations. Recently, I had the privilege of conducting compassion fatigue workshops for an animal rescue organization. I was reminded that many other helping occupations experience high levels of direct and indirect trauma exposure, often without education on the risks of vicarious trauma. This realization coupled with the wonderful gratitude for the training from the employees inspired me to look for other opportunities to serve.

As an advocate, the clinician aims to promote systemic changes that foster trauma-informed practices and accommodate for trauma considerations, and these advocacy efforts are often accompanied by attention to prevention as well. In the trauma field, **prevention** work seeks to mitigate, reduce, or eliminate the occurrence or impact of trauma. The impact of trauma is a public health issue, and advocacy as well as prevention work should be a part of every clinician's professional identity (Goodman, Morgan, Hodgson, & Caldwell, 2017). According to a recent teleconference conducted by Dr. Schuchat from the Centers for Disease Control, the prevention of adverse childhood events (ACEs) could drastically impact Americans' health by potentially averting 1.9 million cases of coronary heart disease, 2.5 million cases of obesity, 21 million cases of depression, and 1.5 million students from dropping out of school (CDC, 2019b). Dr. Schuchat also listed six prevention strategies, which include:

(1) Intervening to lessen harms of ACEs with treatment, services, and support
(2) Connecting youth with caring adults and activities through mentoring and other after-school programs
(3) Improving youth and parent skills, such as increased positive communication and problem-solving habits, in order to manage stress and everyday challenges
(4) Providing high-quality, affordable child care and early education to bolster positive patterns developed during early childhood
(5) Promoting social norms that protect against violence and adversity
(6) Strengthening families' economic stability to reduce family stress and conflict

The treatment and prevention of trauma should no longer be viewed through a narrow, individualistic lens. Macro level issues, such as intergenerational poverty, discrimination, and racism, play a significant role in the cyclical nature and potential mitigation of many traumatic events. As clinicians, we must expand our understanding of the impact of trauma on the larger community and advocate for systemic change (Coddington, 2017). Cultural competency and promotion of human rights go hand in hand with trauma-informed care. Participation in advocacy and prevention work may not stop all traumatic events from occurring, but these efforts can make a significant difference in the health and well-being of many individuals and communities, including opportunities of empowerment for the clinician. Undoubtedly, advocacy and prevention is a standard for best practice in trauma work, and beginning trauma clinicians must consider specific ways in which they aim to integrate this aspect into their practice.

Conclusion

Professional development is an ongoing process across a career, not a destination at which one finally arrives. As clinicians, we are ever-growing, ever-developing, and ever-changing. This perpetual growth means that we will always have professional goals before us and will always seek to challenge and enrich ourselves for our clients. As a beginning trauma clinician, the next step in your journey likely involves assessing and enhancing your competency in trauma work, developing your trauma-specific skills within a theoretical context, and integrating advocacy and prevention efforts into your practice.

Recently, after meeting at a conference, a colleague and I began to discuss the rewards and challenges of serving as trauma specialists. We shared our professional experiences and reflections, and by the end of our talk, we landed on a profound theme regarding our work: generosity. Among all of the truly remarkable attributes of trauma clinicians, including courage, passion, commitment, and empathy, a posture of generosity seemed to be the core quality and value that carried us through as professionals. Generosity finds its way into our sessions when we choose to engage in a therapeutic relationship fraught with challenges; generosity rises up when we willingly share our knowledge of trauma and its impacts with others; and generosity keeps us going even when we know the needs are tremendous. As trauma clinicians, we are known, most definitively, by our willingness to generously share our gifts, talents, resources, time, compassion, and knowledge with those who need it most. When we enter our sessions open-handed, ready to receive from our clients and ready to give respect, attunement, and care, we set the table for healing and recovery. On this unending journey of growth, professional development will always call us to reach higher, and a posture of generosity will always hearten us to go deeper. As you move forward as a trauma clinician, we send you off with the encouragement to develop your gifts and then to give them away to the world.

KEYWORD ASSESSMENT

Write definitions in your own words, describe the concept's role in trauma work, list any questions, or make notes of important aspects that you want to remember.

Professional Competencies

Competency in Scientific Knowledge about Trauma

Competency in Psychosocial Trauma-Focused Assessment

Competency in Trauma-Focused Psychosocial Intervention

Competency in Trauma-Informed Professionalism

Competency in Trauma-Informed Relational and Systems Issues

Theory-Based Skills

Advocacy

Prevention

EXPERIENTIAL ACTIVITIES: INTERACTING WITH THE CHAPTER CONTENT

Expand Self-Awareness

1) Consider the idea of generosity in trauma work. Trace each of your hands on a piece of paper and lay the papers side by side so that you can see one hand next to the other. Reflect on the image of being "open-handed" in trauma work and, inside one hand, draw or list the therapeutic qualities you hope to generously give to your clients. On the other hand, draw or list the intangible experiences, positive impacts, or internal rewards that you hope to receive or create as a result of your work with clients.

Expand Knowledge

2) Carefully review and consider the specific professional competencies identified for trauma clinicians in the New Haven Competencies, which can be found here:

Cook, Newman et al. (2014). A consensus statement on trauma mental health: The New Haven competency conference process and major findings. *Psychological Trauma: Theory, Research, Practice, and Policy, 6*(4), 300–307. doi:10.1037/a0036747

Expand Skills

3) Create an advocacy or prevention plan that you can integrate into your professional work. Identify the population and problem that your plan specifically addresses.

SUPERVISORY DISCUSSION: SHARING PERSONAL INSIGHTS AND IDENTIFYING AREAS FOR GROWTH

1) Describe three insights that you gained from the "open hand" drawing activity.

2) In your review of the New Haven Competencies, identify: 1) the specific competencies that you believe you have adequately mastered and why, 2) the specific competencies that you need continued growth and development in, and 3) the specific competencies which you feel unsure or have questions about. Invite your supervisor to provide you with feedback on your competencies as well.

3) Describe a professional plan (perhaps with a timeline) that outlines your specific goals for theory-based skill development in trauma work.

4) The cover of this text depicts a lantern, which metaphorically reflects many of the powerful attributes of the trauma clinician. The lantern's flame is protected from the outside elements so that it cannot be easily blown out, and its fire is fueled from an internal resource. Serving as a companion for the traveler journeying through dark places, the lantern's light illuminates each step of the way. Share your final reflections, thoughts, and feelings about your journey as a trauma clinician. What have you gained, how have you changed, and where are you going next? How do you hope to share your light with the world?

APPENDICES

Trauma-Related Assessments

Please check the qualifications needed to administer these tools as well as cost and permissions needed for use.

Title	Assessment Focus	Population
Adult Attachment Interview (AAI) Kaplan & Main, 1985	Attachment style	Adult
Adult Attachment Scale (AAS) Hazen & Shaver, 1987	Attachment Style	Adult
Alcohol Use Disorders Identification Test (AUDIT) Saunders et al., 1993	Alcohol consumption and behaviors	Adult
Beck Anxiety Index (BAI) Beck & Steer, 1993	Anxiety symptom severity	Ages 17– adult
Beck Depression Inventory (BDI-II) Beck et al., 1996	Depressive symptom severity	Ages 13– adult
Child PTSD Symptom Scale (CPSS) Foa, Johnson, Feeny, & Treadwell, 2001	Traumatic stress symptoms	Children
Clinician-Administered PTSD Scale (CAPS-5) Weathers, Blake et al., 2013	Diagnostic for PTSD based on *DSM-5*	Adult (child version available)
Columbia–Suicide Severity Rating Scale (C-SSRS) Posner et al., 2008	Suicidal ideation and risk	Adolescents and adults
Connor Davidson Resilience Scale (CD-RISC) Connor & Davidson, 2003	Ego resiliency	Ages 10– adult
Ego-Resiliency Scale (ER89) Block & Kremen, 1996	Ego resiliency	Adolescents and adults
GAD- 7 Generalized Anxiety Disorder (Anxiety) Spitzer et al., 2006	Anxiety	Adolescents and adults
Impact of Events Scale Revised (IES-R) Weiss & Marmar, 1996	Subjective distress caused by traumatic events	Adults
Inventory of Complicated Grief (ICG) Prigerson et al., 1995	Complicated grief	Adults
Life Events Checklist for *DSM-5* (LEC-5) Weathers, Litz et al., 2013	Traumatic events history (often used in conjunction with CAPS)	Adults
Posttraumatic Cognitions Inventory (PTCI) Foa, Ehlers, Clark, Tolin, & Orsillo, 1999	Trauma-related thoughts and beliefs	Adults

Title	Assessment Focus	Population
Posttraumatic Growth Inventory Tedeschi & Calhoun, 1996	Posttraumatic growth	Adults
Posttraumatic Growth Inventory–Short Form (PTGI-SF) Cann et al., 2010	Posttraumatic growth, abbreviated scale	Adults
Posttraumatic Symptom Inventory for Children (PT-SIC) Eisen, 1997	Traumatic stress symptoms	Children 4–8
PTSD Checklist for *DSM-5* (PCL-5) Weathers, Litz et al., 2013	Provisionally diagnostic for PTSD	Adults
Session Rating Scale Johnson, Miller, & Duncan, 2000	Therapeutic alliance between client and therapist	Adolescents and adults
Trauma History Questionnaire (THQ) Green, 1996	Traumatic events history	Adults
Trauma Symptom Checklist–40 (TSC–40) Elliot & Briere, 1992	Traumatic stress symptoms	Adults
Trauma Symptom Checklist for Children (TSCC) Briere, 1996; Briere et al., 2001	Traumatic stress symptoms	Children 8–16
Trauma Symptom Checklist for Young Children (TSCYC) Briere, 1996; Briere et al., 2001	Traumatic stress symptoms	Children 3–12
Traumatic Grief Inventory, Self-Report Version (TGI-SR) Boelen & Smid, 2017	Persistent complex bereavement and prolonged grief	Adults
Witnessing of Disenfranchised Grief Scale (WDG) St. Claire, 2013	Disenfranchised grief	Adults
World Assumptions Scale (WAS) Janoff-Bulman, 1989	Core beliefs	Adolescents and adults

Professional Organizations for Creative Modalities and Approaches

Modality	Parent Organization	Website	Specialized Certification
Play Therapy	Association for Play Therapy	www.a4pt.org	Registered Play Therapist (RPT), School Based-Registered Play Therapist (SB-RPT) Registered Play Therapist-Supervisor (RPT-S)
Sand Tray	Association for Play Therapy, World Association for Sand Therapy Professionals	www.a4pt.org www.worldsand therapy.org	None specific for sandtray but often overlaps with play therapy certification
Art Therapy	American Art Therapy Association	www.arttherapy.org	Registered Art Therapist (ATR), Board Certified Art Therapist (ATR-BC), Art Therapy Certified Supervisor (ATCS)
Animal Assisted Therapy	Human-Animal Interaction, Division 17 of the American Psychological Association; Animal Assisted Intervention International	www.apa-hai.org www.aai-int.org	None identified
Dance/Movement Therapy	American Dance Therapy Association	www.adta.org	Registered Dance/ Movement Therapist (R-DMT), Board Certified Dance/ Movement Therapist (BC-DMT)
Drama Therapy	North American Drama Therapy Association	www.nadta.org	Registered Drama Therapist (RDT)
Adventure Therapy	Association of Experiential Education	www.aee.org	Accreditation for Organizations: Adventure & Outdoor Behavioral Healthcare Programs
Yoga Therapy	International Association of Yoga Therapists	www.iayt.org	Certified Yoga Therapist (C-IAYT)

Modality	Parent Organization	Website	Specialized Certification
Music Therapy	American Music Therapy Association	www.musictherapy.org	Music Therapist—Board Certified (MT-BC)
Expressive Writing and Poetry	International Federation for Biblio/Poetry Therapy, National Association for Poetry Therapy	www.ifbpt.org www.poetrytherapy.org	Certified Applied Poetry Facilitator (CAPF), Certified Poetry Therapist (CPT), Registered Poetry Therapist (PTR)
Professional Organizations That Provide Education and Training in Various Types of Creative Therapy Modalities	Association for Creativity in Counseling (Division of American Counseling Association), Society for the Psychology of Aesthetics, Creativity, & the Arts (Division 10 of the American Psychological Association), Expressive Therapies Summit	www.creativecounselor. org www.div10.org www.summit. expressivemedia.org	

References

Adams, K. M. (1999). Sexual harassment as cycles of trauma reenactment and sexual compulsivity. *Sexual Addiction & Compulsivity: The Journal of Treatment and Prevention, 6*, 177–193. doi:10.1080/10720169908400191

Ainsworth, M. D. S., Blehar, M. C., Waters, E., & Wall, S. (1978). *Patterns of attachment: A psychological study of the strange situation.* Hillsdale, NJ: Erlbaum.

Alford, C. F. (2015). Subjectivity and the intergenerational transmission of historical trauma: Holocaust survivors and their children. *Subjectivity, 8*, 261–282. doi:10.1057/sub.2015.10

American Psychiatric Association. (1980). *Diagnostic and statistical manual of mental disorders* (3rd ed.). Washington, DC: Author.

American Psychiatric Association. (2013). *Diagnostic and statistical manual of mental disorders* (5th ed.). Washington, DC: Author.

American Psychological Association Presidential Task Force on Evidence-Based Practice. (2006). Evidence-based practice in psychology. *American Psychologist, 61*(4), 271–285. doi:10.1037/0003-066X.61.4.271

Anderson, J. P., Papazoglou, K., & Collins, P. (2018). Association of authoritarianism, compassion fatigue, and compassion satisfaction among police officers in North American: An exploration. *International Journal of Criminal Justice Sciences, 13*, 405–419. doi:110.5281/zenodo.2657663

Armstrong, C. (2015). *The therapeutic "aha!": 10 strategies for getting your clients unstuck.* New York, NY: Norton.

Arnold, D., Calhoun, L., Tedeschi, R., & Cann, A. (2005). Vicarious posttraumatic growth in psychotherapy. *Journal of Humanistic Psychology, 45*, 239–263. doi:10.1177/0022167805274729

Axline, V. (1947). *Play therapy.* New York, NY: Ballantine.

Badenoch, B. (2008). *Being a brain-wise therapist: A practical guide to interpersonal neurobiology.* New York, NY: Norton.

Badger, K., Royse, D., & Craig, C. (2008). Hospital social workers and indirect trauma exposure: An exploratory study of contributing factors. *Health & Social Work, 33*, 63–71. doi:10.1093/hsw/33.1.63

Baker, F. A., Metcalf, O., Varker, T., & O'Donnell, M. (2017). A systematic review of the efficacy of creative arts therapies in the treatment of adults with PTSD. *Psychological Trauma: Theory, Research, Practice, and Policy, 10*, 643–651. doi:10.1073/tra0000353

Balboa, M., Cavallo, F., & Fernandez, I. (2019). Integrating EMDR in psychotherapy. *Journal of Psychotherapy Integration, 29*, 23–31. doi:10.1037/int0000136

Bandura, A. (1982). Self-efficacy mechanism in human agency. *American Psychologist, 37*, 122–147. doi:10.1037/0003-66X.37.2.122

Baranowsky, A. B., Gentry, J. E., & Schultz, D. F. (2005). *Trauma practice: Tools for stabilization and recovery.* Toronto: Hogrefe & Huber.

Barfield, S., Dobson, C., Gaskill, R., & Perry, B. (2012). Neurosequential model of therapeutics in a therapeutic preschool: Implications for work with children with complex neuropsychiatric problems. *International Journal of Play Therapy, 21*(1), 30–44. doi:10.1037/a0025955

Bass, E., & Davis, L. (2008). *The courage to heal: A guide for women survivors of childhood sexual abuse.* New York, NY: Harper Collins.

Bayne, H. B., & Hays, D. G. (2017). Examining conditions for empathy in counseling: An exploratory model. *Journal of Humanistic Counseling, 56*(1), 32–52. doi:10.1002/johc.12043

Beck, A. T., & Steer, R. A. (1993). *Beck anxiety inventory manual*. San Antonio, TX: Psychological Corporation.

Beck, A. T., Steer, R. A., & Brown, G. K. (1996). *Manual for the beck depression inventory-II*. San Antonio, TX: Psychological Corporation.

Beeney, J. E., Wright, A. G. C., Stepp, S. D., Hallquist, M. N., Lazarus, S. A., Beeney, J. R. S., . . . Pilkonis, P. A. (2017). Disorganized attachment and personality functioning in adults: A latent class analysis. *Personality Disorders: Theory, Research, and Treatment, 8*(3), 206–216. doi:10.1037/per0000184

Bell, H. (2003). Strengths and secondary trauma in family violence work. *Social Work, 48*(4), 513–522.

Benito, K. G., & Walther, M. (2015). Therapeutic process during exposure: Habituation model. *Journal of Obsessive-Compulsive and Related Disorders, 6*, 147–157. doi:10.1016/j.jocrd.2015.01.006

Bilgi, M. M., Taspinar, S., Aksoy, B., Oguz, K., Coburn, K., & Gonul, A. S. (2017). The relationship between childhood trauma, emotion recognition, and irritability in schizophrenia patients. *Psychiatry Research, 251*, 90–96. doi:10.1016/j.psychres.2017.01.091

Bingaman, K. A. (2013). The promise of neuroplasticity. *Pastoral Psychology, 62*, 549–560. doi:10.1007/s11089-013-0513-0

Black, T. G. (2006). Teaching without traumatizing: Principles of trauma treatment in the training of graduate counselors. *Traumatology, 12*, 266–271. doi:10.1177/15347656062978216

Booth, R. W. et al. (2019). A relationship between weak attentional control and cognitive distortions, explained by negative affect. *PLoS One, 14*, 1–12. doi:10.1371/journal.pone.0215399

Boudoukha, A. H., Ouagazzal, O., & Goutaudier, N. (2017). When traumatic event exposure characteristics matter: Impact of traumatic event exposure characteristics on posttraumatic and dissociative symptoms. *Psychological Trauma: Theory, Research, Practice, and Policy, 9*(5), 561–566. doi:10.1037/tra0000243

Bowen, M. (1978). *Family therapy in clinical practice*. New York, NY: Jason Aronson.

Bowlby, J. (1969). *Attachment and loss. Vol 1: Attachment*. New York, NY: Basic Books.

Bowlby, J. (1973). *Attachment and loss. Vol. 2: Separation and anxiety*. New York, NY: Basic Books.

Bowlby, J. (1988). *A secure base*. New York, NY: Basic Books.

Bradley, N., Whisenhunt, J., Adamson, N., & Kress, V. E. (2013). Creative approaches for promoting counselor self-care. *Journal of Creativity in Mental Health, 8*, 456–469. doi:10.1080/15401383.2013.844656

Brave Heart, M. Y. H. (2003). The historical trauma response among natives and its relationship with substance abuse: A Lakota illustration. *Journal of Psychoactive Drugs, 35*, 7–13. Retrieved from https://search-proquest-com.ezproxy.regent.edu/docview/208011932?pq-origsite=summon

Bremner, J. D. (2006). Traumatic stress and the brain. *Dialogues in Clinical Neuroscience, 8*, 445–461. Retrieved from www.ncbi.nlm.nih.gov/pmc/articles/PMC3181836/

Brewin, C. R., Cloitre, M., Hyland, P., Shevlin, M., Maercker, Bryant, R. A., . . . Reed, G. M. (2017). A review of current evidence regarding the ICD-11 proposals for diagnosing PTSD and complex PTSD. *Clinical Psychology Review, 58*, 1–15. doi:10.1016/j.cpr.2017.09001

Briere, J., & Lanktree, C. (2013). *Integrative treatment of complex trauma for adolescents treatment guide* (2nd ed.). Retrieved from http://keck.usc.edu/adolescent-trauma-training-center/wp-content/uploads/sites/169/2016/06/ITCT-A-TreatmentGuide-2ndEdition-rev20131106.pdf

Briere, J. N., Hodges, M., & Godbout, N. (2010). Traumatic stress, affect dysregulation, and dysfunctional avoidance: A structural equation model. *Journal of Traumatic Stress, 23*, 767–774. doi:10.1002/jys.20578

Briere, J. N., & Scott, C. (2015). *Principles of trauma therapy* (2nd ed.). Los Angeles: Sage.

Brown, D. W., Anda, R. F., Tiemeier, H., Felitti, V. J., Edwards, V. J., Croft, J. B., & Giles, W. H. (2009). Adverse childhood experiences and the risk of premature mortality. *American Journal of Preventive Medicine, 37*, 389–396. doi:10.1016/j.amepre.2009.06.021

Browning, B. R., McDermott, R. C., & Scaffa, M. E. (2019). Transcendent characteristics as predictors of counselor professional quality of life. *Journal of Mental Health Counseling, 41*, 51–64. doi:10.17744/mehc.41.1.05

Buck, J. N., & Hammer, E. F. (1969). *Advances in house-tree-person techniques: Variations and applications*. Los Angeles: Western Psychological Services.

Burke, N. N., Finn, D. P., McGuire, B. E., & Roche, M. (2017). Psychological stress in early life as a predisposing factor for the development of chronic pain: Clinical and preclinical evidence and neurobiological mechanisms. *Journal of Neuroscience Research, 95*, 1257–1270. doi:10.1002/jnr.23802

Burnett, H. J. (2017). Revisiting the compassion fatigue, burnout, compassion satisfaction, and resilience connection among CISM responders. *Sage Open, 73*. doi:10.1177/2158244017730857

Cairns, K., & Stanway, C. (2004). *Learning the child: Helping looked after children learn, a good guide for social workers, carers, and teachers*. BAAF Adoption & Fostering, The Russell Press (YU), Nottingham.

Caselli, G. et al. (2018). The metacognitions about gambling questionnaire: Development and psychometric properties. *Psychiatry Research, 261*, 367–374. doi:10.1016/j.psychres.2018.01.018

Centers for Disease Control and Prevention. (2015). *Injury prevention and control.* Retrieved from www.cdc.gov/injury/wisqars/overview/key_data.html

Centers for Disease Control and Prevention. (2019a). *Preventing sexual violence.* Retrieved from www.cdc.gov/violenceprevention/sexualviolence/fastfact.html

Centers for Disease Control and Prevention. (2019b). *Transcript of CDC telebriefing: At least 5 of the top 10 leading causes of death are associated with adverse childhood events (ACEs).* Retrieved from www.cdc.gov/media/releases/2019/t1105-aces.html

Centers for Disease Control and Prevention. (2020). *Mortality in the United States, 2018.* Retrieved from www.cdc.gov/nchs/products/databriefs/db355.htm

Chard, K. M., Ricksecker, E. G., Healy, E. T., Karlin, B. E., & Resick, P. A. (2012). Dissemination and experience with cognitive processing therapy. *Journal of Rehabilitation Research and Development, 49,* 667–678.

Chen, J. A., Fortney, J. C., Bergman, H. E., Browne, K. C., Grubbs, K. M., Hudson, T. J., & Raue, P. J. (2019). Therapeutic alliance across trauma-focused and non-trauma-focused psychotherapies among veterans with PTSD. *Psychological Services.* doi:10.1037/ser0000329

Christiansen, D. M., & Elklit, A. (2008). Risk factors predict post-traumatic stress disorder differently in men and women. *Annals of General Psychiatry, 7*(24), 1–12. doi:10.1186/1744-859X-7-24

Christon, L. M., McLeod, B. D., & Jensen-Doss, A. (2015). Evidence-based assessment meets evidence-based treatment: An approach to science informed case conceptualization. *Cognitive and Behavioral Practice, 22,* 36–48.

Cieslak, R., Shoji, K., Douglas, A., Melville, E., Luszczynska, A., & Benight, C. C. (2014). A meta-analysis of the relationship between job burnout and secondary traumatic stress among workers with indirect exposure to trauma. *Psychological Services, 11,* 75–86. doi:10.1037/a0033798

Clabough, E. (2019). *Second nature.* Boulder, CO: Sounds True.

Cloitre, M., Stolbach, B. C., Herman, J. L., van der Kolk, B., Pynoos, R., Wang, J., & Petkova, E. (2009). A developmental approach to complex PTSD: Childhood and adult cumulative trauma as predictors of symptom complexity. *Journal of Traumatic Stress, 22,* 399–408. doi:10.1002/jts.20444

Cloud, H., & Townsend, J. (2017). *Boundaries: When to say yes and how to say no to take control of your life.* Grand Rapids, MI: Zondervan.

Coddington, K. (2017). Contagious trauma: Reframing the spatial mobility of trauma within advocacy work. *Emotion, Space, and Society, 24,* 66–73. doi:10.1016/j.emospa.2016.02.002

Cohen, J. A., Mannarino, A. P., & Deblinger, E. (2006). *Treating trauma and traumatic grief in children and adolescents.* New York, NY: Guilford Press.

Cole, E. R. (2009). Intersectionality and research in psychology. *American Psychology, 64,* 170–180. doi:10.1037/a0014564

Cole, P. M., Martin, S. E., & Dennis, T. A. (2004). Emotion regulation as a scientific construct: Methodological challenges and directions for child development research. *Child Development, 75,* 317–333. Retrieved from www.jstor.org/stable/3696638

Collins, S., & Arthur, N. (2010). Culture-infused counselling: A model for developing multicultural competence. *Counselling Psychology Quarterly, 23*(2), 217–233. doi:10.1080/09515071003798212

Compton, L. (2013). *Compassion fatigue and compassion satisfaction in critical incident stress management (CISM) providers* (Dissertation). Retrieved from http://gradworks.umi.com/35/77/3577317.html

Cook, J. M., Dinnen, S., Simiola, V., Thompson, R., & Schnurr, P. P. (2014). VA residential provider perceptions of dissuading factors to the use of two evidence-based PTSD treatments. *Professional Psychology: Research and Practice, 45*(2), 136–142. doi:10.1037/a0036183

Cook, J. M., Newman, E., & The New Haven Competency Group. (2014). A consensus statement on trauma mental health: The New Haven competency conference process and major findings. *Psychological Trauma: Theory, Research, Practice, and Policy, 6*(4), 300–307. doi:10.1037/a0036747

Copeland, W. E., Shanahan, L., Hinesely, J., Chan, R. F., Aberg, K. A., Fairbank, J. A., . . . Costello, J. (2018). Association of childhood trauma exposure with adult psychiatric disorders and functional outcomes. *JAMA Network Open, 7,* 1/11–11/11. doi:10.1001/jamanetworkopen.2018.4493

Corcoran, K. J. (1982). An exploratory investigation into self-other differentiation: Empirical evidence for a monistic perspective on empathy. *Psychotherapy Theory, Research, and Practice, 19,* 63–68. doi:10.1037/h0088418

Corcoran, K. J. (1989). Interpersonal stress and burnout: Unraveling the role of empathy. *Journal of Social Behavior, 4,* 141–144.

Corey, G. (2017). *Theory and practice of counseling and psychotherapy* (10th ed.). Boston, MA: Cengage Learning.

Corey, M. S., & Corey, G. (2003). *Becoming a helper* (4th ed.). Belmont, CA: Brooks, Cole.

Courtois, C. A., & Ford, J. (2016). *Treatment of complex trauma: A sequenced, relationship-based approach.* New York, NY: Guilford Press.

Courtois, C. A., & Gold, S. N. (2009). The need for inclusion of psychological trauma in the professional curriculum: A call to action. *Psychological Trauma: Theory, Research, Practice, and Policy, 1,* 3–23. doi:10.1037/a0015224

Craske, M. G., Treanor, M., Conway, C., Zbozinek, T., & Verviliet, B. (2014). Maximizing exposure therapy: An inhibitory learning approach. *Behavior Research Therapy, 58,* 1–23. doi:10.1016/j.brat.2014.04.006

Crombie, K. M., Brellenthin, A. G., Hillard, C. J., & Koltyn, K. F. (2018). Psychobiological responses to aerobic exercise in individuals with posttraumatic stress disorder. *Journal of Traumatic Stress, 31,* 134–145. doi:10.1002/jts.22253

Crumpton, S. M. (2017). Trigger warnings, covenants of presence, and more: Cultivating safe space for theological discussions about sexual trauma. *Teach Theological Religion, 20,* 137–147. doi:10.1111/teth.12376

Cureton, J. L., & Clemens, E. V. (2015). Affective constellations for countertransference awareness following a client's suicide attempt. *Journal of Counseling and Development, 93*(3), 352–360. doi:10.1002/jcad.12033

Davis, D. D. (2008). *Terminating therapy: A professional guide to ending on a positive note.* Hoboken, NY: John Wiley & Sons, Inc.

Day, W., Lawson, G., & Burge, P. (2017). Clinicians experiences of shared trauma after the shootings at Virginia Tech. *Journal of Counseling & Development, 95,* 269–278. doi:10.1002/jcad.12141

DeGroot, J. M., & Vik, T. A. (2017). Disenfranchised grief following a traumatic birth. *Journal of Loss and Trauma, 4,* 346–356. doi:10.1080/15325024.2017.1284519

Desmond, K. J., Kindsvatter, A., Stahl, S., & Smith, H. (2015). Creating space for connection: A column for creative practice. *Journal of Creativity in Mental Health, 10,* 439–455. doi:10.1080/15401383.2015.1040938

Doka, K. J. (1989). *Disenfranchised grief: Recognizing hidden sorry.* Lexington, MA: Lexington Books.

Doka, K. J. (2002). *Disenfranchised grief: New directions, challenges, and strategies for practice* (pp. 323–336). Champaign, IL: Research Press.

Drožđek, B. (2010). How do we salve our wounds? Intercultural perspectives on individual and collective strategies of making peace with own past. *Traumatology, 16*(4), 5–16. doi:10.1177/1534765610362800

Dubi, M., Powell, P., & Gentry, J. E. (2017). *Trauma, PTSD, grief, & loss: The 10 core competencies for evidence-based treatment.* Eau Claire, WI: PESI.

Dwyer, S. (2003). Reconciliation for realists. In C. A. L. Prager & T. Govier (Eds.), *Dilemmas of reconciliation: Cases and concepts* (pp. 91–110). Warterloo, ON: Wilfrid Laurier University Press.

Elwood, L. S., Mott, J., Lohr, J. M., & Galovski, T. E. (2011). Secondary trauma symptoms in clinicians: A critical review of the construct, specificity, and implications for trauma-focused treatment. *Clinical Psychology Review, 31,* 25–36. doi:10.1016/j.cpr.2010.09.004

Espeleta, H. C., Brett, E. I., Ridings, L. E., Leavens, E. L. S., & Mullins, L. L. (2018). Childhood adversity and adult health-risk behaviors: Examining the role of emotion dysregulation and urgency. *Child Abuse & Neglect, 82,* 92–101.

Faddis, T. J., & Cobb, K. F. (2016). Family therapy techniques in residential settings: Family sculptures and reflecting teams. *Contemporary Family Therapy, 38*(1), 43–51. doi:10.1007/s10591-015-9373-3

Farina, B., Liotti, M., & Imperatori, C. (2019). The role of attachment trauma and disintegrative pathogenic processes in the traumatic-dissociative dimension. *Frontiers in Psychology, 10,* 1–18. doi:10.3389/fpsyg.2019.00933

Fazakas-DeHoog, L. L., Rnic, K., & Dozois, D. J. A. (2017). A cognitive distortions and deficits model of suicide prevention. *Europe's Journal of Psychology, 13,* 178–193. doi:10.5964/ejop.v13i2.1238

Fazel, M., Wheeler, J., & Danesh, J. (2005). Prevalence of serious mental disorder in 7000 refugees settled in Western countries: A systemic review. *Lancet, 365,* 1309–1314. doi:10.1016/S0140-6736(05)61027-6

Fedele, K. M. (2018). *An investigation of factors impacting vicarious traumatization and vicarious posttraumatic growth in crisis workers: Vicarious exposure to trauma, feminist beliefs, and feminist labeling* (Dissertation). Retrieved from https://search-proquest-com.ezproxy.regent.edu/docview/2128014328?pq-origsite=summon

Felitti, V. J., Anda, R. F., Nordenberg, D., Williamson, D. F., Spitz, A. M., Edwards, V., . . . Marks, J. S. (1998). Relationship of childhood abuse and household dysfunction to many of the leading causes of death in adults: The adverse childhood experiences (ACE) study. *American Journal of Preventive Medicine, 14,* 245–258.

Feng, X., Hooper, E. G., & Jia, R. (2017). From compliance to self-regulation: Development during early childhood. *Social Development, 26,* 981–995. doi:10.1111/sode.12245

Fewster-Thuente, L., & Batteson, T. J. (2018). Kolb's experiential learning theory as a theoretical underpinning for interprofessional education. *Journal of Allied Health, 47,* 3–8.

Figley, C. (2002). *Treating compassion fatigue.* New York, NY: Routledge.

Finlay, L. (2015). Sensing and making sense: Embodying metaphor in relational-centered psychotherapy. *The Humanistic Psychologist, 43*, 338–353. doi:10.1080/08873267.2014.993070

Fisher, J. (2017). *Healing the fragmented selves of trauma survivors: Overcoming internal self-alienation*. New York, NY: Routledge.

Foa, E. B., Keane, T. M., Friedman, M. J., & Cohen, J. A. (2009). *Effective treatments for PTSD: Practical guidelines from the international society for traumatic stress studies* (2nd ed.). New York, NY: Guilford Press.

Foa, E. B., & Rothbaum, B. O. (1998). *Treating the trauma of rape: Cognitive behavioral therapy for PTSD*. New York, NY: Guilford Press.

Forbes, D., Creamer, M., Bisson, J. L., Cohen, J. A., Crow, B. E., Foa, E. B., & Ursano, R. J. (2010). A guide to guidelines for the treatment of PTSD and related conditions. *Journal of Traumatic Stress, 23*, 537–552. doi:10.1002/jts.20565

Fragkaky, I., Thomaes, K., & Sijbrandij, M. (2016). Posttraumatic stress disorder under ongoing threat: A review of neurobiological and neuroendocrine findings. *European Journal of Psychotraumatology, 7*, 1–13. doi:10.3402/ejpt.v7.31593

Frankl, V. E., & Boyne, J. (2017). *Man's search for meaning*. Boston, MA: Beacon Press.

Freud, A. (1946). *The psycho-analytical treatment of children*. New York, NY: International Universities Press.

Freud, S. (1914). Remembering, repeating, and working through. In J. Strachey (Ed.), *The standard edition of the complete works of Sigmund Freud* (Vol. 12, pp. 147–156). London: Hogarth Press.

Frisby, B. N. (2019). The influence of emotional contagion on student perceptions of instructor rapport, emotional support, emotion work, valence, and cognitive learning. *Communication Studies, 70*, 492–506. doi:10.1080/10510974.2019.1622584

Gantt, L., & Tinnin, L. (2009). Support for a neurobiological view of trauma with implications for art therapy. *The Arts in Psychotherapy, 36*, 148–153. doi:10.1016/j.aip.2008.12.005

Gaskill, R. L. (2019). Neuroscience helps play therapists go low so children can aim high. *Play Therapy, 14*(3), 8–10.

Gaskill, R. L., & Perry, B. D. (2012). Child abuse, traumatic experiences, and their impact on the developing brain. In P. Goodyear-Brown (Ed.), *Handbook of child sexual abuse: Identification, assessment, and treatment* (pp. 29–47). Hoboken, NJ: John Wiley & Sons, Inc.

Gaskill, R. L., & Perry, B. D. (2017). A neurosequential therapeutics approach to guide play, play therapy, and activities for children who won't talk. In C. A. Malchiodi & D. A. Crenshaw (Eds.), *What to do when children clam up in psychotherapy: Interventions to facilitate communication* (pp. 38–68). New York, NY: The Guilford Press.

Gawrysiak, M. J., Grassetti, S. N., Greeson, J. M., Shorey, R. C., Pohlig, R., & Baime, M. J. (2017). The many facets of mindfulness and the prediction of change following mindful-based stress reduction (MBSR). *Journal of Clinical Psychology, 74*, 523–535. doi:10.1002/jclp.22521

Gelso, C. J., & Carter, J. A. (1994). Components of the psychotherapy relationship: Their interaction and unfolding during treatment. *Journal of Counseling Psychology, 41*, 296–306. doi:10.1037/0022-0167.41.3.296

Gelso, C. J., & Hayes, J. A. (2002). Management of countertransference. In J. C. Norcross (Ed.), *Psychotherapy relationships that work: Therapist contributions and responsiveness to patients* (pp. 267–284). New York, NY: Oxford University Press.

Gentry, J. E., Baranowsky, A. B., & Dunning, K. (2002). The accelerated recovery program (ARP) for compassion fatigue. In C. R. Figley (Ed.), *Treating compassion fatigue* (pp. 123–138). New York, NY: Routledge.

Gentry, J. E., Baranowsky, A. B., & Rhoton, R. (2017). Trauma competency: An active ingredients approach to treating posttraumatic stress disorder. *Journal of Counseling and Development, 95*(3), 279–287. doi:10.1002/jcad.12142

Geoffrion, S., Morselli, C., & Guay, S. (2016). Rethinking compassion fatigue through the lens of professional identity: The case of child-protection workers. *Trauma, Violence, &Abuse, 17*, 270–283.

Gibbs, J. J., & Goldbach, J. (2015). Religious conflict, sexual identity, and suicidal behaviors among LGBT young adults. *Archives of Suicide Research, 19*, 472–488. doi:10.1080/13811118.2015.1004476

Gingrich, H. D. (2013). *Restoring the shattered self: A Christian counselor's guide to complex trauma*. Downers Grove, IL: InterVarsity Press.

Gingrich, H. D., & Gingrich, F. C. (2017). *Treating trauma in Christian counseling*. Downers Grove, IL: InterVarsity Press.

Goldberg, R. M., & Stephenson, J. B. (2016). Staying with the metaphor: Applying reality therapy's use of metaphors to grief counseling. *Journal of Creativity Mental Health, 11*(1), 105–117. doi:10.1080/15401383.2015.11113396

Goodman, J. M., Morgan, A. A., Hodgson, J. L., & Caldwell, B. E. (2017). From private practice to academia: Integrating social and political advocacy into every MFT identity. *Journal of Martial and Family Therapy, 44*(1), 32–45. doi:10.1111/jmft.12298

Goodman, R. D. (2015). Trauma counseling and interventions: Introduction to the special issue. *Journal of Mental Health Counseling, 37*, 283–294. doi:10.17744/mehc.37.4.01

Goodman, R. D., Versely, C. K., Letiecq, B., & Cleaveland, C. L. (2017). Trauma and resilience among refugee and undocumented immigrant women. *Journal of Counseling and Development, 95*, 309–321. doi:10.1002/jcad.12145

Gostecnik, C., Repik, T., Cvetek, M., & Cvetek, R. (2009). The salvational process in relationships: A view from projective-introjective identification and repetition compulsion. *Journal of Religion and Health, 48*, 496–506. doi:10.1007/s10943-008-9215-9

Gottman, J. M. (1993). A theory of marital dissatisfaction and stability. *Journal of Family Psychology, 7*, 57–75.

Gratz, K. L., & Roemer, L. (2004). Multidimensional assessment of emotional regulation and dysregulation: Development, factor structure, and initial validation of the difficulties in emotional regulation scale. *Journal of Psychopathology and Behavioral Assessment, 26*, 41–54. doi:10.1023/B:JOBA.0000007455.08539.94

Green, J. G., McLaughlin, K. A., Berglund, P. A., Gruber, M. J., Sampson, N. A., Zaslavsky, A. M., & Kessler, R. C. (2010). Childhood adversities and adult psychiatric disorders in the national comorbidity survey replication I: Associations with the first onset of DSM-IV disorders. *Arch General Psychiatry, 67*, 113–123. doi:10.1001/archgnepsychiatry.2009.186

Gregory, R. J. (2013). *Psychological testing: History, principles, and applications* (7th ed.). Wheaton, IL: Pearson.

Haddock, D. B. (2001). *The dissociative identity disorder sourcebook.* New York, NY: McGraw-Hill.

Hambrick, E. P., Brawner, T. W., Perry, B. D., Brandt, K., Hofmeister, C., & Collins, J. O. (2019). Beyond the ACE score: Examining relationships between timing of developmental adversity, relational health, and developmental outcomes in children. *Archives of Psychiatric Nursing, 33*, 238–247. doi:10.1016/j.apnu.2018.11.001

Hancock, L., & Bryant, R. A. (2018). Posttraumatic stress, uncontrollability, and emotional distress tolerance. *Depression and Anxiety, 35*, 1040–1047. doi:10.1002/da.22783

Harlé, K. M., Spadoni, A. D., Norman, S. B., & Simmons, A. N. (2019). Neurocomputational changes in inhibitory control associated with prolonged exposure therapy. *Journal of Traumatic Stress,* 1–11. doi:1002/jts.22461

Hass-Cohen, N., Bokoch, R., Findlay, J. C., & Banford Witting, A. (2018). A four-drawing art therapy trauma and resiliency protocol study. *The Arts in Psychotherapy, 61*, 44–56. doi:10.1016/j.aip/2018.02.003

Hass-Cohen, N., Findlay, C. J., Carr, R., & Vanderlan, J. (2014). Check, change, and/or keep what you need: An art therapy relational neurobiological (ATR-N) trauma intervention. *Art Therapy: Journal of the American Art Therapy Association, 31*, 69–78. doi:10.1080/07421656.2014.903825

Hayuni, G., Hasson-Ohayon, I., Goldzweig, G., Bar Sela, G., & Braun, M. (2019). Between empathy and grief: The mediating effect of compassion fatigue among oncologists. *Psycho-Oncology,* 1–7. doi:10.1002/pon.5227

Hendricks, B., Bradley, L. J., Brogan, W. C. III, & Brogan, C. (2009). Shelly: A case study focusing on ethics and counselor wellness. *The Family Journal: Counseling and Therapy for Couples and Families, 17*(4), 355–359. doi:10.1177/1066480709348034

Hensel, J. M., Ruiz, C., Finney, C., & Dewa, C. S. (2015). Meta-analysis of risk factors for secondary traumatic stress in therapeutic work with trauma victims. *International Society for Traumatic Stress Studies, 28*, 83–91. doi:10.1002/jts.21998

Herman, J. L. (1992a). Complex PTSD: A syndrome in survivors of prolonged and repeated trauma. *Journal of Traumatic Stress, 5*, 377–391. http://doi-org.exproxy.regent.edu/10.1002/jts.2490050305

Herman, J. L. (1992b). *Trauma and recovery.* New York, NY: Basic Books.

Hernandez, P., Gangsei, D., & Engstrom, D. (2007). Vicarious resilience: A new concept in work with those who survive trauma. *Family Process, 46*, 229–241. doi:10.1111/j.1545-5300.2007.00206.x

Hicks, L. M., & Dayton, C. J. (2019). Mindfulness and trauma symptoms predict child abuse potential in risk-exposed, men and women during pregnancy. *Child Abuse & Neglect, 90*, 43–51. doi:10.1016/j.chiabu.2019.01.018

Hinton, D. E., & Lewis-Fernández, R. (2010). Idioms of distress among trauma survivors: Subtypes and clinical utility. *Culture, Medicine, and Psychiatry, 34*, 209–218. doi:10.1007/s11013-010-9175-x

Homeyer, L. E., & Sweeney, D. S. (2017). *Sandtray therapy: A practical manual* (3rd ed.). New York, NY: Routledge.

Hooper, A., Spann, C., Tiyahri, M., & Kimberly, C. (2017). Revisiting the basics: Understanding potential demographic differences with John Gottman's four horsemen and emotional flooding. *The Family Journal: Counseling and Therapy for Couples and Families, 25*, 224–229. doi:10.1177/1066480717710650

Hopper, J. W., Spinazzola, J., Simpson, W. B., & van der Kolk, B. A. (2006). Preliminary evidence of parasympathetic influence of basal heart rate in posttraumatic stress disorder. *Journal of Psychosomatic Research, 60*(1), 83–90. doi:10.1016/j.jpscyhores.2005.06.002

Horowitz, M. J. (2015). Effects of trauma on sense of self. *Journal of Loss and Trauma, 20,* 189–193. doi:10.1080/15325024.2014.897578

Horvath, A. O., Del Re, A. C., Fluckiger, C., & Symonds, D. (2011). Alliance in individual psychotherapy. *Psychotherapy, 48,* 9–16. doi:10.1037/a0022186

Hunter, S. V. (2012). Walking in sacred spaces in the therapeutic bond: Therapist's experiences of compassion satisfaction coupled with the potential for vicarious traumatization. *Family Process, 51*(2), 179–192.

Ivey, A. E., Ivey, M. B., & Zalaquett, C. P. (2014). *Intentional interviewing and counseling: Facilitating client development in a multicultural society* (8th ed.). Pacific Grove, CA: Brooks, Cole.

Janoff-Bulman, R. (1992). *Shattered assumptions: Towards a new psychology of trauma.* New York, NY: Free Press.

Jeffrey, G. (2016). The talking cure of avoidant personality disorder: Remission through earned-secure attachment. *American Journal of Psychotherapy, 70*(3), 233–246. doi:10.1176/appi.psychotherapy.2016.70.3.233

Jongsma, A. E. (2014). *The crisis counseling and traumatic events treatment planner, with DSM-5 updates* (2nd ed.). Hoboken, NJ: John Wiley & Sons, Inc.

Jung, C. G. (1954). The development of personality. In H. Read, M. Fordham, G. Adler, & W. McGuire (Eds.), *The collected works of C. G. Jung, Vol. 17: The development of personality* (pp. 165–186). Princeton, NJ: Princeton University Press.

Kaiser, E., Gillette, C., & Spinazzola, J. (2010). A controlled pilot-outcome study of sensory integration (SI) in the treatment of complex adaptation to traumatic stress. *Journal of Aggression, Maltreatment & Trauma, 19,* 699–720. doi:10.1080/10926771.2010.51562

Kalff, D. M. (1980). *Sandplay: A psychotherapeutic approach to the psyche.* Santa Monica, CA: Sigo Press.

Keck, B. (2018). *Attachment, social support, and disenfranchised grief in adult third culture kids* (Doctoral dissertation). ProQuest Dissertations (Accession No. 13420825).

Keck, B., Compton, L., Schoeneberg, C., & Compton, T. (2017). Trauma recovery: A heroic journey. *Heroism Science, 2,* 1–17.

Kern, E., & Perryman, K. (2016). Leaving it in the sand: Creatively processing military combat trauma as a means for reducing risk of interpersonal violence. *Journal of Creativity in Mental Health, 11*(3–4), 446–457. doi:10.1080/15401383.2016.1172995

Kick, K. A., & McNitt, M. (2016). Trauma, spirituality, and mindfulness: Finding hope. *Social Work & Christianity, 43*(3), 97–108.

Killian, K. D. (2008). Helping till it hurts? A multimethod study of compassion fatigue, burnout, and self-care in clinicians working with trauma survivors. *Traumatology, 14,* 32–44.

Kilpatrick, D. G., Resnick, H. S., Milanak, M. E., Miller, M. W., Keyes, K. M., & Friedman, M. J. (2013). National estimates of exposure to traumatic events and PTSD prevalence using DSM-IV and DSM-5 criteria. *Journal of Traumatic Stress, 26,* 537–547. doi:10.1002/jts.21848

Kisiel, C., Summersett-Ringgold, F., Weil, L. E. G., & McClelland, G. (2017). Understanding strengths in relation to complex trauma and mental health symptoms within child welfare. *Journal of Child and Family Studies, 26,* 437–451. doi:10.1007/s10826-016-0569-4

Klein, M. (1932/1975). *The psychoanalysis of children.* London: Hogarth Press.

Kliem, S., Kroger, C., & Kosfelder, J. (2010). Dialectical behavioral therapy for borderline personality disorder: A meta-analysis using mixed effects modeling. *Journal of Consulting and Clinical Psychology, 78,* 936–951. doi:10.1037/a0021015

Kolb, D. A. (1984). *Experiential learning: Experience as the source of learning and development.* Englewood Cliffs, NJ: Prentice Hall.

Koltz, R. L., Odegard, M. A., Feit, S. S., Provost, K. P., & Smith, T. (2012). Parallel process and isomorphism: A model for decision making in the supervisory triad. *The Family Journal: Counseling Therapy for Couples and Families, 20,* 233–238.

Kopacz, M. S., Lockman, J., Lusk, J., Bryan, C. J., Park, C. L., Sheu, S. C., & Gibson, W. C. (2019). How meaningful is meaning-making? *New Ideas in Psychology, 54,* 76–81. doi:10.1016/j.newideapsych.2019.02.001

Korn, D. L. (2009). EMDR and the treatment of complex PTSD: A review. *Journal of EMDR Practice and Research, 3*(4), 264–278. doi:10.1891/1933-3196.3.4.264

Kosanke, G. C., Puls, B., Feather, J., & Smith, J. (2016). Minimizing intense relational dynamics to enhance safety: A thematic analysis of literature on sandtray work with adult trauma survivors. *British Journal of Psychotherapy, 32*(4), 502–516. doi:10.1111/bjp.12242

Kredlow, M. A., Eichenbaum, H., & Otto, M. W. (2018). Memory creation and modification: Enhancing the treatment of psychological disorders. *American Psychologist, 73*, 269–285. doi:10.1037/amp0000185

Krupnik, V. (2019). Trauma or adversity? *Traumatology, 25*, 256–261. doi:10.1037/trm0000169

Kurtz, S. P., Pagano, M. E., Buttram, M. E., & Ungar, M. (2019). Brief interventions for young adults who use drugs: The moderating effects of resilience and trauma. *Journal of Substance Abuse Treatment, 101*, 18–24. doi:10.1016/j.jsat.2019.03.009

Landreth, G. L. (2012). *Play therapy: The art of the relationship* (3rd ed.). New York, NY: Routledge.

Langberg, D. M. (2003). *Counseling survivors of sexual abuse.* Maitland, FL: Xulon Press.

Lemma, A. (2010). The power of relationship: A study of key working as an intervention with traumatized young people. *Journal of Social Work Practice, 24*(4), 409–427. doi:10.1080/02650533.2010.496965

Lerias, D., & Byrne, M. K. (2003). Vicarious traumatization: Symptoms and predictors. *Stress and Health, 19*, 129–138. doi:10.1002/smi.969

Levine, P. (1997). *Waking the tiger: Healing trauma.* Berkeley, CA: North Atlantic Books.

Levy, M. S. (1998). A helpful way to conceptualize and understand reenactments. *Journal of Psychotherapy Practice and Research, 7*, 227–235.

Lewey, J. H., Smith, C. L., Burcham, B., Saunders, N. L., Elfallal, D., & O'Toole, S. K. (2018). Comparing the effectiveness of EMDR and TF-CBT for children and adolescents: A meta-analysis. *Journal of Child & Adolescent Trauma, 11*, 457–472. doi:10.1007/s40653-018-0212-1

Liddel, B. J., & Jobson, L. (2016). The impact of cultural differences in self-representation on the neural substrates of posttraumatic stress disorder. *European Journal of Psychotraumatology, 7*(1), 1–13. doi:10.3402/ejpt.v7.30464

Lim, B. H., Adams, L. A., & Lily, M. M. (2012). Self-worth as a mediator between attachment and posttraumatic stress in interpersonal trauma. *Journal of Interpersonal Violence, 27*(10), 2039–2061. doi:10.1177/0886260511431440

Lin, Y.-W., & Bratton, S. C. (2015). A meta-analytic review of child-centered play therapy approaches. *Journal of Counseling and Development, 93*(1), 45–58. doi:10.1002/j.1556-6676.2015.00180.x

Linehan, M. M. (1993). *Cognitive-behavioral treatment of borderline personality disorder.* New York, NY: Guilford Press.

Lowenfeld, M. (1979). *The world technique* (2nd ed.). London: Allen Unwin.

Lu, H., Zhou, Y., & Pillay, Y. (2017). Counselor education students' exposure to trauma cases. *International Journal of Advanced Counseling, 39*, 322–332. doi:10.1007/s10447-017-9300-4

Luedke, A. J., Peluso, P. R., Diaz, P., Freund, R., & Baker, A. (2016). Predicting dropout in counseling using affect coding of the therapeutic relationship: An empirical analysis. *Journal of Counseling and Development, 95*, 125–134. doi:10.1002/jcad.12125

MacKay, L. M. (2017). Differentiation of self: Enhancing therapist resilience when working with relational trauma. *Australian and New Zealand Journal of Family Therapy, 38*, 637–656. doi:10.1002/anzf.1276

MacLeod, L. (2012). Making SMART goals smarter. *Physician Executive, 38*, 68–70. Retrieved from http://eres.regent.edu: 2048

Maercker, A., & Horn, A. B. (2013). A socio-interpersonal perspective on PTSD: The case for environments and interpersonal processes. *Clinical Psychology and Psychotherapy, 20*, 465–481. doi:10.1002/cpp.1805

Malchiodi, C. (2003). *Handbook of art therapy.* New York, NY: Guilford Press.

Manning-Jones, S., de Terte, I., & Stephens, C. (2017). The relationship between vicarious posttraumatic growth and secondary traumatic stress among health professionals. *Journal of Loss & Trauma, 22*, 256–270. doi:10.1080/15325024.2017.1284516

Marlowe, J., & Adamson, C. (2011). Trauma teaching: Critically engaging a troublesome term. *Social Work Education, 30*, 623–634.

Mathieu, F. (2018). Running on empty: Compassion fatigue in mental health professionals. *Rehabilitation and Community Care Medicine.* Retrieved from https://www.tendacademy.ca/wp-content/uploads/2018/11/Solutions-article-revised-2018-1.pdf

May, R. R. (1983). *The discovery of being: Writings in existential psychology.* New York, NY: Norton.

McAuliffe, G. (Ed.). (2013). *Culturally alert counseling: A comprehensive introduction* (2nd ed.). Thousand Oaks, CA: Sage.

McCann, I. L., & Pearlman, L. A. (1990). Vicarious traumatization: A framework for understanding the psychological effects of working with victims. *Journal of Traumatic Stress, 3*, 131–149.

McLaughlin, A. A., Keller, S. M., Feeny, N. C., Youngstrom, E. A., & Zoellner, L. A. (2014). Patterns of therapeutic alliance: Rupture-repair episodes in prolonged exposure for posttraumatic stress disorder. *Journal of Consulting and Clinical Psychology, 82*(1), 112–121. doi:10.1037/a0034696

Meany-Walen, K. K., Teeling, S., Cobie-Nuss, A., Eittreium, E., Wilson, S., & Xander, C. (2018). Play therapist's perceptions of wellness and self-care practices. *International Journal of Play Therapy, 27*(3) 176–186. doi:10.1037.pla0000067

Metcalf, O., Varker, T., Forbes, D., Phelps, A., Dell, L., Dibattista, A., Ralph, N., & O'Donnell, M. (2016). Efficacy of fifteen emerging interventions for the treatment of post-traumatic stress disorder: A systemic review. *Journal of Traumatic Stress, 29*(1), 88–92. doi:10.1002/jts.22070

Michalchuk, S., & Martin, S. L. (2019). Vicarious resilience and growth in psychologists who work with trauma survivors. *Professional Psychology: Research and Practice, 50*, 145–154. doi:10.1037/pro0000212

Milan, S., Zona, K., Acker, J., & Turcios-Cotto, V. (2013). Prospective risk factors for adolescent PTSD: Sources of differential exposure and differential vulnerability. *Journal of Abnormal Child Psychology, 41*, 339–353. doi:10.1007/s10802-012-9677-9

Miller, D. (2002). Addictions and trauma recovery: An integrated approach. *Psychiatric Quarterly, 73*, 157–170.

Miller, S. D., Hubble, M. A., Chow, D. L., & Seidel, J. A. (2013). The outcome of psychotherapy: Yesterday, today, and tomorrow. *Psychotherapy, 50*, 88–97. doi:10.1037/a0031097

Mitchell, C. W. (2007). *Effective techniques for dealing with highly resistant clients* (2nd ed.). Johnson City, TN: Clifton W. Mitchell Publishing.

Moon, P. K. (2006). Sand play therapy with U.S. soldiers diagnoses with PTSD and their families. In G. R. Walz, J. C. Yep, & R. K. Yep's (Eds.), *Vistas: Compelling perspectives on counseling 2006*. Alexandria, VA: American Counseling Association.

Morin, A. (2011). Self-awareness part 1: Definition, measures, effects, functions, and antecedents. *Social and Personal Psychology Compass, 5*, 807–823. doi:10.1111/j.1751-9004.2011.00387.x

Morsy, L. (2019). Toxic stress and clinical teaching. *The Clinical Teacher, 17*, 1–3. doi:10.1111/tct.13112

Mozdzierz, G., Peluso, P. R., & Lisiecki, J. (2014). *Principles of counseling and psychotherapy: Learning the essential domains and nonlinear thinking of master practitioners* (2nd ed.). New York, NY: Routledge.

Nagata, D. K., Kim, J. H. J., & Nguyen, T. U. (2015). Processing cultural trauma: Intergenerational effects of the Japanese American incarceration. *Journal of Social Issues, 71*, 356–370. doi:10.1111/josi.12115

Najavits, L. M. (2002). *Seeking safety: A treatment manual for PTSD and substance abuse*. New York, NY: Guilford Press.

National Association of State Mental Health Program Directors. (2012). *Fact sheet on reducing the behavioral health impact of trauma: The SBHA role*. Retrieved from www.nasmhpd.org/sites/default/files/Integration_Fact%20Sheet%20on%20Reducing%20BH%20Impact%20of%20Trauma.pdf

Naumburg, M. (1950). *An introduction to art therapy: Studies of the free art expression of behavior problems of children and adolescents as a means of diagnosis and therapy*. New York, NY: Teachers College Press.

Nichter, M. (1981). Idioms of distress: Alternatives in the expression of psychological distress: A case from South India. *Culture, Medicine, and Psychiatry, 5*, 379–408.

Nooner, K. B., Linares, O., Batinjane, J., Kramer, R. A., Silva, R., & Cloitre, M. (2012). Factors related to posttraumatic stress disorder in adolescence. *Trauma, Violence, and Abuse, 13*(3), 153–166. doi:10.1177/1524838012447698

Norcross, J. C., Krebs, P. M., & Prochaska, J. O. (2011). Stages of change. *Journal of Clinical Psychology in Session, 67*(2), 143–154. doi:10.1002/jclp.20758

Norcross, J. C., & Wampold, B. E. (2011). Evidence-based therapy relationships: Research conclusions and clinical practices. *Psychotherapy, 48*, 98–102. doi:10.1037/a0022161

Norman, G. J., Hawkley, L., Ball, A., Bernston, G. G., & Cacioppo, J. T. (2011). Perceived social isolation moderates the relationship between childhood trauma and pulse pressure in older adults. *International Journal of Psychophysiology, 88*, 334–338. doi:10.1016/j.ijpsycho.2012.12.008

Obrist, B., Pfeiffer, C., & Henley, R. (2010). Multi-layered social resilience: A new approach in mitigation research. *Progress in Development Studies, 10*, 283–293. doi:10.1177/146499340901000402

Ogden, P., Minton, K., & Pain, C. (2006). *Trauma and the body: A sensorimotor approach to psychotherapy*. New York, NY: Norton.

Ogle, C. M., Rubin, D. C., & Siegler, I. C. (2016). Maladaptive trauma appraisals mediate the relation between attachment anxiety and PTSD symptom severity. *Psychological Trauma: Theory, Research, Practice, and Policy, 8*(3), 301–309. doi:10.1037.tra0000112

Owen, C. (2017). Obscure dichotomy of early childhood trauma in PTSD versus attachment disorders. *Trauma, Violence, and Abuse*, 1–14. doi:10.1177/1524838017742386

Pelon, S. B. (2017). Compassion fatigue and compassion satisfaction in hospital social work. *Journal of Social Work in End-of-Life & Palliative Care, 13*, 134–150. doi:10.1080/15524256.2017.1314232

Peltonen, K., & Kangaslampi, S. (2019). Treating children and adolescents with multiple traumas: A randomized clinical trial of narrative exposure therapy. *European Journal of Psychotraumatology, 10*, 1–13. doi:10.1080/20 008198.2018.1558708

Perryman, K., Blisard, P., & Moss, R. (2019). Using creative arts in trauma therapy: The neuroscience of healing. *Journal of Mental Health Counseling, 4*(1), 80–94. doi:10.17744/mehc.41.1.07

Phinney, J. S., & Ong, A. D. (2007). Conceptualization and measurement of ethnic identity: Current status and future directions. *Journal of Counseling Psychology, 54*, 271–281. doi:10.1037/0022-0167.54.3.271

Pierce, L. M. (2016). Overwhelmed with the burden of being myself: A phenomenological exploration of the existential experiences of counselors-in-training. *Journal of Humanistic Counseling, 55*, 136–150. doi:10.1002/johc.12030

Pipher, M. (2019). *Women rowing North*. New York, NY: Bloomsbury.

Place, P. J., Ling, S., & Patihis, L. (2018). Full statistical mediation of the relationship between trauma and depressive symptoms. *International Journal of Psychology, 53*, 142–149. doi:10.1002/ijop.12279

Powers, A., Dixon, H. D., Conneely, K., Gluck, R., Munoz, A., Rochat, C., . . . Gillespie, C. F. (2019). The differential effects of PTSD, MDD, and dissociation on CRP in trauma-exposed women. *Comprehensive Psychiatry, 93*, 33–40. doi:10.1016/j.comprsych.2019.06.007

Prikhidko, A., & Swank, J. M. (2018). Emotional regulation for counselors. *Journal of Counseling & Development, 96*, 206–212. doi:10.1002/jcad.12193

Prochaska, J. O., & Norcross, J. C. (2010). *Systems of psychotherapy: A transtheoretical analysis* (7th ed.). Belmont, CA: Brooks, Cole.

Quake-Rappy, C., Miller, B., Ananthan, G., & Chiu, E.-C. (2008). Direct observation as a means of assessing frequency of maladaptive behavior in youths with severe emotional and behavioral disorder. *The American Journal of Occupational Therapy, 62*(2), 206–211.

Quiros, L., Kay, L., & Montijo, A. M. (2012). Creating emotional safety in the classroom and in the field. *Reflections: Narratives of Professional Heling, 18*, 42–47.

Radey, M., & Figley, C. R. (2007). The social psychology of compassion. *Clinical Social Work Journal, 35*, 207–214. doi:10.1007/s10615-007-0087-3

Raju, R., Corrigan, F. M., Davidson, A. J. W., & Johnson, D. (2012). Assessing and managing mild to moderate emotion dysregulation. *Advances in Psychiatric Treatment, 18*, 82–93. doi:10.1192/apt.bp.107.005033

Ray, D. C. (2015). Research in play therapy: Empirical support for practice. In D. A. Crenshaw & A. L. Stewart's (Eds.), *Play therapy: A comprehensive guide to theory and practice* (pp. 467–482). New York, NY: Guilford Press.

Read, J., Fosse, R., Moskowitz, A., & Perry, B. (2014). The traumagenic neurodevelopmental model of psychosis revisited. *Neuropsychiatry, 4*, 65–79. doi:10.2217/npy.13.89

Renkel, R. E. (1983). *Reader's digest*. Pleasantville, NY: The Reader's Digest Association, Inc.

Resick, P. A., & Schnicke, M. K. (1992). Cognitive processing therapy for sexual assault victims. *Consulting and Clinical Psychology, 60*, 747–756.

Reynolds, C., Simms, J., Webb, K., Corry, M., McDermott, B., Ryan, M., . . . Dyer K. F. (2017). Client factors that predict the therapeutic alliance in a chronic, complex trauma sample. *Traumatology, 23*(4), 294–302.

Robjant, K., & Fazel, M. (2010). The emerging evidence for narrative exposure therapy: A review. *Clinical Psychology Review, 30*, 1030–1039. doi:10.1016/j.cpr.2010.07.004

Roelofs, K. (2017). Freeze for action: Neurobiological mechanisms in animal and human freezing. *Philosophical Transactions Royal Society, 372*, 1–10. doi:10.1098/rstb.2016.0206

Roisman, G. L., Padron, E., Sroufe, L. A., & Egeland, B. (2002). Earned-secure attachment status in retrospect and prospect. *Child Development, 73*(4), 1204–1219.

Rorschach, H. (1942). *Psychodiagnostics: A diagnostics test based on perception*. Bern: Huber. (Original work published 1921).

Rosin, J. (2015). The necessity of counselor individuation for fostering reflective practice. *Journal of Counseling and Development, 93*, 88–95. doi:10.1002/j.1556-6676.2015.00184.x

Sackett, C. R., & Jenkins, A. M. (2015). Photovoice: Fulfilling the call for advocacy in the counseling field. *Journal of Creativity in Mental Health, 10*(3), 376–385. doi:10.1080/15401383.2015.1025173

Saeri, A. K., Cruwys, T., Barlow, F. K., Stronge, S., & Sibley, C. G. (2018). Social connectedness improves public mental health: Investigating bidirectional relationships in the New Zealand attitudes and values survey. *Australian & New Zealand Journal of Psychiatry, 52*(4), 365–374. doi:10.1177/0004867417723990

Sansbury, B. S., Graves, K., & Scott, W. (2015). Managing traumatic stress responses among clinicians: Individual and organizational tools for self-care. *Trauma, 17*, 114–122. doi:10.1177/1460408614551978

Sareen, J. (2014). Posttraumatic stress disorder in adults: Impact, comorbidity, risk factors, and treatment. *Canadian Journal of Psychiatry, 59*(9), 460–467.

Schaefer, C. E., & Drewes, A. A. (Eds.). (2014). *The therapeutic powers of play: 20 core agents of change* (2nd ed.). Hoboken, NJ: John Wiley & Sons, Inc.

Schauer, M., Neuner, F., & Elbert, T. (2005). *Narrative exposure therapy (NET): A short-term intervention for traumatic stress disorders after war, terror, and torture.* Gottingen: Hogrefe & Huber.

Schimmel, C. J., & Jacobs, E. E. (2013). Creative interventions using chairs: Going beyond gestalt. *Journal of Creativity in Mental Health, 8*, 428–443. doi:10.1080/15401383.2013.852456

Schiraldi, G. R. (2009). *The Post-traumatic stress disorder sourcebook.* New York, NY: McGraw-Hill.

Schmelzer, G. L. (2018). *Journey through trauma: A trail guide to the five-phase cycle of healing repeated trauma.* New York, NY: Avery.

Schoedl, A. F., Costa, M. P., Fossaluza, V., Mari, J. J., & Mell, M. F. (2014). Specific traumatic events during childhood as risk factors for posttraumatic stress disorder development in adults. *Journal of Health Psychology, 19*(7), 847–857. doi:10.1177/1359105313481074

Schoeneberg, C., Forth, N., & Seto, A. (2011). Using metaphor in facilitating self-awareness. In S. Degges-White & N. L. Davis (Eds.), *Integrating the expressive arts into counseling practice: Theory-based interventions* (pp. 172–173). New York, NY: Springer.

Schoeneberg, C., & Zaporozhets, O. (2018). Child-parent relationship therapy: Responding to the needs of attachment in childhood. *Journal of Kyiv Institute of Business and Technologies, 3*(37), 76–81.

Schomaker, S. A., & Ricard, R. J. (2015). Effect of mindfulness-based intervention on counselor-client attunement. *Journal of Counseling and Development, 93*(4), 491–498. doi:10.1002/jcad.12047

Schon, D. A. (1983). *The reflective practitioner: How professionals think in action.* New York, NY: Basic Books.

Schoultz, M., Macaden, L., & Hubbard, G. (2016). Participants perspectives on mindfulness- based cognitive therapy for inflammatory bowel disease. *Pilot and Feasible Studies, 2*, 3. doi:10.1186/s40814-015-0041-z

Schouten, K. A., de Niet, G. J., Knipscheer, J. W., Kleber, R. J., & Hutschemaekers, G. J. M. (2015). The effectiveness of art therapy in the treatment of traumatized adults: A systemic review of art therapy and trauma. *Trauma, Violence, and Abuse, 16*(2), 220–228. doi:10.1177/1524838014555032

Schubert, C. F., Schmidt, U., & Rosner, R. (2016). Posttraumatic growth in populations with posttraumatic stress disorder- A systematic review on growth-related psychological constructs and biological variables. *Clinical Psychology and Psychotherapy, 23*, 469–486. doi:10.1002/cpp.1985

Schwartz, H. L. (2000). *Dialogue with forgotten voices: Relational perspective on child abuse trauma and treatment of dissociative disorders.* New York, NY: Basic Books.

Schwartz, M. F., & Masters, W. H. (1994). The masters and Johnson treatment program for sex offenders: Intimacy, empathy, and trauma resolution. *Sexual Addiction & Compulsivity, 1*, 57–76.

Sege, R., Bethell, C., Linkenbach, J., Jones, J., Klika, B., & Pecora, P. J. (2017). *Balancing adverse childhood experiences with hope: New insights into the role of positive experience on child and family development.* Boston: The Medical Foundation. Retrieved from www.cssp.org

Shapiro, F. (1989). Efficacy of the eye movement desensitization procedure in the treatment of traumatic memories. *Journal of Traumatic Stress, 2*, 199–223. doi:10.1002/jts.2490020207

Shapiro, F. (2018). *Eye movement desensitization reprocessing (EMDR) therapy: Basic principles, protocols, and procedures* (3rd ed.). New York, NY: Guilford Press.

Shear, K. M. (2015). Complicated grief. *The New England Journal of Medicine, 372*, 153–160. doi:10.1056/NEJMcp1315618

Shelby, J. (2019). Too tired to play? Play therapists and secondary traumatic stress. *Play Therapy™ Magazine, 14*(2), 16–19.

Sherman, M. D., Harris, J. I., & Erbes, C. (2015). Clinical approaches to addressing spiritual struggle in veterans with PTSD. *Professional Psychology, 46*, 203–212. doi:10.1037/pro0000020

Siegel, D. J. (2004). Attachment and self-understanding: Parenting with the brain in mind. *Journal of Prenatal and Perinatal Psychology and Health, 18*(4), 273–285.

Siegel, D. J. (2012). *Pocket guide to interpersonal neurobiology: An integrative handbook of the mind.* New York, NY: Norton.

Siegel, D. J. (2015). *The developing mind: How relationships and the brain interact to shape who we are* (2nd ed.). New York, NY: Guilford Press.

Siegel, D. J., & Bryson, T. P. (2012). *The whole brain child.* New York, NY: Bantam Books.

Silveira, F. S., & Boyer, W. (2015). Vicarious resilience in counselors of child and youth victims of interpersonal trauma. *Qualitative Health Research, 25*, 513–526. doi:10.1177/1049732314552284

Silver, J., Caleshu, C., Casson-Parkin, S., & Ormond, K. (2018). Mindfulness among genetic counselors is associated with increased empathy and work engagement and decreased burnout and compassion fatigue. *Journal of Genetic Counseling, 27*, 1175–1186. doi:10.1007/s10897-018-0236-6

Skorikov, V. B., & Vondracek, F. W. (2011). Occupational identity. In S. J. Schwartz, K. Luyckx, & V. L. Vignoles (Eds.), *Handbook of identity theory and research* (pp. 693–714). New York, NY: Springer.

Spinazzola, J., van der Kolk, B., & Ford, J. D. (2018). When nowhere is safe: Interpersonal trauma and attachment adversity as antecedents of posttraumatic stress disorder and developmental trauma disorder. *Journal of Traumatic Stress, 31*, 631–642.

Stamm, B. H. (2002). Measuring compassion satisfaction as well as fatigue: Developmental history of the Compassion Satisfaction and Fatigue Test. In C. Figley (Ed.), *Treating compassion fatigue* (pp. 107–119). New York, NY: Routledge.

Stamm, B. H. (2010). *The concise ProQOL manual* (2nd ed.). Pocatello, ID: ProQOL.org.

Stanley, B., Brown, G., Brenner, L. A., Galfalvy, H. C., Currier, G. W., Knox, K. L., . . . Green, K. L. (2018). Comparison of the safety planning intervention with follow-up vs usual care of suicidal patients in the emergency department. *JAMA Psychiatry, 75*, 894–900. Retrieved from https://jamanetwork.com

Stinson, J. D., Robbins, S. R., & Crow, C. W. (2011). Self-regulatory deficits as predictors of sexual, aggressive, and self-harm behaviors in a psychiatric sex offender population. *Criminal Justice and Behavior, 38*, 885–895. doi:10.1177/0093854811409872

Substance Abuse and Mental Health Services Administration. (2014). *SAMHSA's concept of trauma and guidance for a trauma-informed approach.* HHS Publication No. (SMA) 14-4884. Rockville, MD: Substance Abuse and Mental Health Services Administration. Retrieved from https://store.samhsa.gov/system/files/sma14-4884.pdf

Sue, D. W., Arrendondo, P., & McDavis, R. J. (1992). Multicultural counseling competencies and standards: A call to the profession. *Journal of Counseling and Development, 70*, 481–483.

Sugiyama, H., Oshida, A., Thueneman, P., Littell, S., Katayama, A., Kashiwaga, M., . . . Herz, R. S. (2015). Proutisian products are preferred: The relationship between odor-evoked memory and product evaluation. *Chemosensory Perception, 8*, 10. http://dx.doi.org.exproxy.regent.edu:1048/10.1007/s12078-015-9182-y

Tay, D. (2012). Applying the notion of metaphor types to enhance counseling protocols. *Journal of Counseling and Development, 90*(2), 142–149. doi:10.1111/j.1556-6676.2012.00019.x

Taylor, J. G., & Baker, S. B. (2007). Psychosocial and moral development of PTSD-diagnosed combat veterans. *Journal of Counseling and Development, 85*, 364–369.

Tedeschi, R. G., & Calhoun, L. G. (1996). The posttraumatic growth inventory: Measuring the positive legacy of trauma. *Journal of Traumatic Stress, 9*, 455–471. doi:10.1002/jts.2490090305

Tedeschi, R. G., & Calhoun, L. G. (2004). Posttraumatic growth: Conceptual foundations and empirical evidence. *Psychological Inquiry, 15*, 1–18. Retrieved from www.jstor.org/stable/20447194

Terr, L. C. (1991). Childhood traumas: An outline and overview. *American Journal of Psychiatry, 148*, 10–20.

Thompson-Hollands, J., Jun, J., & Sloan, D. (2017). The association between peri-traumatic dissociation and PTSD symptoms: The mediating role of negative beliefs about self. *Journal of Traumatic Stress, 30*, 190–194. doi:10.1002/jts.22179

Turner, R. B. (2019). Play heals us, too! *Play Therapy Magazine, 14*, 32–35.

Underwood, L. G. (2011). The daily spiritual experience scale: Overview and results. *Religions, 2*, 29–50. doi:10.3390/rel2010029

Underwood, L. G., & Teresi, J. A. (2002). The daily spiritual experience scale: Development, theoretical description, reliability, exploratory factor analysis, and preliminary construct validity using health-related data. *Annals of Behavioral Medicine, 24*, 22–33. doi:10.1207/S15324796ABM2401_04

van der Kolk, B. A. (1989). The compulsion to repeat the trauma: Re-enactment, revictimization, and masochism. *Treatment of Victims of Sexual Abuse, 12*, 389–411.

van der Kolk, B. A. (2005). Developmental trauma disorder: Towards a rational diagnosis for children with complex trauma histories. *Psychiatric Annals, 35*, 401–408. doi:10.3928/00485713-20050501-06

van der Kolk, B. A. (2006). Clinical implications of neuroscience research in PTSD. *Annals of the New York Academy of Sciences, 1071*, 277–293.

van der Kolk, B. A. (2015). *The body keeps score: Brain, mind, and body in the healing of trauma* (reprinted ed.). New York, NY: Penguin Books.

Van Petegem, S., Beyers, W., Brenning, K., & Vansteenkiste, M. (2013). Exploring the association between insecure attachment styles and adolescent autonomy in family decision making: A differentiated approach. *Journal of Youth and Adolescence, 42*, 1837–1846. doi:10.1007/s10964-012-9886-0

Voinov, B., Richney, W. D., & Bailey, R. K. (2013). Depression and chronic diseases: It is time for a synergistic mental health and primary care approach. *Primary Care Companion for CNS Disorders, 15*. doi:10.4088/PCC.12r01468

von Diwans, B., Trueg, A., Kirschbaum, C., Fishbaucher, U., & Henirichs, M. (2018). Acute social and physical stress interact to influence social behavior: The role of social anxiety. *PLoS One, 13*, 1–21. doi:10.1371/journal.pone.0204665

Wagoner, B. (2017). There is more to memory than inaccuracy and distortion. *Behavioral and Brain Sciences, 40,* 65. http//doi.org.ezproxy.regent.edu:2048/10.1017/S0140525X15002435

Walsh, F. (2016). Family resilience: A developmental systems framework. *European Journal of Developmental Psychology, 13,* 313–324. doi:10.1080/17405629/2016.1154045

Walton, J. L., Cuccurullo, L. J., Raines, A. M., Vidaurri, D. N., Allan, N. P., Maiertisch, K. P., & Franklin, C. L. (2017). Sometimes less is more: Establishing the core symptoms of PTSD. *Journal of Traumatic Stress, 30,* 254–258. doi:10.1002/jts.22185

Waszczuk, M., Li, X., Bromet, E., Gonzalez, A., Zvolensky, M., Ruggero, C., . . . Kotov, R. (2017). Pathway from PTSD to respiratory health: Longitudinal evidence from a psychosocial intervention. *Health Psychology, 36*(5), 429–437. doi:10.1037/hea0000472

Watson, L. B., DeBlaere, C., Langrehr, K. J., Zelaya, D. G., & Flores, M. J. (2016). The influence of multiple oppression on women of color's experiences with insidious trauma. *Journal of Counseling Psychology, 63*(6), 656–667. doi:10.1037/cou0000165

Wei, M., Tsai, P., Lannin, D., Du, Y., & Tucker, J. R. (2015). Mindfulness, psychological flexibility, and counseling self-efficacy: Hindering self-focused attention as a mediator. *The Counseling Psychologist, 43,* 39–63. doi:10.1177/0011000014560173

Weinberg, M., & Gil, S. (2016). Trauma as an objective or subjective experience: The association between types of traumatic events, personality traits, subjective experience of the event, and posttraumatic symptoms. *Journal of Loss and Trauma, 21*(2), 137–146. doi:10.1080/153250224.2015.1011986

Wharton, T., Whitworth, J., MacCauley, E., & Malone, M. (2019). Pilot testing a manualized equine-facilitated cognitive processing therapy (EF-CPT) intervention for PTSD in veterans. *Psychiatric Rehabilitation Journal, 42,* 268–276. doi:10.1037/prj0000359

Whiston, S. C. (2017). *Principles and applications of assessment in counseling* (5th ed.). Boston, MA: Cengage Learning.

Whitford, H. S., Olver, I. N., & Peterson, M. J. (2008). Spirituality as a core domain in the assessment of quality of life in oncology. *Psycho-Oncology, 17,* 1121–1128. doi:10.1002/pon.1322

Wicks, R. J. (2012). *Riding the dragon.* Notre Dame, IN: Sorin Books.

Wilks, C. R., Korslund, K. E., Harned, M. S., & Linehan, M. M. (2016). Dialectical behavior therapy and domains of functioning over two years. *Behaviour Research and Therapy, 77,* 162–169. doi:10.1016/j.brat.2015.12.013

Wilson, B., & Nojachski, T. (2016). Evaluating the impact of trauma–informed care (TLC) perspective in social work curriculum. *Social Work Education, 35,* 589–602.

Wolfelt, A. D. (2003). *Understanding your grief: Ten essential touchstones for finding hope and healing your heart.* Fort Collins, CO: Companion Press.

Wolpe, J., & Lazarus, A. A. (1966). *Behavior therapy techniques: A guide to the treatment of neuroses.* New York, NY: Pergamon.

Wong-Wylie, G. (2010). *Counsellor "know thyself": Growing ourselves, shaping our professional practice, and enhancing education through reflection.* Saarbrücken, Germany: VDM Verlag Press.

Worden, W. (2008). *Grief counseling and grief therapy: A handbook for the mental health practitioner* (4th ed.). New York, NY: Springer.

Wu, Z., Xu, J., & Sui, Y. (2016). Posttraumatic stress disorder and posttraumatic growth coexistence and the risk factors in Wenchuan earthquake survivors. *Psychiatry Research, 237,* 49–54. doi:10.1016/j.psychres.2016.01.041

Yoo, Y., Park, H.-J., Park, S., Cho, M. J., Cho, S.-J., Lee, J. Y., . . . Lee, J. (2018). Interpersonal trauma moderates the relationship between personality factors and suicidality of individuals with posttraumatic stress disorder. *PLoS One, 13*(1), 1–15. doi:10.1371/journal.pone.0191198

Youngstrom, E. A. (2012). Future directions in psychological assessment: Combining evidence-based medicine innovations with psychology's historical strengths to enhance utility. *Journal of Clinical Child and Adolescent Psychology, 42,* 139–159. doi:10.1080/15374416.2012.736358

Zerubavel, N., & Wright, M. O. (2012). The dilemma of the wounded healer. *Psychotherapy, 48,* 482–491. doi:10.1037/a0027824

Index

abuse 3–6, 15–19, 21, 30, 42, 57, 61–62, 73–74, 79,
    81, 91, 93–95, 97–99, 107–108, 111, 121–122,
    136, 138, 140, 144, 146, 180–182, 188, 191, 193,
    198, 208
action stage 123–124
acute stress disorder (ASD) 17, 109
Adaptive Information Processing (AIP) 158
addictions 5, 15, 18, 91
adjustment disorder (AD) 20, 109
adventure therapy 183, 218
adverse childhood events (ACEs) 21, 26–27, 209
adversity 17, 19–21, 25–26, 48–50, 57, 209
advocacy 62, 196, 205–206, 208–209, 211–212
affect 139
Ainsworth, M. 73
ambivalence 79, 81, 123, 172, 174, 180
amygdala 105–106, 140, 146
animal-assisted therapy 183
anxious attachment style 74, 83
appropriate level of emotional separation 44, 51
arousal 18, 20, 45, 76, 106, 109, 14, 143, 163–164,
    192, 195
art therapy 172, 176, 181–183, 185, 218
assessment 30, 47, 56, 90–91, 94, 100, 104–105,
    107–122, 125, 127, 144, 154, 156–175, 166, 183,
    189, 206–207, 216–217
attachment 5, 7, 19, 55, 58, 68–69, 72–85, 95, 97–98,
    109, 137, 140–142, 144, 177, 188, 191, 216
attachment disruption 73, 83, 137
attention deficit hyperactivity disorder (ADHD)
    5, 110
attunement 42, 63, 68, 70–72, 75–77, 79–80, 82, 89,
    153, 155, 175–176, 184, 210
avoidance 6, 18, 62, 77–78, 93, 109–111, 142, 152,
    157, 159, 161, 175, 180, 198
avoidant attachment style 73–74, 83
Axline, V. 176

Bandura, A. 198
Baranowsky, A. 40, 128, 154, 163
Beck, A. 114, 125, 216

Beck Anxiety Inventory (BAI) 114, 216
Beck Depression Inventory (BDI) 114, 125, 216
bereavement 155
biases 36, 55, 61, 63, 160, 162
borderline personality disorder (BPD) 5, 80, 110, 159
boundaries 16, 45–48, 138, 145, 191–192, 194–195,
    200, 202
Bowen, M. 191
Bowlby, J. 72–73, 78, 140
Brave Heart, M. 56
Briere, J. 23, 72, 79, 111, 142, 217
Brown, D. 21, 49, 114, 141
burnout 31, 38, 43–47, 51–53

capacity 4, 6, 45, 49, 139, 159, 175, 189, 195, 197
case conceptualization 6–7, 23, 41, 63, 87, 89–90,
    92, 94, 96, 98–101, 104–106, 108, 110, 112–114,
    116, 120–122, 124, 126–128, 131, 156, 182
Centers for Disease Control (CDC) 16, 21, 94, 209
cognitive behavioral therapy (CBT) 157–159, 161
cognitive distortions 39, 111, 160, 168–170, 181, 193
cognitive processing therapy (CPT) 157–158, 219
cognitive restructuring 45, 154, 158–161, 168–169
cognitive schema 39, 78
Cohen, J. 125, 158
cohesive narratives 154, 162, 169
collateral information 112–113, 117
collectivistic 59–61
comorbid 78, 93, 110, 117, 172, 183
compassion fatigue 31, 38, 41–47, 49, 51–53, 208
compassion satisfaction 47–49, 51, 53
complex trauma 58, 79, 94, 106, 110, 182, 190
complicated grief 155, 168, 216
confrontation 193–194
containment 162, 164, 168–170
contemplation stage 122–124
contingent communication 72–73, 82
Cook, J. 172, 206, 212
Corey, M. 31, 136, 160
countertransference 7, 29, 31, 40–41, 51, 72, 78, 82,
    124, 142, 148, 154, 165

Courtois, C. 16, 21, 92, 164
creative interventions 172–176, 183, 185
cultural awareness 61–62, 65, 67
cultural factor(s) 54–57, 135
culture 7, 23, 42, 47, 54–56, 58–67, 91, 110, 114, 125–126, 157, 187, 192, 206

dance and movement therapy 183
defenses 6, 95, 97, 107, 139, 154, 162, 164
degree of personal threat 99, 101
degree of proximity to the trauma 99, 101
depression 6, 18, 39–41, 59, 73, 80, 93, 96–97, 110–111, 114, 122, 125, 146, 158, 173, 209, 216
developmental age 97, 101
developmental trauma 19–21, 25–26, 74–75, 78
dialectical behavioral therapy (DBT) 157, 159
differentiation of self (DOS) 191, 194
direct observation 112–113, 177
disempowered cultural groups 56, 65
disenfranchised grief 155–156, 168, 217
disenfranchised groups 58, 65
disinhibited social engagement disorder (DSED) 19, 75, 109
disorganized attachment style 73–75, 83
dissociation 18, 56–57, 59, 77, 99, 107–108, 140, 142, 146, 165–166, 193
dissociative identity disorder (DID) 107
double jeopardy 57, 65
drama therapy 183, 218
Drożdek, B. 60
dual awareness 158, 162, 165, 168, 170
dysregulation 23, 47, 55–56, 75–77, 83, 108, 111, 140–144, 147, 151, 165, 175, 190, 193, 195

earned secure attachment 82–83, 191
emotional contagion 145, 149
emotional dysregulation 56, 108, 140–143, 191
emotional flooding 149, 165
emotional regulation 18–19, 45, 76–78, 128, 140, 142, 146, 149, 154, 159, 191, 195
empathy 31, 41–44, 46, 50, 68, 70–72, 76, 123, 155, 162, 192, 197–200, 209
empowerment 5, 49, 56–58, 96, 121, 123, 127, 137–139, 147, 150–151, 153, 165, 174, 178, 188, 192, 194, 198, 208–209
equilibrium 20–21, 23, 29, 140–141, 143–144
ethnic identity strength 58, 64–65, 67
etiology 113, 156
evidence-based practice (EBP) 157
evidence-based treatment (EBT) 157
existential crises 6, 12
experiential learning theory 9
explicit memory 162, 168
exposure 7–9, 15, 17, 38–41, 43–46, 48, 51, 60, 74, 76, 91, 106, 110, 121, 126, 128, 135, 146, 154, 157–159, 161–165, 168–170, 174, 181–182, 207–208
expressive writing and poetry therapy 183

externalizing memories 182, 185
external resources 19, 22, 111, 122, 139, 151
eye movement desensitization reprocessing (EMDR) 157–158, 162, 164–165, 176

faith 6, 47, 55, 60, 63, 68, 77, 99, 111, 121, 152, 154, 197
Felitti, V. 21
fight or flight response 105–106
fight response 105–106, 117–118, 140
Figley, C. 41, 49
flashbacks 18, 106–107, 111, 144, 156, 182, 193
flight response 105–106, 117–118, 140
Foa, E. 125, 157, 216
forgiveness 6, 61, 191, 193–194
four-factor conceptualization 127
fragmented or fragmentation 18, 106–107, 110, 154, 158, 162
Frankl, V. 161
freeze response 56–57, 105–108, 117–118, 140, 175

Gaskill, R. 19, 75, 78, 106, 175
Gentry, J. 40, 128, 154–155, 207
Gottman, J. 140
grief 6, 47, 91, 111, 128, 153–156, 168, 171, 182, 193, 197, 200, 216–217
grounding 128, 141–142, 145–147, 149–150, 163–165, 193, 195

habituation 162–163, 168
helplessness 4, 7, 57, 138, 140, 161, 199–200, 208
Herman, J. 18, 43, 128
historical trauma 56, 65
homeostasis 21
Homeyer, L. 179–180
hopelessness 7, 122, 140
House-Tree-Person (HTP) 114–115
hyperarousal 5, 106, 108, 110–111, 121, 140–144, 164
hypervigilance 18, 23, 26, 38, 74, 78, 93, 106, 108, 111, 122, 137, 156, 162, 180, 195
hypoarousal 94, 107, 111, 140–144, 146, 150, 164

idioms of distress 58–59, 65
imaginal exposure 157
immediacy 147, 149
implicit memory 162, 168
impostor syndrome 119
indirect trauma exposure 38, 41, 46, 48, 51, 208
insidious trauma 57, 65
intake interview 90–94, 96–101, 104–105, 112–113, 123
internal family systems (IFS) 166
internal resources 19, 38, 48, 111, 139, 196
interpersonal trauma 19, 57, 60–61, 75, 98, 101, 138, 191, 203
intrusive thoughts 18, 40, 106, 110, 146, 165
in vivo exposure 157
Ivey, A. 147

Janoff-Bulman, R. 6, 159, 196, 217
Jongsma, A. 125
Jung, C. 28, 177, 179
justice 61

Kalff, D. 179
Kolb, D. 9

Landreth, G. 72, 176
letter of impact 194, 203–204
Levine, P. 166
loss 4, 7, 16, 39, 40, 59, 63, 71, 91–92, 96, 111, 123,
    128, 138, 153–154, 156, 165, 182, 189, 191, 192,
    197, 199, 200
Lowenfeld, M. 179

MacLeod, L. 125
maintenance stage 123, 190, 194
Malchiodi, C. 10
marginalized groups 57–58, 65, 208
McAulifee, G. 54–55, 61–62
meaning-making 47, 128, 143, 161, 197
mental map 29, 39, 104
mental status exam 90, 114
metaphor 10, 13, 20, 46, 48, 68, 120, 139, 150–153,
    163–164, 171–174, 176, 180–181, 184–187, 197,
    204, 213
mindfulness 45–46, 48, 146–147, 149–150, 159, 195
mourning 128, 152–153, 155–156, 167–168, 183
multiculturalism 54, 61, 64, 67
music therapy 172, 183, 219

narrative exposure therapy (NET) 157–159,
    161–162, 229
neglect 16, 19, 28, 61, 73–74, 79, 95–96, 98,
    137–138, 140
neurobiology 105–106, 108
neuroplasticity 9, 108, 117
neuroscience 9, 174
New Haven Trauma Competencies 206, 212–213
non-intrusiveness 70
Norcross, J. 69, 122–123
normative stress 4, 9, 20–21, 26

objective instrument 113–114, 117, 166
occupational benefits 48, 53
occupational hazards 37–38, 44, 48, 52–53
Ogden, P. 164, 166

parallel process 8, 12–14, 32, 37, 39, 41, 43, 45,
    47–49, 126, 129, 200
pathologize 22, 25
perpetuating or maintaining factors 121–122, 131
Perry, B. 19, 75, 106
phase 1: safety and stabilization 128–129, 135–136,
    138–139, 141, 145, 147, 152, 164–165, 181, 188
phase 2: remembrance and mourning 128, 152–153,
    155, 167, 183

phase 3: reconnection 128, 175, 188–190, 196,
    199–200
physical abuse 5, 16–18, 21, 57, 61–62, 73–74, 79,
    91, 97, 99, 107–108, 111, 122, 136, 140, 146,
    180–182, 191
play therapy 71, 97, 172, 176–179, 181, 183,
    185, 218
posttraumatic growth 6, 48–51, 53, 115, 123, 189,
    196–198, 202, 204, 217
Posttraumatic Growth Inventory (PTGI) 196, 217
posttraumatic stress disorder (PTSD) 5, 16–18, 22–23,
    26, 30, 38, 56–58, 75, 80, 93, 96, 98–99, 105,
    109–111, 116, 137, 156–159, 161, 166, 194, 198,
    216–217
power differentials 78
powerlessness 39, 138, 154
precipitating or causal factors 121–122, 127, 131
precontemplation stage 122–124
predictability 70, 137–138, 147
predisposing factors 121–122, 127, 131
prefrontal cortex 106–107
preparation stage 123, 153, 189
prevention 16, 44–45, 52, 194–195, 208–209,
    211–212
Prochaska, J. 122
professional development 8–9, 11, 28, 32–35, 44,
    209–210, 213
professional disposition 11, 45, 69–72, 79–80, 82,
    83–85, 206
professional growing pains 32, 34–36
professional identity 4, 41–42, 207, 209
Professional Quality of Life Scale (ProQOL) 47, 52
projection 173–174, 179–181, 185
projective instruments 114–115
prolonged exposure therapy (PE) 157, 162–163
protective factor(s) 6, 44, 54–55, 58, 94, 99,
    121–123, 131
psychoeducation 8, 59–60, 62, 95, 97, 123, 127, 144,
    153, 156, 158, 162, 165, 193–194, 208
psychological distance 173–174, 185
psychotropic medication 114

reactive attachment disorder (RAD) 19, 75, 109
reactive state 109, 142–143
receptive state 144–145
reconciliation 61, 193
reflection-in-action 29–30, 34
reflection-on-action 29–30, 34
reflection-on-self 29–30, 34
reflexive practice 28–36, 50, 69
reframe 23–24, 45, 47, 51, 112, 138, 144–145, 161,
    172, 181, 189, 200
regulation 18–19, 23, 45, 47, 55–56, 74–78, 128,
    139–143, 146–147, 149, 154, 158–159, 166, 175,
    177, 188–191, 194–196, 200
relational discernment 192, 195, 202
relational triggers 78–79, 83, 96
relationship ruptures 5, 80–81, 85, 141

repetition compulsion 95
resilient/resiliency/resilience 6–7, 19, 22, 48–51, 53, 73, 96, 99, 100, 111, 138, 154, 175, 189, 196, 202, 206, 216
resources 19, 22–23, 27, 38, 43, 47–49, 56, 58, 63, 76, 90, 91, 97, 99, 104, 111, 121–122, 139, 151, 176, 189–190, 193, 195–196, 198–199, 208, 210
retraumatization 129–130, 146, 163, 165, 192
rupture repair 80–83, 85, 141, 191

safety 5–7, 18–19, 23, 32, 38–39, 42, 60, 70, 75, 79, 82, 91, 93–95, 98, 102–103, 107, 128–129, 135–139, 141, 144–149, 151–152, 158, 161, 163–165, 167, 172–174, 180–181, 188, 194, 206
Safety Planning Interventions (SPI+) 94, 102
sandtray 141, 172, 176, 179–183, 185–186, 218
Schaefer, C. 176
Schauer, M. 158
schema 39, 78
secondary posttraumatic stress 51
secure attachment 7, 73, 75–79, 82–83, 140, 191
self-awareness 7–8, 10, 12, 28–33, 42, 45–47, 62–63, 112, 128, 136, 139, 143–145, 147–148, 165, 189, 191, 195
self-care 10, 37, 39, 42, 44–53, 122, 143, 145, 200, 206
self-disclosure 41, 62–63
self-doubt 3, 8, 28, 32–33, 36, 139
self-efficacy 18, 49, 77, 198
self-harm 18, 77, 91, 94, 103, 121, 142, 159, 182
self-medicate 93
self-soothing 77, 141, 143
sexual abuse 3, 5, 15–17, 21, 61, 91, 95, 97, 99, 108, 140, 180–181, 191, 193, 198
shame 19, 23, 55, 58–60, 77, 81, 93, 96–97, 108, 111, 125, 139, 144, 152, 154, 158, 160–161, 163, 192–193
Shapiro, F. 158
Siegel, D. 7, 9, 72, 74, 76, 140
silencing response 40
SMARTER approach for goal setting 125, 130
somatic 39, 59, 75, 111–112, 146, 163, 166, 180
stabilization 98, 128–129, 135–163, 138–145, 147–149, 151–155, 164–165, 181, 188
stage of change 122–125, 127, 129–130, 132, 166
Stamm, B. 47, 49
startle response 18, 59, 106
stereotyping 55, 65
strengths-based 16, 22–23, 25–27
Subjective Units of Distress Scale (SUDS) 143–144, 150–151, 157, 195
substance use/abuse 21, 30, 40, 73, 77, 90–91, 93–94, 110–111, 121, 146

suicidality/suicide 18, 21, 94, 97, 102–103, 110, 155, 216
synthesizing 105, 113, 120–121, 129

Tedeschi, R. 49, 196–197, 217
termination 6, 22, 93, 115, 128, 189, 194–196, 199–200, 202
theory-based skills 207–208, 211
therapeutic alliance/therapeutic relationship 4–8, 22, 28–29, 32, 39, 40–41, 54, 59, 61–62, 68–73, 75–82, 91, 98, 103, 121–123, 127, 128, 135–138, 141, 145, 152, 154–156, 160–162, 166, 171, 175, 177–179, 188–191, 193–196, 199–200, 206–207, 209, 217
titration 162–164, 168, 180
toxic stress 20–21, 25–26, 57, 121
transference 7, 29, 31, 40–41, 51, 72, 78, 80, 82, 142, 145, 148, 154, 165, 179, 188
transparency 5, 70
trauma-focused cognitive behavioral therapy (TF-CBT) 158, 176
trauma-informed care 5–6, 12, 16, 92, 156, 199, 209
trauma-informed lens 3, 5, 92, 95
trauma narrative 38, 98, 138, 154, 157–159, 161, 164, 168, 175, 182
trauma reenactment 95–96, 101, 121
treatment goals 7, 14, 44, 69–70, 104–105, 108, 112, 120–126, 128–132, 135–136, 139, 148, 152–154, 156–157, 159, 166–167, 172, 175, 179, 181, 188–191, 194–195, 199, 207
treatment objectives 104, 124–126, 128, 130, 179
treatment plan 89, 104–105, 108, 112, 114–115, 120–121, 123–135, 156, 176, 199
triad of trauma-work 3–4, 6–8, 14–15
triggers 78–79, 83, 93, 95–96, 121, 126, 128, 137, 140–142, 144–145, 148–149, 157–158, 163, 188, 190, 195, 197–198
tri-phasic model 120, 128–129, 131, 183, 189, 207
trust 5–7, 19, 37–38, 69, 72, 78–82, 100, 136–138, 147, 152, 154, 158, 188, 192, 194
type 1 trauma 17–21, 25–26
type 2 trauma 17–21, 25–26

unconditional positive regard 70, 145, 171

van der Kolk, B. 21, 93, 96, 110, 138, 145
vicarious posttraumatic growth 48–51, 53
vicarious resiliency 48–51, 53
vicarious traumatization 38–47, 51–53, 208

window of tolerance 162, 164, 168, 175, 195
wounded healer 31, 34

yoga therapy 46, 166, 183, 218

Made in the USA
Las Vegas, NV
24 August 2021